AF541061

SHAPING INDIA'S ARSENAL

The Path to Self-Reliance in Ammunition Manufacturing

SHAPING INDIA'S ARSENAL

The Path to Self-Reliance in Ammunition Manufacturing

Brig. (Dr.) Biju Jacob, VSM

PENTAGON PRESS LLP

Copyright © BRIG. (DR.) BIJU JACOB, VSM, 2026

All rights reserved. No part of this publication may be reproduced, stored in a retrieval system, or transmitted in any form or by any means, electronic, mechanical, photocopying, recording or otherwise, without the prior written permission of the Publisher.

First Published in 2025
Revised Edition 2026
by
PENTAGON PRESS LLP
206, Peacock Lane, Shahpur Jat
New Delhi-110049, India
Contact: 011-26490600

Printed at Aegean Offset Printers, Greater Noida

ISBN 978-81-982857-4-4 (HB)

Disclaimer: The views and opinions expressed in the book are the individual assertion of the Author. The Publisher does not take any responsibility for the same in any manner whatsoever. The same shall solely be the responsibility of the Author.

www.pentagonpress.in

CONTENTS

1. Introduction 1

2. Analysing India's Strategic Initiatives for Self-Reliance in Defence Manufacturing 9

Introduction 9
Policy Framework for Self-Reliance 12
India's Strategic Vision and Goals in Defence Manufacturing 16
Technology Acquisition and Development 18
Institutional Framework and Key Stakeholders 20
Technological and Industrial Base: Challenges and Opportunities 22
Complexities in Setting up an Ammunition Manufacturing Factory 25
Comparative Analysis of Ammunition Industries in the United Kingdom and India 27
Case Studies of Strategic Initiatives: Indigenous Defence Projects 35
International Collaborations and Joint Ventures 37
Impact on National Security and Economy 38
Conclusion 42

3. Defence Exports: A Strategic Pathway to Self-Reliance 44

Introduction 44
Historical Context of India's Defence Exports 47
Evolution of Policy Framework 49
Current Trends in India's Defence Ammunition Exports 50
Policy Framework for Promoting Defence Resilience 54
Analysis of Defence Equipment Export Trends 58
Role of Defence Exports in Fostering Self-Reliance 63
Technological Innovations and Investments 65
Challenges and Opportunities 67
Strategic Implications for Self-Reliance 70
Conclusion 72

4. Advancing Ammunition Tech: Pathways to Self-Reliance in Indian Defence Production 75
Introduction 75
Role of DRDO in India's Defence Production Scenario 79
Academic Contributions to Technological Advancements in India's Defence Sector 81
Role of Private Sector in India's Defence Production before 1991 83
Challenges of Private Sector in India's Defence Sector Post 1991 85
Position of India's Defence Exports in the Past Decade 86
Exploring the Viability of Joint Defence Production in India 87
Self-Reliance in the Indian Defence Industry: Is It Possible? 89
Conclusion 92

5. Synergies and Stumbling Blocks: The Role of Public and Private Sectors in Ammunition Production 94
Introduction 94
Historical Development of Ammunition Production in India 97
Technological Base for Ammunition Production 101
Comparison with Global Standards and Practices 103
Technological Challenges 107
Industrial Base for Ammunition Production 109
Key Private Sector Players 110
Supply Chain and Logistics 112
Production Capacity and Output 113
SWOT Analysis of India's Technological and Industrial Base 115
Conclusion 118

6. Securing Ammunition Supply Chains: Reliable Sourcing of Raw Materials and Components 120
Introduction 120
Ammunition Supply Chain: An Overview 121
Challenges in Sourcing Raw Materials and Components 124
Strategic Approaches to Secure the Ammunition Supply Chain 127
Policy Recommendations for Strengthening Ammunition Supply Chains 128
Conclusion 130

7. Modernising Ammunition Acquisitions: Transition from Qualitative Requirement Based to Technology-Based Model for Procurement 131
Introduction 131
Analysis of QR-Based Procurement Process 132
Transition to Technology-Based Procurement 135
Implementation Framework for Technology-Based Procurement 136
Risk Mitigation Strategies 140
Conclusion 141

8. Envisioning the Way Ahead: A Blueprint for Ammunition Self-Reliance 142
Introduction 142
India's Current Position in the Ammunition Ecosystem 143
Priority Sectors and Key Focus Areas 146
Defence Export Competitiveness 146
Structural and Operational Complexities in Establishing Ammunition Manufacturing 150
Charting the Path Forward 152
Building a Collaborative Ammunition Ecosystem 158
Conclusion 163

9. Roadmap and Innovation Pathways 165
Introduction 165
Emerging Technologies in Ammunition Manufacturing 166
Pioneering R&D Models for Cutting-Edge Ammunition Innovations 177
Conclusion 185

Endnotes 187

Appendices 205

Chapter One
Introduction

> "*We are becoming self-reliant in the defence sector. Today, we have our own identity in defence manufacturing. India is emerging as a defence manufacturing hub.*"
>
> —Prime Minister Shri Narendra Modi in 78th Independence Day Address, New Delhi

Self-reliance in national defence is fundamental to sovereignty and security. It represents a nation's capacity to independently protect its interests, uphold its principles, and ensure its citizens' safety, free from excessive dependence on external forces, thereby reinforcing autonomy and resilience against external pressures or influences. The importance of self-reliance in defence cannot be overstated, as it not only ensures a nation's autonomy but also fosters resilience, innovation, and strategic flexibility in the face of evolving threats and geopolitical dynamics. Firstly, self-reliance in defence is instrumental in preserving a nation's sovereignty. Relying excessively on external sources for military capabilities can undermine a nation's autonomy, subjecting it to the influence and interests of foreign powers. By cultivating indigenous defence capabilities, a nation asserts its independence and maintains control over its security apparatus. This self-determination is fundamental to safeguarding national interests and preserving the integrity of governance structures. Moreover, self-reliance enhances a nation's security by mitigating vulnerabilities associated with dependency on foreign arms supplies or military assistance. In an interconnected world where geopolitical alliances can shift unpredictably, relying solely on external support exposes a nation to the risk of strategic vulnerability and manipulation.

Speaking at the 'Aatmanirbhar Bharat' defence dialogue hosted by the STRIVE think tank in June 2024, Raksha Mantri Rajnath Singh emphasised the need for self-sufficiency in the defence manufacturing sector, particularly given that India is currently dealing with a double threat on its borders and evolving forms of warfare. He continued by saying that India must create its own cutting-edge technology platforms and equipment if it is to safeguard its sovereignty.[1] A country can strengthen its defences, lessen its dependency on outside actors, and guarantee that operations continue even during periods of geopolitical unrest by cultivating its own defence industries and technological capabilities.

The 'Make in India' initiative, inaugurated by Prime Minister Narendra Modi in 2014, sought to catalyse India's transition into a formidable manufacturing hub across various sectors.[2] Among the 25 sectors earmarked for development, Defence Manufacturing emerged as a pivotal area of focus, alongside others such as Aviation, Construction, and Chemicals. This initiative aimed to foster self-sufficiency within India's defence sector, prompting the implementation of a comprehensive set of reforms to bolster indigenous design, development, and production capabilities. Central to this initiative were a series of strategic measures. Firstly, the Defence Acquisition Procedure (DAP)-2020 prioritised the procurement of capital items from domestic sources, underscoring the government's commitment to bolstering indigenous defence manufacturing. Secondly, the announcement of 18 major defence platforms for industry-led design and development underscored the government's efforts to promote innovation and collaboration within the domestic defence industry. Thirdly, the introduction of 'Positive Indigenisation Lists' for both the Services and Defence Public Sector Undertakings (DPSUs) signalled a clear intent to reduce dependence on imports, with embargoes placed on specified items beyond designated timelines. Additionally, the simplification of the industrial licensing process and the liberalisation of the Foreign Direct Investment (FDI) policy, allowing up to 74 per cent FDI under the automatic route, aimed to create a more conducive environment for domestic and foreign investment in the defence sector. Further initiatives included the streamlining of the Make Procedure, the launch of Innovations for the Defence Excellence (iDEX) scheme to engage start-ups and MSMEs, and the implementation of the Public

Procurement (Preference to Make in India) Order 2017, all of which were designed to stimulate domestic production and innovation. Moreover, the establishment of an indigenisation portal named SRIJAN and reforms in the Offset policy, focusing on attracting investment and Transfer of Technology, reflected the government's commitment to fostering collaboration and technology transfer within the domestic defence industry. Lastly, the establishment of two defence industrial corridors, located in Uttar Pradesh and Tamil Nadu, aimed to create dedicated manufacturing ecosystems to support the growth of the defence manufacturing sector. Complementing these initiatives, the Department of Defence Production, Ministry of Defence, introduced the Draft 'Defence Production & Export Promotion Policy (DPEPP) 2020,' serving as an overarching guiding framework to enhance defence production capabilities, promote self-reliance, and facilitate exports within the defence sector, including aerospace and naval shipbuilding sectors.[3]

The significance of the defence sector is underscored by various economic indicators. In the fiscal year 2023-2024, the share of GDP allocated to defence expenditure reached 3.3 per cent, reflecting a substantial allocation of resources to national security. Moreover, there has been a notable 13 per cent increase in the defence budget from the fiscal year 2022-2023, indicating a continued commitment to strengthening the country's defence capabilities. Furthermore, India's defence exports surged to an unprecedented level, reaching approximately $ 160 billion in the fiscal year 2022-2023.[4] Despite these advancements, India's position in the global arms trade landscape presents a contrasting picture. According to the 'Trends in International Arms Transfers, 2023' report, India does not rank among the top 25 largest exporters of major arms, but it stands as the largest importer globally. The data indicates a notable percentage change from the period of 2014-2018 to 2019-2023, with a 4.7 per cent increase in India's share of global arms imports. From 2019 to 2023, India accounted for 9.8 per cent of global arms imports, compared to 9.1 per cent from 2014-2018. Notably, Russia, France, and the USA emerged as the primary sources of India's arms imports, constituting significant portions of the total imports, with Russia alone contributing around 36 per cent, followed by France with 33 per cent and the USA with 13 per cent.[5] The driving force behind India's substantial imports in the defence sector primarily stems from geopolitical tensions with neighbouring countries such as Pakistan.[6] These tensions necessitate a robust defence apparatus, leading to heightened procurement activities to bolster India's defence capabilities and ensure national security.

In a country like India, characterised by volatile geopolitical dynamics and threats along its borders, the concept of self-reliance or 'Atmanirbharta' holds significant relevance. This approach is crucial as it cultivates resilience, empowering nations to adapt to evolving security challenges and technological advancements effectively. In an era marked by rapid technological innovation and asymmetric threats, the capacity to innovate and customise defence solutions according to specific needs becomes paramount. Moreover, self-reliance in the defence sector enhances strategic flexibility, providing nations with the autonomy to pursue independent foreign policies and respond adeptly to regional or global security crises. Relying on external military assistance or alliances may constrain a nation's freedom of action, potentially obliging it to align with the interests of its partners, even if they deviate from its own objectives. By fostering indigenous defence capabilities, nations retain the sovereignty to shape their strategic priorities, establish alliances based on mutual interests, and pursue diplomatic resolutions to conflicts. This approach not only strengthens a country's defence posture but also reinforces its position as a sovereign entity capable of safeguarding its national interests in a dynamic and unpredictable international landscape.

India's pursuit of self-reliance in defence has been shaped by the experiences of wars it has encountered since independence. Following the Chinese aggression in 1962, the Department of Defence Production (DDP) was established to cultivate a self-reliant and self-sufficient indigenous defence production base. This department focuses on matters related to defence production and the indigenisation of imported stores, equipment, and spares. However, it was the Kargil conflict in 1999 that brought to light the Indian Army's inadequacy in conventional warfare under high altitude and extreme climate conditions. In response, a committee of 'Group of Ministers on National Security' was formed shortly after the war. This committee, in its report submitted to the Prime Minister on 26 February 2001, recommended the establishment of a separate and dedicated institutional structure to handle the complete spectrum of procurement functions. The objective was to inject a higher level of professionalism and reduce delays in the acquisition process. Consequently, following the acceptance of the report, a new acquisition set-up was instituted within the Ministry of Defence (MoD) in October 2001.[7]

In pursuit of achieving self-reliance in defence, the government established a committee in 2004 under Mr. Vijay Kelkar's leadership. One of its main objectives was to examine and recommend strategies for integrating the user, the Ministry of Defence (MoD), and Indian industry (both private and public) in the acquisition process and defence production.[8] This committee submitted its report in two parts: the first part in April 2005, which primarily focused on defence procurement procedures and proposed various measures to promote indigenous production. While certain recommendations from the Kelkar committee, such as the creation of a 15-year equipment acquisition plan and the introduction of offsets in defence purchases, were accepted, many others were not. Notably, the crucial recommendation for accrediting and nurturing Raksha Udyog Ratnas, or industrial 'jewels', in the private sector to undertake significant defence manufacturing projects and joint ventures, was shelved. The second part of the report, submitted later in the same year, advocated greater autonomy for India's nine Defence Public Sector Undertakings (DPSUs) to form joint ventures and consortiums with overseas original equipment manufacturers, aimed at enhancing their efficiency.[9] Additionally, the committee recommended the corporatisation of the Ordnance Factory Board, a proposal that had previously been suggested by the T.K.A. Nair committee in 2000. This recommendation was reiterated by subsequent committees, including the Vice Admiral Raman Puri (retd.) committee in 2015 and the Lieutenant General D.B. Shekatkar (retd.) committee. However, it wasn't until 2021 that this recommendation was finally implemented.[10]

The Kelkar Committee made a significant recommendation concerning projects involving indigenous development under the 'Make' procedure, which was subsequently incorporated into the Defence Procurement Procedure (DPP) of 2006. This recommendation aimed to focus the Defence Research and Development Organisation (DRDO) solely on projects requiring sophisticated technology of strategic, complex, and security-sensitive nature. However, it wasn't until 2014 with the launch of the 'Make in India' initiative that the government aimed to incentivise both indigenous and foreign companies to invest in manufacturing in India, making it an attractive destination for capital and technological investments.

To align the Defence Procurement Procedure (DPP) with the objectives of 'Make in India,' the Ministry of Defence (MoD) constituted an expert committee under Dhirendra Singh in May 2015. This committee emphasised the integration of the private sector, advocating two well-defined partnership models depending on strategic needs, quality criticality, and cost competitiveness. One such model suggested was the 'Strategic Partnership' to create capacity in the private sector for platforms of strategic importance, and supplementing the capacity and infrastructure existing in the public sector.

The recommendations of the expert committee led to the promulgation of DPP-2016, effective from 1 April 2016. This procedure adopted a three-pronged approach to support the 'Make in India' initiative, including institutionalisation, streamlining, and simplification of the procedure to promote indigenous design, development, and manufacturing of defence equipment. Notably, it introduced a new category called 'Buy (Indian-IDDM)' with overriding preference, followed by 'Buy (Indian)' and 'Buy & Make (Indian)' categories. Furthermore, DPP-2016 streamlined the 'Make' procedure, aiming at developing long-term indigenous defence capabilities. Under the revised 'Make' procedure, projects are categorised into 'Make-I' and 'Make-II,' with government funding of 90 per cent for 'Make-I' projects and no government funding for 'Make-II' projects. Additionally, to support Micro, Small, and Medium Enterprises (MSMEs), preference is given to them for 'Make-1' and 'Make-2' projects costing less than Rs. 10 crore and Rs. 3 crore, respectively, for prototype development.[11]

According to the data provided by the Ministry of Defence in its Annual Report 2022-2023, the export-import profile of the Indian defence industry spanning from 2014-2015 to 2022-2023 reveals a discernible upward trend in defence exports over the specified period, with notable fluctuations observed from year to year. Total exports have demonstrated more than a twofold increase from the initial recorded figures in 2014-2015 to the latest data available in 2022-2023. While certain years exhibit substantial growth in exports, such as the periods from 2016-2017 to 2017-2018 and from 2019-2020 to 2020-

2021, there are also instances of decline, notably from 2018-2019 to 2019-2020. This observed fluctuation in export figures underscores the influence of the pandemic which led to fluctuations in international demand for Indian defence products, geopolitical dynamics, and shifts in domestic industry capabilities and competitiveness. The significant growth witnessed in recent years, particularly from 2019-2020 onwards, suggests the potential successful implementation of policies or initiatives aimed at bolstering defence exports during this period. Nonetheless, sustained monitoring and strategic planning are imperative to navigate the nuances of the defence export landscape and foster continued growth and resilience in the Indian defence industry.

Export promotion is instrumental in bolstering defence resilience through market diversification, revenue generation, and technological exchange. Governments can facilitate defence exports by leveraging trade agreements, export financing mechanisms, and diplomatic efforts to ease market access and overcome trade barriers. International cooperation and collaboration with strategic partners further enhance interoperability, knowledge sharing, and technology transfer, thereby strengthening defence capabilities. Efficient regulatory frameworks and procurement processes are essential for promoting transparency and accountability in defence acquisitions. Policy reforms aimed at simplifying bureaucratic procedures, reducing red tape, and accelerating decision-making can improve efficiency and effectiveness. Embracing best practices like competitive bidding and performance-based contracting fosters innovation and ensures value for money in defence acquisitions. Investing in human capital development is crucial for building a skilled workforce to support defence resilience efforts. Policymakers can promote education and training programs tailored to the defence industry's needs, including specialised training in manufacturing, quality assurance, and cyber security. Creating incentives for talent retention and career advancement within the defence sector addresses skill shortages and strengthens workforce resilience. In an increasingly digitised world, cyber security and protection of critical infrastructure are paramount for defence resilience. Governments must prioritise cyber security initiatives to safeguard defence networks, systems, and data from cyber threats. Additionally, investing in resilience measures for critical infrastructure, such as manufacturing facilities and supply chains, ensures continuity of operations in the face of cyber attacks or other disruptions. By implementing a coherent and proactive policy framework addressing these areas, governments can enhance defence resilience, promote self-reliance in ammunition manufacturing, and safeguard national security interests in a complex and uncertain global landscape.

In the face of evolving security threats, geopolitical uncertainties, and economic vulnerabilities, establishing a robust policy framework is imperative to promote defence resilience and cultivate self-reliance in ammunition manufacturing. This framework should encompass a comprehensive array of policies and initiatives aimed at bolstering indigenous capabilities, enhancing competitiveness, and safeguarding national security interests. Central to this framework is the need for a clear strategic vision and national security objectives that take into account the changing threat landscape, geopolitical dynamics, and technological advancements. A cohesive and forward-looking strategy forms the bedrock upon which specific policies and initiatives can be devised and executed. One crucial aspect of this framework is investment in research and development (R&D) to drive innovation and technological progress. Governments should allocate resources towards R&D endeavours focused on developing cutting-edge technologies, refining manufacturing processes, and addressing technological gaps in ammunition production. Public-private partnerships, along with collaboration with academia and research institutions, can further harness expertise and resources to accelerate innovation in the defence sector. Promoting the growth of indigenous manufacturing capabilities is paramount for reducing reliance on foreign suppliers and bolstering defence resilience. Policymakers can incentivise domestic production through measures such as tax incentives, subsidies, and preferential procurement policies. Moreover, fostering collaboration between defence industries and small and medium-sized enterprises (SMEs) can spur innovation, generate employment opportunities, and fortify the domestic defence industrial base. By embracing these strategies, nations can strengthen their defence posture and enhance their ability to address emerging security challenges effectively.

Chapter Two

Analysing India's Strategic Initiatives for Self-Reliance in Defence Manufacturing

Introduction

The strategic imperative for self-reliance in defence manufacturing has become increasingly significant for India, given the complex and evolving security environment. The pursuit of self-reliance in defence manufacturing aims to reduce dependency on foreign arms suppliers, enhance national security, and foster indigenous technological and industrial capabilities. This chapter delves into the various measures and strategies implemented by India to achieve this critical objective. It also seeks to provide a comprehensive understanding of the policy framework, institutional mechanisms, technological advancements, and challenges associated with this ambitious goal. It includes an examination of the historical context and evolution of India's defence manufacturing capabilities, an analysis of the key policies and initiatives aimed at promoting self-reliance in terms of the role of government agencies, DPSUs, and private sector participation as well as identifying the challenges and opportunities in achieving self-reliance. This chapter is a critical component of the book, which explores the broader theme of India's strategic imperatives in defence and security. Understanding the drive for self-reliance in defence manufacturing is essential for comprehending India's defence policies, its quest for strategic autonomy, and its positioning in the global defence market. The insights gained from this analysis will contribute to a broader discourse on how India can effectively navigate the challenges of defence modernisation while fostering a robust, indigenous defence industry. Achieving self-reliance in defence manufacturing is a multifaceted endeavour that involves coordinated efforts across policy, industry, and technology domains. By analyzing India's strategic initiatives in this area, this chapter aims to shed light on the progress made, the hurdles encountered, and the path forward for realising the vision of an '*Atmanirbhar Bharat*' in defence manufacturing.

In the past two decades, India has been one of the largest importers of arms globally. According to the Stockholm International Peace Research Institute (SIPRI), India accounted for nearly 9.5 per cent of the global arms imports between 2016 and 2020, highlighting the country's heavy reliance on foreign defence equipment.[12] This dependency poses significant risks, including supply chain vulnerabilities and strategic leverage exercised by exporting nations. It should also be noted that achieving self-reliance in defence manufacturing has been a priority for India.

In terms of defining the concept of self-reliance in defence manufacturing, it refers to any nation's ability to design, develop, produce, and maintain its own defence equipment and technologies with minimal dependence on foreign entities. This concept has become crucial for ensuring national security, strategic autonomy, and economic benefits. Nations around the world have adopted various strategies to achieve self-reliance in defence manufacturing, reflecting their unique geopolitical, economic, and technological needs and interests in this context. Furthermore, self-reliance in defence manufacturing encompasses several dimensions such as indigenous research and development (R&D) capabilities, robust industrial base, skilled workforce, and efficient supply chains. It also comprises the capacity to modernise as well as produce an extensive range of defence equipment indigenously along with maintaining operational readiness without relying on external sources. This idea of self-sustenance in defence manufacturing is critical for national security as it helps in allaying the risks associated with foreign supply disruptions, enhances strategic autonomy, and supports the local economy by creating jobs and fostering technological advancements.[13]

Numerous nations exemplify self-reliance in defence manufacturing through strategic initiatives and policies. For instance, the USA, through its Defence Advanced Research Projects Agency (DARPA), emphasises cutting-edge innovation and maintaining technological superiority. DARPA's efforts have led to significant advancements in stealth technology, unmanned systems, and cyber capabilities. Israel is another notable example, with its robust defence industry focussed on companies like Israel Aerospace Industries (IAI) and Rafael Advanced Defence Systems. Israel's focus on developing indigenous technologies such as the Iron Dome missile defence system and advanced drone capabilities underscores its commitment to self-reliance.[14] (Katz, 2020). Another example of China in terms of its significant strides made to achieve self-reliance in defence manufacturing through its Made in China 2025 initiative is also noteworthy. The Chinese policy aimed to reduce dependency on foreign technology by fostering domestic innovation and industrial capabilities, particularly in advanced weaponry and military technologies (Cheung, 2019). The experiences of the USA, Israel, and China illustrate diverse approaches to achieving this critical goal, highlighting the importance of strategic planning and sustained investment in defence R&D and manufacturing.

The concept of self-reliance in defence is not new to India. The foundation for this was laid soon after independence, with the establishment of defence public sector undertakings (DPSUs) and the Defence Research and Development Organisation (DRDO). Over the decades, these institutions have made notable contributions; however, the desired level of self-sufficiency in terms of defence manufacturing remains elusive in the case of India. The evolution of India's defence sector can be traced back to its post-independence era when the country focused on building a robust defence infrastructure. As, for instance, DRDO has been instrumental in developing various defence technologies, including missile systems, aircraft, and electronic warfare systems.[15]

India's defence sector is a pivotal component of its strategic and security architecture. Being one of the largest armed forces across the globe, India's defence sector encompasses a broad spectrum of activities, including defence procurement, R&D, manufacturing, and strategic defence initiatives. Furthermore, this sector's growth is driven by geopolitical imperatives, economic considerations, and technological advancements. In the past few years, the Indian government has initiated various strategic projects with the aim to revitalise the indigenous defence manufacturing sector. These initiatives are aligned with Prime Minister Modi's vision of '*Atmanirbhar Bharat*' or 'Make in India' initiative which seeks to transform India into a global manufacturing hub.

India's defence sector also comprises public sector undertakings (PSUs) and private industries apart from research institutions like DRDO. Significant PSUs include Hindustan Aeronautics Limited (HAL), Bharat Electronics Limited (BEL), and the erstwhile Ordnance Factory Board (OFB). These organisations have played a crucial role in manufacturing a range of defence equipment, from aircraft and avionics to electronic systems and munitions.[16] In recent years, the private sector's involvement in defence manufacturing has increased manifold. It is mostly driven by the much-needed policy reforms and the Make in India initiative. Also, companies such as Tata Advanced Systems, Mahindra Defence Systems, and Larsen & Toubro are now significant players in the defence landscape, contributing to diverse projects from land systems to naval vessels.[17] India has undertaken several strategic initiatives to enhance its defence capabilities and achieve self-reliance. For example, the Defence Procurement Policy (DPP) and Defence Production and Export Promotion Policy (DPEPP) are key frameworks designed to rationalise the procurement processes, encourage indigenous production, and encourage exports. Moreover, the introduction of strategic partnerships and increased foreign direct investment (FDI) aim to magnetise global defence companies to set up manufacturing bases in India.[18]

Policy Framework for Self-Reliance

In India, achieving self-reliance in defence manufacturing is a strategic imperative due to the need to reduce dependence on imports, augment national security, and encourage indigenous innovation and industrial capabilities. To achieve these aims, the Indian government has framed a comprehensive policy outline including various initiatives and guidelines designed to promote indigenous production, encourage private sector participation, and facilitate technology transfer. The sections below are India's initiatives to achieve self-reliance in defence manufacturing.

Defence Procurement Policy (DPP)

India's defence procurement policy has experienced significant transformations in the past few years with the aim to modernise its military capabilities and reduce dependency on foreign arms imports. DPP 2016 and its successor—the Defence Acquisition Procedure (DAP) 2020—are significant frameworks steering these efforts. The DAP 2020 introduced several reforms to streamline procurement processes and promote indigenous manufacturing. One of the fundamental changes is the emphasis on '*Atmanirbhar Bharat*', which promotes domestic production and reduces reliance on imports. The policy requires a higher indigenous requirement and promotes the 'Make in India' initiative, enabling Indian firms to play a more substantial role in defence manufacturing. Furthermore, DAP 2020 includes provisions for faster decision-making, increased transparency, and the involvement of private sector entities in defence production. Another significant feature of DAP 2020 is the introduction of the 'Leasing' category, which allows the Indian military to lease equipment for operational flexibility and cost-effectiveness. This approach is particularly valuable for acquiring high-cost platforms like ships and aircraft without the need for outright purchases. Furthermore, the policy emphasises the 'Buy Indian (IDDM)' category, which highlights procurement from Indian vendors, fostering local innovation and manufacturing capabilities.

Despite these progressive measures, the implementation of defence procurement policies faces several challenges such as bureaucratic hurdles, delays in decision-making, and the complexities of technology transfer agreements, which impede the efficiency of the procurement process. Also, aligning the defence industry's capabilities with the evolving requirements of the armed forces needs sustained investment in R&D. So, India's defence procurement policy aims to create a robust and self-reliant defence manufacturing ecosystem. While DAP 2020 marks a significant step towards achieving these goals, addressing the implementation challenges remains crucial for realising the full potential of these reforms. DAP serves as the guiding framework for defence acquisitions in India. It sketches procedures and guidelines for procurement, emphasising indigenisation and preference for domestically manufactured products.[19]

Defence Production Policy (DPrP)

DPrP aims to promote self-reliance in defence manufacturing by enhancing indigenous production capabilities, fostering innovation, and promoting private sector participation. It emphasises the development of a robust defence industrial base through measures such as technology collaboration, investment incentives, and offset policies. DPrP seeks to create an ecosystem conducive to indigenous defence production by streamlining regulations, facilitating ease of doing business, and promoting innovation clusters. Various policy measures have been adopted by the Government to ease approval/certifications for Indian industries for defence production. The Defence Products list requiring Industrial Licences has been rationalised and the manufacture of most parts or components does not require an Industrial Licence. The initial validity period of the Industrial Licence granted under the Industries (Development & Regulation)-I (D&R) Act has been increased from three years to 15 years with a provision to further extend it by three years on a case-to-case basis. A new online portal has been developed for facilitating the filing of online applications for Industrial Licences under the Industries (Development & Regulation)-IDR Act 1951/Arms Act 1959 with effect from 2018. Furthermore, the Indian government has also launched a scheme for awarding self-certification status to DPSUs and private industries wherein these have been delegated the responsibility of certifying the quality of products.[20]

Make in India Initiative

The 'Make in India' initiative was launched by Prime Minister Modi in September 2014. It is a major programme designed to transform India into a global manufacturing hub. The initiative focuses on encouraging multinational as well as domestic companies to manufacture their products in India, thereby enhancing employment, promoting innovation, and augmenting skill development across the country. The primary objectives of the 'Make in India' initiative include: increasing the manufacturing sector's growth rate to 12-14 per cent annually; creating additional manufacturing jobs; and ensuring the manufacturing sector's contribution to about 25 per cent of GDP by 2025 (an increase from 16 per cent in 2014). To achieve this, the initiative emphasises streamlining the regulatory framework, enhancing infrastructure, and promoting FDI along with promoting significant reforms including the introduction of a single-window clearance system, deregulation of several sectors, and the liberalisation of FDI policies, allowing 100 per cent FDI in most sectors, including defence, railways, and e-commerce.[21] The 'Make in India' initiative has earmarked 25 sectors, including automobiles, pharmaceuticals, textiles, chemicals, IT, aviation, and defence. Each sector has specific policies and initiatives to enhance manufacturing capabilities and attract investment. In the defence sector, this initiative fosters domestic production of military equipment. The 'Make in India' initiative, despite its ambitious goals, faces several challenges. One major stumbling block is the complexity of India's regulatory environment, which can discourage investors. Also, the bureaucratic red tape continues to pose challenges. However, there have been improvements in this regard also. According to the World Bank's Ease of Doing Business rankings, India improved from 142nd in 2014 to 63rd in 2020, indicating substantial progress but also emphasising the need for further improvement.

Impact of Policies on Defence Manufacturing

The implementation of these key policies and initiatives has had a significant impact on defence manufacturing in India. These policies have contributed to the growth of the domestic defence industry by creating opportunities for indigenous manufacturers and fostering a conducive environment for private sector participation. The emphasis on indigenisation and preference for domestically manufactured products has incentivised investment in indigenous R&D, technology development, and manufacturing capabilities. Furthermore, policies like DPP and DPrP have accelerated the integration of the private sector into defence production, leading to increased competition, innovation, and efficiency in manufacturing processes. The introduction of measures such as offset policies has encouraged technology transfer and collaboration between domestic and foreign companies, thereby enhancing indigenous capabilities and reducing dependence on imports. In this regard, the 'Make in India' initiative has also played a decisive role in promoting defence manufacturing by providing a platform for showcasing domestic capabilities, attracting investments, and fostering partnerships between domestic and foreign firms. The initiative's focus on skill development, infrastructure enhancement, and ease of doing business reforms has created a conducive environment for manufacturing growth.

India's Strategic Vision and Goals in Defence Manufacturing

The Defence Production and Export Promotion Policy (DPEPP) outlines the strategic vision and goals for increasing self-reliance in defence manufacturing and promoting defence exports. It emphasises the importance of indigenisation, innovation, and technology absorption in building a robust defence industrial base. The policy aims to achieve a turnover of $ 25 billion in defence manufacturing by 2025, including exports of $ 5 billion.[22] It lays down measures to promote indigenous design and development, enhance ease of doing business, and facilitate defence exports through proactive marketing and promotion efforts.[23]

The long-term vision for self-reliance in defence manufacturing revolves around building a technologically advanced, indigenous defence industrial base capable of meeting the country's defence requirements and contributing to global supply chains.[24] The primary goal is to reduce dependence on imports and enhance indigenous capabilities across the defence manufacturing value chain, including design, development, production, and maintenance. There is a focus on fostering a culture of innovation, research, and development to develop cutting-edge technologies and solutions tailored to India's defence needs. The strategic vision needs to foster partnerships between the government, defence forces, academia, and the private sector to leverage synergies, pool resources, and drive innovation in defence manufacturing. The long-term objective includes expanding the footprint of Indian defence products in international markets through proactive marketing, promotion, and support measures to enhance export competitiveness. The Indian government has enhanced FDI in the defence sector by 74 per cent through the automatic route for companies seeking new defence industrial licences and up to 100 per cent by the government route wherever it is likely to result in access to modern technology.[25]

An innovation ecosystem for defence titled "Innovations for Defence Excellence (iDEX)" has also been launched by the Indian government in April 2018. iDEX is aimed at the creation of an ecosystem to foster innovation and technology development in defence and aerospace by engaging industries including MSMEs, start-ups, individual innovators, R&D institutes, and academia and provide them grants/funding, and other support to carry out

R&D which has the potential for future adoption for Indian defence and aerospace needs. Furthermore, the government has also set up the Technology Development Fund (TDF) to encourage the participation of public/private industries. All this helps to create an ecosystem for enhancing cutting-edge technology capability for defence applications.

The Indian government reported the 'Strategic Partnership' Model in 2017, which envisages the establishment of long-term strategic partnerships with Indian entities through a transparent and competitive process. Through this, they can tie up with global original equipment manufacturers (OEMs) to obtain technology transfers to set up domestic manufacturing infrastructure and supply chains. Similarly, the 'offset portal' was launched in 2019 to ensure 'greater transparency, efficiency, and accountability in the process'. Reforms in the offset policy have been included in DAP 2020, with a focus on attracting investment and transfer of technology for defence manufacturing, by assigning higher multipliers to them.[26] In 2019, the government announced a 'Policy for indigenisation of components and spares used in defence platforms' to create an industry ecosystem that can indigenise imported components (including alloys and special materials) and sub-assemblies for defence equipment and platforms manufactured in India.[27] An indigenisation portal, namely, Srijan was also launched in 2020 for DPSUs/services with an industry interface to provide development support to MSMEs/start-ups/industry for import substitution. Till now, over 36,000 defence items—which were earlier imported—have been displayed on the Srijan portal. Furthermore, more than 12,300 items have been indigenously produced in the last three years.[28]

The government has established two defence industrial corridors, one each in Uttar Pradesh and Tamil Nadu to attract investments of Rs. 10,000 crore in each corridor by 2024-25. So far, investment of approximately Rs. 3,750 crore in both the corridors by public and private sector companies have been made. Moreover, respective state governments have also published their aerospace and defence policies to attract industries including foreign companies in these two corridors.[29] An Inter-Governmental Agreement (IGA) on "Mutual Cooperation in Joint Manufacturing of Spares, Components, Aggregates and other material related to Russian/Soviet Origin Arms and Defence Equipment" was signed in September 2019. The objective of the IGA is to enhance the after-sales support and operational availability of Russian-origin equipment currently in service in the Indian Armed Forces by organising the production of spares and components in the territory of India by Indian industry by way of the creation of joint ventures/partnerships with Russian original equipment manufacturers (OEMs) under the framework of the 'Make in India' initiative. The defence products list requiring an industrial licence has been rationalised and the manufacture of most parts or components does not require an industrial licence. The initial validity of the industrial licence granted under the IDR Act has been increased from three years to 15 years with a provision to further extend it by three years based on each case.

India's policy framework for self-reliance in defence manufacturing is anchored in key policies and initiatives such as the Defence Procurement Policy, Defence Production Policy, and Make in India initiative. These policies have had a significant impact on defence manufacturing by promoting indigenous production, fostering private-sector participation, and encouraging technology transfer. The strategic vision outlined in documents like the DPEPP underscores India's commitment to enhancing self-reliance and promoting defence exports. However, achieving self-reliance in defence manufacturing requires concerted efforts to address challenges related to infrastructure, technology absorption, skill development, and regulatory reforms. By pursuing a holistic approach encompassing policy reforms, industry collaboration, and innovation promotion, India can realise its long-term vision of a self-reliant and globally competitive defence industrial base.

Technology Acquisition and Development

India's aspiration to become a global leader in ammunition manufacturing is intrinsically linked to its ability to acquire and develop cutting-edge technologies. The modernisation of the defence sector, particularly in ammunition production, necessitates a multi-faceted approach, encompassing advancements in precision-guided munitions (PGMs), smart ammunition, next-generation propellants, and materials science. A key focus in this modernisation is the development of advanced guidance systems for PGMs, integrating technologies like laser guidance, GPS, and image-based systems, which are crucial for enhancing accuracy and minimising collateral damage.[30]

The miniaturisation of these guidance components further enables their integration into various ammunition types, thus enhancing versatility and adaptability in combat scenarios.[31] Additionally, sensor integration for real-time target acquisition and tracking improves the effectiveness of munitions, particularly in complex environments, reinforcing the need for indigenous advancements in this field.[32]

Complementing PGMs is the development of smart ammunition, which relies heavily on advanced sensor technology for target recognition and battlefield assessment. The incorporation of miniaturised computers for real-time data processing allows these munitions to make autonomous decisions, adjusting their trajectory to ensure precision strikes.[33] Moreover, enabling communication between smart ammunition and other systems is critical for coordinated military operations, emphasising the need for secure and reliable communication technologies within India's defence sector.[34]

Next-generation propellants represent another critical area of technological advancement, focusing on enhanced performance through higher energy density, improved burn rates, and reduced smoke signatures. These improvements are vital for achieving superior ballistic characteristics, such as longer ranges and higher velocities, which are essential for modern warfare.[35] The role of material science in developing advanced formulations for propellants cannot be overstated, as it directly influences the stability, energy output, and environmental impact of these substances.[36] Ensuring the safety and stability of these propellants under various conditions is also paramount, necessitating rigorous testing and innovation in chemical formulations.[37] Material science extends beyond propellants to the development of lightweight, high-strength materials for ammunition components. These materials, including advanced alloys and composites, are crucial for improving the mobility and logistical efficiency of munitions, which is increasingly important in modern combat scenarios.[38] Furthermore, the focus on wear-resistant and corrosion-resistant materials ensures the longevity and reliability of ammunition, even in harsh environmental conditions, thereby extending its operational viability.[39, 40]

However, India faces significant challenges in technology acquisition and development, including navigating the complex intellectual property (IP) landscape. Balancing the acquisition of foreign technologies with the development of indigenous innovations while safeguarding IP rights is a delicate task that requires strategic management.[41] Additionally, the need to build a skilled workforce in areas such as materials science, physics, chemistry, and engineering is critical. Investment in education and training programs is essential to cultivate the talent necessary for advancing technology in the defence sector.[42] Infrastructure development is another critical challenge, with the need for world-class research and development facilities equipped with advanced technology. Collaboration between government, industry, and academia is essential to create an ecosystem that supports technological innovation.[43] Such partnerships can accelerate the development of new technologies, positioning India competitively on the global stage.[44]

In conclusion, technology acquisition and development are fundamental to India's ambition to become a global leader in the ammunition manufacturing sector. By prioritising advancements in PGMs, smart ammunition, next-generation propellants, and material science, India can significantly enhance its defence capabilities. Addressing challenges related to intellectual property, talent acquisition, and infrastructure development through collaboration among various stakeholders will be key to realising this vision and ensuring India's leadership in the global defence industry.

Institutional Framework and Key Stakeholders

India's defence manufacturing sector is supported by a robust institutional framework and involves multiple key stakeholders working together to strengthen its defence capabilities. This ecosystem is designed to foster indigenous production, reduce dependency on imports, and enhance self-reliance in defence technology. The Ministry of Defence (MoD) is the primary body responsible for formulating policies related to defence procurement and manufacturing. It oversees various departments and agencies that coordinate defence manufacturing activities. As part of the MoD, the Department of Defence Production (DDP) has become a vital organisation in promoting and regulating the manufacturing of defence equipment in India. It executes policies related to indigenous production and manages state-owned defence enterprises. Another organisation, DRDO, plays a fundamental role in research and development for defence technologies. It operates a network of laboratories and institutions that work on various aspects of defence technology, from basic research to advanced systems. Furthermore, the Directorate General of Quality Assurance (DGQA) ensures that all defence equipment produced meets stringent quality standards. It plays a crucial role in the quality control and certification processes for defence products. Next is the Ordnance Factory Board (OFB) which has been recently restructured into seven new defence public sector undertakings (DPSUs). The erstwhile OFB has been a cornerstone of India's defence manufacturing. It is involved in the production of a wide range of defence equipment, including arms, ammunition, and other military hardware.

Besides, there are various public sector undertakings (PSUs) such as Hindustan Aeronautics Limited (HAL) and Bharat Electronics Limited (BEL) that also play a pivotal role in India's defence manufacturing sector. These organisations have significantly contributed to the country's self-reliance in defence production and technology development. HAL was established in 1940 and is one of the oldest and largest aerospace companies in India. It is involved in the design, development, manufacture, and maintenance of aircraft, helicopters, avionics, and related systems. HAL has developed a range of aircraft, including the Tejas Light Combat Aircraft (LCA), Dhruv Advanced Light Helicopter (ALH), and various trainer aircraft. It should be noted that Tejas is an indigenously designed fighter jet, representing a significant achievement in India's aerospace capabilities. The helicopters developed by HAL serve in various roles in the Indian Armed Forces, including transport, reconnaissance, and search–and-rescue operations. Besides, HAL is also developing a light combat helicopter (LCH) and light utility helicopter (LUH). HAL has also collaborated with global aerospace companies like Boeing, Airbus, and Sukhoi for technology transfer, joint production, and maintenance projects, enhancing its technical capabilities and global presence. Bharat Electrical Limited (BEL) was founded in 1954 and is a leading electronics company that supplies advanced electronic equipment to the Indian defence forces. BEL's product range includes radar systems, communication equipment, electronic warfare systems, and missile systems. BEL has developed and manufactured a wide range of radar systems, including the central acquisition radar (CAR), weapon locating radar (WLR), and coastal surveillance radar. These systems enhance the surveillance and defence capabilities of the Indian Armed Forces. BEL also provides advanced communication systems, including secure communication radios, network-centric warfare systems, and electronic warfare suites. These technologies are crucial for modern battlefield management and operational effectiveness. BEL has also been involved in the development and production of various missile systems like the Akash surface-to-air missile system. The Akash missile is a significant indigenous success, providing a robust air defence solution for the Indian armed forces.

Other PSUs include Bharat Dynamics Limited (BDL) which specialises in manufacturing guided missiles and allied defence equipment. It produces various missile systems, including anti-tank guided missiles (ATGMs), surface-to-air missiles (SAMs), and torpedoes. Similarly, Mazagon Dock Shipbuilders Limited (MDL) and Garden Reach Shipbuilders & Engineers have emerged as leading shipyards involved in the construction of warships and submarines for the Indian Navy. It has built numerous vessels, including the P-15B destroyers and the Scorpene-class submarines. GRSE shipyard develops a wide range of vessels, including frigates, corvettes, and offshore patrol vessels which has significantly contributed to the modernisation of the Indian Navy's fleet. The contributions of these PSUs have been instrumental in enhancing India's defence capabilities. Their efforts in indigenisation and technological innovation have helped in reducing the nation's dependence on foreign suppliers and enhanced self-reliance. The collaboration with private sector entities and international partners has further strengthened their capabilities. PSUs like HAL, BEL, BDL, MDL, and GRSE have become the backbone of India's defence manufacturing sector. Their continuous efforts in research, development, and production have significantly reinforced India's defence preparedness and technological self-sufficiency. As India aims to become a global defence manufacturing hub, the role of these PSUs remains crucial in achieving this vision.

Technological and Industrial Base: Challenges and Opportunities

India's technological and industrial base in the defence sector has been growing steadily. The Indian defence industry has witnessed major advancements in the past few decades which are facilitated by government initiatives, increased private sector participation, and strategic collaborations. However, the defence sector still faces several challenges that need to be addressed to fully realise its potential. The Indian defence industry has developed considerable capabilities in various areas, including missile systems, naval vessels, combat aircraft, and space technology. DRDO has been at the forefront of these advancements, developing key technologies such as the Agni and Prithvi missile systems, the LCA Tejas, and the Arihant-class nuclear submarines.

India has achieved significant milestones in missile technology, with a diverse arsenal that includes ballistic missiles (Agni series), cruise missiles (BrahMos), and anti-ballistic missile systems. The successful development and deployment of these systems highlight India's growing expertise in missile technology. In terms of naval capabilities India has also seen substantial growth. The Indian Navy operates on various indigenously built vessels, including the *INS Vikrant*, the country's first indigenous aircraft carrier, and various stealth frigates and submarines. These developments underscore India's shipbuilding and maritime engineering capabilities. In the aerospace sector also, India has made notable progress with the indigenously developed Tejas LCA being the best example. Furthermore, India has a burgeoning space program, with the Indian Space Research Organisation (ISRO) achieving significant success in satellite launches and interplanetary missions. Additionally, the defence electronics sector has also expanded with advancements in radar systems, electronic warfare, and communications systems. India's focus on cyber security has led to the development of robust cyber security protocols and infrastructure to protect critical defence assets.

Despite these advancements, the Indian defence industry faces several challenges. These include dependency on foreign suppliers for critical technologies, delays in project execution, and bureaucratic hurdles. To address these issues, the Indian government has launched initiatives like 'Make in India' and '*Atmanirbhar Bharat*' to promote indigenous production and reduce reliance on imports. Enhancing the indigenisation of defence production is crucial. This requires investment in domestic R&D, technology acquisition, and fostering partnerships between public and private sectors. Also, streamlining procurement processes, reducing bureaucratic red tape, and enhancing transparency can significantly boost the efficiency of defence projects. Added to this, it is necessary to develop a skilled workforce through specialised training programs and education which become crucial in supporting advanced manufacturing and R&D activities. Another major step is to strengthen international collaborations and joint ventures that can facilitate technology transfer and access to advanced technologies.

The Indian defence industry has made significant advances in developing indigenous capabilities and infrastructure. However, addressing existing challenges through strategic policy measures, investment in R&D, and fostering public-private partnerships still remain critical to achieving self-reliance and enhancing India's defence capabilities. The gaps persist in the realm of technological advancements and R&D efforts, which deter the defence sector's full potential. These issues include inadequate funding, talent shortages, regulatory constraints, and reliance on foreign technology.

Another major challenge is the insufficient allocation of funds for defence R&D. The percentage of India's GDP spent on defence R&D is relatively low as compared to other major military powers. It is a mere 0.7 per cent of the GDP allocated, in sharp contrast with China's substantial investment.[45] This financial limitation restricts the scope and scale of research projects, leading to delays in the development of new technologies. DRDO, which is the backbone of India's defence R&D, often faces budgetary constraints that limit its ability to undertake high-risk, high-reward projects.

Regulatory hurdles pose another significant challenge to technological advancements and R&D in the Indian defence sector. The complex and often cumbersome procurement processes, coupled with stringent regulatory requirements, can stifle innovation. Lengthy approval cycles and bureaucratic red tape delay the adoption of new technologies and impede the rapid prototyping and testing of defence systems. This slow pace of regulatory adaptation is particularly problematic in a rapidly evolving technological landscape. Despite efforts to promote indigenisation, India's defence sector remains heavily reliant on foreign technology. A significant portion of advanced defence equipment and systems are either imported or developed through collaborations with foreign entities. This dependence not only increases costs but also poses strategic vulnerabilities. The transfer of technology agreements often come with limitations that restrict India's ability to fully exploit and further develop the acquired technologies.

To address these challenges, a multifaceted approach is required. Enhancing funding for defence R&D is crucial. It is necessary that the Indian government allocate more resources to DRDO and incentivise private sector investment through grants, tax breaks, and public-private partnerships. This increased financial support can enable more ambitious and innovative projects. Investing in education and training programs is essential to build a skilled workforce. Initiatives to improve STEM (Science, Technology, Engineering, and Mathematics) education, along with specialised training for defence technologies, can help bridge the talent gap. Additionally, creating more attractive career paths and incentives within the defence sector can help retain skilled professionals. Regulatory reforms are also needed to streamline procurement processes and reduce bureaucratic hurdles. Adopting more agile and flexible regulatory frameworks can facilitate faster development and deployment of new technologies. This includes simplifying approval processes, enhancing transparency, and encouraging a more innovation-friendly environment.

Finally, it is important to reduce reliance on foreign technology for a sustained focus on indigenisation. Promoting domestic manufacturing, fostering innovation through research collaborations between industry and academia, and supporting start-ups in the defence sector can drive self-reliance. Additionally, strategic international collaborations should focus on genuine technology transfer and joint development rather than on mere procurement.

Complexities in Setting up an Ammunition Manufacturing Factory

Establishing an ammunition manufacturing facility in India presents a multifaceted challenge, requiring a deep understanding of the country's regulatory, logistical, economic, and technological landscape. At the heart of these challenges is the stringent regulatory environment. India's defence sector is governed by complex laws such as the Arms Act, 1959, and the Arms Rules, 2016, which impose rigorous security protocols, regular audits, and inspections to ensure national security. Companies must also navigate the nuanced foreign direct investment (FDI) policies, which, despite allowing up to 74 per cent FDI under the automatic route and up to 100 per cent with government approval, often involve cumbersome bureaucratic processes that can deter foreign investors.[46], [47] Additionally, the environmental and safety regulations that oversee the handling of hazardous materials necessitate clearances from multiple government bodies, adding another layer of complexity to the process.[48]

These regulatory challenges are compounded by India's vast and diverse geography, which significantly impacts the logistical aspects of setting up a manufacturing facility. The selection of a site for the factory must consider factors such as proximity to raw materials, the availability of skilled labour, and access to reliable transportation networks. Furthermore, regions prone to natural disasters require additional infrastructure investments to mitigate risks, underscoring the need for a strategic approach to site selection.[49] The logistical complexities extend to the transportation of hazardous materials across the country, requiring secure and compliant supply chain management to ensure the safe and timely delivery of raw materials and finished products.[50] Additionally, the energy and water resources necessary for ammunition production further influence site selection, especially in remote or underdeveloped areas.[51]

Economic considerations are also crucial in the decision-making process. The significant capital investment required to establish an ammunition manufacturing facility—covering everything from plant and machinery to regulatory compliance and infrastructure—can be a deterrent, particularly in a competitive global market. The ongoing costs associated with regulatory compliance, such as security measures and environmental monitoring, are particularly challenging for small and medium-sized enterprises (SMEs).[52, 53] Moreover, the fluctuating costs of raw materials like metals and chemicals add another layer of economic uncertainty, necessitating careful cost management and strategic sourcing to maintain profitability.[54]

In addition to regulatory and economic challenges, technological and workforce considerations play a pivotal role in the complexity of setting up an ammunition manufacturing facility. The adoption of advanced manufacturing technologies, including precision machining and automation, requires not only substantial investment in state-of-the-art equipment but also the availability of a skilled workforce capable of operating such technologies. However, India faces a shortage of skilled labour in specialised fields such as material science and explosives handling, particularly in remote areas where these facilities are often located. This shortage underscores the importance of investing in training and development to ensure the facility's operational success.[55, 56] Furthermore, maintaining a competitive edge in the global market necessitates ongoing research and development (R&D), which involves additional investment and strategic planning to balance innovation with production demands.[57]

Finally, political and strategic considerations are integral to the establishment of an ammunition manufacturing facility. India's defence procurement policies, outlined in the Defence Procurement Procedure (DPP), directly influence the demand for ammunition and, consequently, the viability of such manufacturing ventures. Understanding and aligning with these policies is crucial for long-term success. Additionally, regional security concerns in South Asia create a heightened sense of urgency for maintaining a robust and self-sufficient defence manufacturing sector, placing additional pressure on manufacturers to ensure continuous operations.[58, 59] While government initiatives like the Make in India campaign and the Defence Production and Export Promotion Policy (DPEPP) 2020 provide incentives and support, they also impose specific targets and obligations, further complicating the process.[60] In conclusion, the establishment of an ammunition manufacturing facility in India involves navigating a complex web of challenges that span regulatory, logistical, economic, technological, and political domains. Despite the significant opportunities for growth in this sector, particularly given India's strategic defence needs, the complexities involved necessitate careful planning, substantial investment, and a comprehensive understanding of the broader defence landscape.

Comparative Analysis of Ammunition Industries in the United Kingdom and India

The ammunition industries in the United Kingdom (UK) and India are pivotal to their respective defence sectors, serving as crucial components in ensuring national security, economic stability, and military readiness. Both countries have rich histories in defence production, but their trajectories, current capabilities, challenges, and future prospects exhibit notable differences due to their distinct geopolitical contexts, defence strategies, and industrial policies. This expanded analysis delves deeper into the historical evolution, key players, challenges, and opportunities facing the ammunition industries in the UK and India, providing a comprehensive comparison that highlights their unique strengths and areas for potential collaboration.

The UK's Ammunition Industry: A Legacy of Innovation and Adaptation

The UK's ammunition industry has a deep-rooted history that traces back to the British Empire when the nation was a global military superpower. During the 19th and early 20th centuries, the UK was a leader in producing military hardware, including ammunition, which was critical to the success of its military campaigns across the globe. The Royal Ordnance Factories, established in the early 20th century, became the backbone of the UK's ammunition production, especially during the World Wars. These factories played a crucial role in supplying the British military and its allies with vast quantities of ammunition, ranging from small arms cartridges to large-calibre artillery shells.

However, the post-World War II era marked a significant shift in the UK's defence production landscape. With the end of the British Empire and a reduction in global military engagements, the UK's need for large-scale ammunition production declined. This decline was further accelerated by the end of the Cold War, which led to substantial defence budget cuts and a re-evaluation of the UK's military strategy. Consequently, many Royal ordnance factories were either privatised or closed, and the industry transitioned towards producing specialised, high-tech munitions rather than focusing on mass production.[61] This shift reflected the broader trend of modernisation and specialisation in the UK's defence industry, where quality and technological sophistication began to take precedence over quantity.

Today, the UK's ammunition industry is characterised by advanced manufacturing capabilities and a focus on producing high-quality, specialised munitions that meet the demands of modern warfare. BAE Systems, one of the world's largest defence contractors, stands as the dominant player in this industry. BAE Systems' munitions division operates several state-of-the-art facilities across the UK, where it produces a wide range of munitions, including small arms ammunition, medium-calibre rounds, and large-calibre artillery shells. The company has made substantial investments in research and development (R&D) to maintain its competitive edge in the global market, ensuring that the UK remains at the forefront of ammunition production.

Another significant player in the UK's ammunition industry is the Chemring Group, which specialises in niche markets such as countermeasures, explosives, and pyrotechnics. Chemring's expertise in these areas makes it a crucial component of the UK's defence industrial base, particularly in providing solutions for improvised explosive device (IED) detection and disposal, which are critical in modern asymmetric warfare. In addition to BAE Systems and Chemring Group, the UK hosts several smaller companies and joint ventures that contribute to specific segments of the ammunition market, including Nammo, a Norwegian company with a significant presence in the UK, which specialises in small arms ammunition and rocket motors.[62]

Despite its strengths, the UK ammunition industry faces several significant challenges that threaten its long-term sustainability and growth. One of the primary challenges is the fluctuating demand for military ammunition, which is largely driven by changes in defence policy and military engagements. For instance, the UK's involvement in overseas conflicts, such as those in Afghanistan and Iraq, led to a temporary surge in demand for ammunition. However, the subsequent withdrawal from these theatres has resulted in a reduction in orders, creating instability within the industry.

Moreover, the UK ammunition industry is under increasing pressure from international competition. Countries like the USA, France, and Germany have well-established ammunition industries, with their companies benefiting from economies of scale that allow them to offer lower prices. This competition is particularly challenging for the UK, given its ongoing defence budget constraints, which force the Ministry of Defence (MoD) to seek cost-effective solutions, often favouring international suppliers over domestic production.

Brexit has also introduced new uncertainties for the UK's ammunition industry, particularly concerning trade regulations, tariffs, and supply chains. Many components and raw materials used in ammunition production are sourced from European Union (EU) countries, and any disruption to these supply chains could increase production costs and lead to delays. Additionally, the industry faces technological challenges as modern warfare continues to evolve. The development of advanced weapons systems, such as precision-guided munitions and autonomous weapons, requires new types of ammunition that are more complex and expensive to produce. To stay competitive, the UK ammunition industry must invest heavily in R&D to innovate and adapt to these emerging trends.[63]

Notwithstanding these challenges, the UK ammunition industry has several opportunities for growth and development. One of the most promising areas lies in the export market, where global demand for ammunition remains strong due to ongoing conflicts, rising defence budgets, and the modernisation of military forces in various countries. The UK has a well-established reputation for producing high-quality, reliable ammunition, making its products attractive to international buyers.

The UK government has recognised the importance of supporting the defence industry, including ammunition production, through strategic initiatives like the Defence and Security Industrial Strategy (DSIS), published in 2021. The DSIS outlines the government's commitment to maintain a robust and competitive defence sector, emphasising the need for collaboration between the government and industry. This includes investments in R&D, the development of new technologies, and support for exports, all of which are critical to ensure the UK's ammunition industry remains competitive on the global stage.

In addition to government support, advances in technology present new opportunities for the UK ammunition industry. The rise of digital manufacturing techniques, such as 3D printing and automation, offers the potential to reduce production costs and increase efficiency. These technologies also enable the production of more complex and customised ammunition, which is increasingly in demand as military forces around the world seek to enhance their capabilities with precision-guided and specialised munitions. Furthermore, the growing demand for environmentally friendly ammunition presents another area of opportunity. As concerns about the environmental impact of military activities grow, there is increasing interest in developing ammunition that is less harmful to the environment, such as lead-free bullets, biodegradable components, and munitions designed to reduce collateral damage. The UK, with its strong R&D capabilities, is well-positioned to lead in this emerging market.[64]

India's Ammunition Industry: A Journey towards Self-Reliance

India's ammunition industry has its roots in its colonial past, with the British establishing some of the earliest ordnance factories on the subcontinent to support the military needs of the British Empire. Following India's independence in 1947, the country inherited this industrial infrastructure and sought to expand and modernise it as part of its broader strategy to achieve self-reliance in defence production. The Cold War era was a period of significant growth for India's defence industry, driven by the need to secure the nation against external threats and reduce dependence on foreign suppliers. The Ministry of Defence's erstwhile Ordnance Factory Board (OFB) became the cornerstone of India's ammunition production, overseeing a network of state-owned factories that produced a wide range of munitions for the Indian armed forces. However, the erstwhile OFB has been criticised for inefficiencies, including delays in production, cost overruns, and quality control issues. These challenges have hindered India's efforts to fully achieve self-sufficiency in defence production, leading to growing concerns about the reliability and effectiveness of domestically produced ammunition.[65]

India's ammunition industry is significantly larger in scale than the UK's, reflecting the country's larger armed forces and ongoing security concerns, particularly with neighbouring countries like Pakistan and China. The erstwhile OFB has historically been the backbone of India's ammunition production, operating over 40 factories across the country. These factories produce a wide array of munitions, ranging from small arms ammunition to large-calibre artillery shells, and play a critical role in supplying the Indian military.

In recent years, the Indian government has undertaken significant reforms to address the inefficiencies within the OFB. In 2021, the OFB was corporatised, leading to the establishment of new entities like Advanced Weapons and Equipment India Limited (AWEIL). This move was part of a broader effort to improve the efficiency and competitiveness of India's defence industry by introducing private sector management practices and increasing accountability.[66]

In addition to these state-owned enterprises, India's defence sector has seen growing involvement from private companies, which are increasingly participating in ammunition production. Companies like Bharat Forge,

Reliance Defence, and Larsen & Toubro have entered the market, often in collaboration with foreign defence firms to enhance their technological capabilities and production capacity. These private players are expected to play a larger role in the future, particularly as the Indian government continues to encourage private sector participation through policy initiatives like the 'Atmanirbhar Bharat' (Self-Reliant India) initiative.[67]

Despite the progress made in recent years, India's ammunition industry continues to face several significant challenges. The legacy issues associated with the erstwhile OFB, including inefficiencies in production and quality control, remain a major concern. These challenges have been a key driver behind the corporatisation of the OFB and the push for greater private sector involvement, as the Indian government seeks to improve the reliability and effectiveness of its defence production.

Another major challenge for India's ammunition industry is its reliance on imports for certain advanced technologies and components. While India has made significant strides in increasing domestic production, it still depends on foreign suppliers for critical technologies, particularly in areas like precision-guided munitions and advanced artillery systems. This reliance on imports highlights the need for greater investment in domestic R&D to develop indigenous capabilities and reduce dependency on foreign suppliers.

India's ammunition industry also faces the challenge of scaling up private sector involvement to meet the growing demands of the Indian military. While the corporatisation of the OFB and policy initiatives like 'Atmanirbhar Bharat' have opened up opportunities for private companies, there are still barriers to entry, including bureaucratic red tape, regulatory challenges, and the need for significant capital investment. Additionally, India's geopolitical tensions with neighbouring countries, particularly Pakistan and China, place pressure on the industry to rapidly modernise and expand its capabilities to ensure the country's military readiness.[68]

The future of India's ammunition industry is closely tied to the country's broader defence modernisation efforts and its goal of achieving self-reliance in defence production. The Indian government's 'Atmanirbhar Bharat' initiative, which aims to reduce dependence on foreign suppliers and promote domestic manufacturing, is expected to drive significant growth in the defence sector, including ammunition production. The corporatisation of the OFB and increased private sector involvement are key elements of this strategy. These reforms are expected to address some of the inefficiencies and quality issues that have plagued India's ammunition industry in the past, making it more competitive and capable of meeting the demands of the Indian military. Furthermore, India's large and growing defence budget, coupled with its strategic partnerships with countries like the USA, Israel, and France, offers opportunities for technology transfer and joint ventures that could further enhance the capabilities of the domestic ammunition industry.[69]

India's focus on developing indigenous capabilities, particularly in areas like precision-guided munitions, advanced artillery systems, and environmentally friendly ammunition, is likely to drive further growth in the industry. Additionally, India's efforts to become a global defence exporter could see the country emerge as a significant player in the international ammunition market. The government's emphasis on promoting defence exports, coupled with the country's competitive labour costs and growing manufacturing capabilities, positions India to capitalise on the global demand for ammunition and other defence products.[70]

Comparative Analysis of Challenges and Opportunities

When comparing the ammunition industries of the UK and India, several key differences and similarities emerge, reflecting their unique historical contexts, current capabilities, and future trajectories. The UK's ammunition industry is characterised by its technological sophistication and focus on specialised, high-quality products. With a strong R&D infrastructure and significant government support, the UK has positioned itself as a leader in producing advanced munitions, such as precision-guided munitions and countermeasures. The UK's expertise in these niche markets has made it a key player in the global ammunition market, with a strong export focus.[71]

In contrast, India's ammunition industry is marked by its larger scale of production, driven by the needs of its vast armed forces and ongoing security concerns. While India is still working to overcome inefficiencies within its state-owned enterprises, the country has made significant progress in recent years, particularly with the corporatisation of the OFB and increased private sector involvement. India's focus on achieving self-reliance in defence production, coupled with its large defence budget, provides significant opportunities for growth and modernisation.[72]

Both the UK and Indian ammunition industries face significant challenges, but these challenges differ in nature. The UK is grappling with issues related to fluctuating demand, international competition, and the uncertainties introduced by Brexit. These challenges require the UK industry to remain agile, investing in R&D and adapting to changing global defence needs. The UK's ability to innovate and maintain its competitive edge in specialised markets will be critical to its future success.[73] India, on the other hand, faces challenges related to inefficiencies in production and quality control within its state-owned enterprises, as well as the need to scale up private sector involvement. However, India's government is actively addressing these challenges through reforms, such as the corporatisation of the OFB and the promotion of private sector participation. India's large defence budget and strategic partnerships also present significant opportunities for growth, particularly in developing indigenous capabilities and expanding its presence in the global defence market.[74]

Looking to the future, both the UK and Indian ammunition industries have the potential to strengthen their positions through strategic investments and partnerships. The UK's focus on high-tech, niche markets complements India's broader strategy of self-reliance and large-scale production. Collaboration between the two countries, particularly in areas like R&D, technology transfer, and joint ventures, could further enhance their respective capabilities and position them as key players in the global ammunition market. For instance, the UK's expertise in precision-guided munitions and advanced manufacturing techniques could provide valuable insights and technologies for India as it seeks to modernise its defence industry. Conversely, India's growing manufacturing capabilities and competitive labour costs could offer opportunities for UK companies to expand their production capacity and reduce costs. Such collaborations could also help address some of the challenges both industries face, such as the need for innovation and the pressures of international competition.[75]

The ammunition industries of the UK and India, though different in scale and focus, are both critical to their respective national defence strategies.

The UK's industry is characterised by advanced technology, specialisation, and a strong export market, while India's industry is marked by its scale, ongoing modernisation efforts, and focus on achieving self-reliance in defence production. Both countries face unique challenges and opportunities, and their ability to adapt to changing defence needs and capitalise on emerging markets will determine their future success.

As the global defence landscape continues to evolve, the UK and India will need to leverage their strengths, address their respective challenges, and explore opportunities for collaboration. By doing so, they can not only maintain but also enhance their positions in the international ammunition market, ensuring that they remain key players in the global defence industry for years to come.

Case Studies of Strategic Initiatives: Indigenous Defence Projects

India has made significant progress in developing indigenous defence projects to enhance its self-reliance in military capabilities. Important projects like the LCA Tejas, the Arjun main battle tank (MBT), and the *INS Vikrant* aircraft carrier showcase the country's growing prowess in defence technology and manufacturing. The sections below discuss in detail India's success stories in terms of these military capabilities:

LCA Tejas

The LCA Tejas is a single-engine, multi-role light fighter aircraft developed by the Aeronautical Development Agency (ADA) and manufactured by Hindustan Aeronautics Limited (HAL). The idea for this was conceived in the 1980s, and the Tejas program aimed to replace the aging MiG-21 aircraft of the Indian Air Force (IAF). The Tejas showcases advanced avionics, fly-by-wire control systems, and composite materials to reduce weight and enhance performance. It is designed for air superiority, ground attack, and reconnaissance missions. The aircraft is equipped with modern radar, electronic warfare systems, and a variety of air-to-air and air-to-ground munitions.

The IAF inducted the first squadron of Tejas—No. 45—known as the 'Flying Daggers' in 2016. The aircraft has since participated in several air exercises, demonstrating its capabilities. The Indian Navy is also considering a naval variant for its aircraft carriers. The Tejas program faced numerous delays and cost overruns. However, it marked a significant achievement in India's aerospace sector, demonstrating the ability to develop a state-of-the-art fighter aircraft indigenously. Continuous improvements and the development of the Tejas Mark 2 aim to address initial limitations and enhance performance.[76]

Arjun Main Battle Tank (MBT)

The Arjun MBT is designed and developed by the DRDO to provide superior firepower, protection, and mobility. The project began in the 1970s to replace older tanks and meet the Indian Army's requirements. The Arjun features a 120-mm rifled gun, advanced composite armour, and a hydro-pneumatic suspension system. It is equipped with a computerised fire control system, thermal imaging sights, and a laser rangefinder, enhancing its combat capabilities in various terrains and conditions. The Arjun entered service in 2004, and the Indian Army has inducted two regiments. The upgraded Arjun Mk.1A variant, with over 90 improvements, was cleared for induction in 2021. The Arjun faced delays and performance issues, including weight and maintenance concerns. Despite these challenges, the tank's successful deployment and ongoing upgrades highlight India's capability to develop advanced armoured vehicles. The project has also provided valuable experience for future tank development programs.

INS Vikrant

The *INS Vikrant*, India's first indigenous aircraft carrier, symbolises the nation's growing maritime capabilities. The project, executed by Cochin Shipyard Limited (CSL) under the guidance of the Indian Navy, aims to enhance India's blue-water naval operations. The Vikrant is a 40,000-ton carrier designed to operate a mix of fixed-wing aircraft and helicopters. It features a ski-jump for short take-off, arrestor wires for landing, and advanced radar and electronic warfare systems. The ship is powered by four gas turbines, providing a top speed of 28 knots. This project was launched in 2013 and commissioned in 2022. This aircraft carrier represents a significant milestone in India's naval history. It can carry up to 30 aircraft, including the MiG-29K fighters and various helicopters for anti-submarine warfare, reconnaissance, and search-and-rescue missions. Again, the Vikrant project faced multiple delays and cost escalations. Nevertheless, it stands as a testament to India's shipbuilding capabilities. The experience gained from building the Vikrant is expected to benefit future indigenous carrier projects, such as the proposed *INS Vishal.*[77]

International Collaborations and Joint Ventures

International collaborations and joint ventures (JVs) play a critical role in enhancing the capabilities of India's defence sector. These partnerships facilitate technology transfer, boost indigenous manufacturing, and help develop cutting-edge defence systems. Several successful collaborations have significantly advanced India's defence capabilities. International collaborations bring in advanced technology, expertise, and best practices, which are essential for the development of sophisticated defence systems. These partnerships help India bridge the technology gap and reduce dependency on imports. They also create opportunities for co-development and co-production, fostering self-reliance in defence manufacturing. One of the most successful international collaborations in India's defence sector is the BrahMos missile project. This joint venture between India's DRDO and Russia's NPO *Mashinostroyenia* (NPOM) has resulted in the development of the BrahMos supersonic cruise missile, which is considered the fastest operational system of its kind. Named after the Brahmaputra and Moskva rivers, this missile can be launched from land, sea, sub-sea, and air platforms with a range of approximately 290 kilometres and a top speed of Mach 3.[78] The missile is capable of carrying various types of warheads and is designed for precision strikes. Brahmos has been inducted in all the streams of the Indian armed forces, that is, Army, Navy, and Air Force. The project has not only helped in enhancing India's strike capabilities but also positioned India as a missile technology leader. The joint venture model adopted for the development of BrahMos has been lauded for its effectiveness in combining Russian missile technology with Indian production capabilities. There are plans to extend the range of the BrahMos missile and develop new variants, including hypersonic versions. The success of BrahMos has paved the way for further Indo-Russian defence collaborations.

Besides, India has entered into several joint ventures with leading foreign defence firms to strengthen its defence manufacturing base and acquire advanced technologies. Tata Advanced Systems Limited (TASL) and Lockheed

Martin have signed a joint venture agreement to produce components and structures for the C-130J Super Hercules transport aircraft and the S-92 helicopter. This collaboration has increased India's aerospace manufacturing capabilities as well as facilitated technology transfer. Similarly, Mahindra Defence Systems and Airbus Defence and Space have formed a joint venture to manufacture military helicopters in India. This partnership aspires to fulfil the requirements of the Indian armed forces and boost indigenous helicopter production capabilities. Kalyani Rafael Advanced Systems (KRAS) is a joint venture between Bharat Forge and Israel's Rafael Advanced Defence Systems. KRAS manufactures Spike anti-tank guided missiles (ATGMs) in India, significantly enhancing India's indigenous missile production capabilities.

India's defence procurement policies mandate foreign defence contractors to invest a certain percentage of the contract value in India, known as the offset policy. This policy has been instrumental in promoting joint ventures and technology transfer. For instance, the procurement of Rafale fighter jets from France's Dassault Aviation included significant offset obligations, leading to technology transfer and collaboration with Indian companies. Despite the success of various joint ventures, there are challenges such as bureaucratic red tape, regulatory hurdles, and delays in project execution. To maximise the benefits of international collaborations, India needs to streamline its regulatory framework, ensure timely project implementation, and enhance its industrial infrastructure. Streamlining approval processes and providing a more conducive environment for foreign investments can attract more international defence firms to collaborate with Indian entities. Investing in skill development and training programs is crucial to support advanced manufacturing and R&D activities. This can help India absorb and further develop the technologies acquired through collaborations. Strengthening the domestic R&D ecosystem is essential to build on the technologies transferred through international partnerships and develop indigenous innovations.

Impact on National Security and Economy

Self-reliance in defence manufacturing is a crucial aspect of national security for any country, and it is particularly significant for India. Given India's geopolitical landscape and the array of security challenges it faces, achieving self-sufficiency in defence production can profoundly enhance its national security. This analysis explores the various ways in which self-reliance in defence manufacturing bolsters India's security. One of the primary benefits of self-reliance in defence manufacturing is the reduction of dependence on foreign suppliers. Historically, India has relied heavily on imports for its defence needs, making it vulnerable to external pressures and supply chain disruptions. By developing indigenous capabilities, India can ensure a steady and uninterrupted supply of critical defence equipment. This independence is vital during times of conflict or diplomatic tensions, where foreign suppliers might be unwilling or unable to provide necessary support.

Self-reliance grants India greater strategic autonomy, allowing it to make independent defence and foreign policy decisions without being influenced by the policies of exporting nations.[79] This autonomy is crucial for maintaining sovereignty and responding effectively to security threats. Indigenous defence manufacturing enhances the operational readiness of the armed forces. Locally produced equipment can be tailored to meet specific operational requirements and environmental conditions, thereby improving efficiency and effectiveness. Additionally, the ability to quickly repair and maintain equipment without waiting for parts from abroad ensures that the military remains combat-ready at all times. Indigenous production allows for customisation and rapid adaptation of defence technologies to meet the unique needs of India's armed forces. This capability ensures that the equipment is more suitable for the specific operational theatres in which the Indian military operates.[80] Developing a robust defence manufacturing sector has significant economic benefits. It creates jobs, stimulates economic growth, and fosters technological advancements. The spill-over effects of defence R&D into civilian industries can lead to broader technological innovation and industrial development. Investing in defence manufacturing can stimulate economic growth by creating high-skilled jobs and fostering innovation. The development of advanced technologies in defence can also benefit other sectors, leading to overall economic progress.[81] A strong defence industrial base enhances national security by ensuring that the country has the necessary infrastructure and expertise to develop, produce, and maintain advanced defence systems. This capability reduces the risk of technological surprises from adversaries and ensures that the military is equipped with state-of-the-art technologies. A robust defence industrial base provides the infrastructure and expertise necessary to support the continuous development and production of advanced defence systems. This capability is essential for maintaining a technological edge over potential adversaries.[82]

India's defence sector has witnessed significant growth and modernisation in recent years, leading to a notable increase in its export potential and global market presence. It is further promoted by initiatives such as 'Make in India' and '*Atmanirbhar Bharat.*' This helps in highlighting India's role as a key player in the global defence market. India has developed a range of indigenous defence products, from small arms to advanced missile systems, which have significant export potential. Various indigenous defence projects, such as the BrahMos missile, LCA Tejas, and Arjun main battle tank (MBT), have demonstrated India's ability to produce high-quality defence equipment. Furthermore, the Indian government has implemented several policies to promote defence exports and enhance global market presence. The 'Make in India' initiative helps in boosting domestic manufacturing as well as reducing dependence on imports, thereby creating a surplus for exports. The government has also streamlined defence export procedures and provided financial incentives to private sector companies to engage in defence production and exports. MoD has also introduced the Defence Export Promotion Scheme, which provides financial assistance to defence companies for marketing their products abroad.[83] This scheme is designed to increase India's defence exports by supporting participation in international defence exhibitions and trade fairs. India has also entered into strategic partnerships with several countries to enhance defence cooperation and export opportunities. These collaborations not only facilitate technology transfer but also create joint ventures that can cater to global markets (MEA, 2022). For instance, the BrahMoS Aerospace joint venture with Russia has opened up several international markets for the BrahMos missile.

However, all this progress is not without challenges. These challenges include stringent international regulatory frameworks, competition from established global defence players, and the need for continuous technological innovation. Navigating the complex web of international arms trade regulations and export control regimes can be challenging for Indian defence. Ensuring compliance with these regulations requires robust export control mechanisms and a thorough understanding of international laws. Furthermore, the global defence market is highly competitive, with established players like the USA, Russia, and European countries dominating the market. Indian defence products must continuously innovate to meet the evolving needs of global customers and compete effectively on price, quality, and performance. To maintain and enhance its export potential, India must invest in cutting-edge research and development. Continuous innovation in defence technologies is essential to keep up with global trends and meet the sophisticated requirements of international buyers.[84] India's defence sector is poised for significant growth in the global market, driven by successful indigenous projects and supportive government policies. The export potential of defence products like the BrahMos missile, Tejas LCA, and Arjun MBT is considerable. However, realising this potential requires addressing regulatory challenges, competing effectively with established players, and investing in continuous technological innovation. With strategic efforts, India can strengthen its position as a key exporter in the global defence market. Table 2.1 highlights the growth in India's defence exports in the past four years, showcasing the increasing reach and influence of India's defence industry on the global stage.

Table 2.1: India's Defence Exports by Countries

(USD in Millions)

S. No.	*Country*	*2021*	*2022*	*2023*	*2024*
1.	Vietnam	30	35	40	45
2.	The Philippines	50	60	70	80
3.	The UAE	20	25	30	35
4.	Sri Lanka	10	15	20	25
5.	Mauritius	15	18	20	25
6.	Myanmar	5	7	10	12
7.	Israel	25	28	30	35
8.	USA	40	45	50	55
9.	South Korea	10	15	20	25
10.	Indonesia	20	25	30	35

Source: Data compiled through the Ministry of Defence, Government of India.[85]

Conclusion

Despite significant progress, the Indian defence sector faces challenges such as bureaucratic delays, inadequate infrastructure, and technological dependencies. However, opportunities abound with increasing defence budgets, modernisation plans, and international collaborations. The focus on indigenous innovation and the development of advanced technologies like artificial intelligence, cyber warfare, and unmanned systems will help in enhancing India's defence sector's future growth.[86] India's pursuit of self-reliance in defence manufacturing has both opportunities and challenges for its broader strategic objectives and defence policies. As India navigates through an increasingly complex global security environment, the motivation towards self-reliance in defence production is both a strategic necessity and an economic imperative.

Furthermore, self-reliance in defence manufacturing directly contributes to India's strategic autonomy. By reducing dependence on foreign suppliers, India can make more independent defence and foreign policy decisions, free from the influence of international arms suppliers and geopolitical pressures. This autonomy is critical for safeguarding national security, especially given the volatile security environment in South Asia and India's extended neighbourhood which is also characterised by persistent tensions. Moreover, the indigenous defence capabilities ensure a more secure and reliable supply of military equipment. This reliability is crucial during times of conflict when external suppliers might impose restrictions due to various reasons. Thus, enhancing indigenous manufacturing capabilities aligns with India's strategic objective of ensuring operational readiness and resilience in the face of potential threats. Also, the drive towards self-reliance in defence manufacturing has profound economic implications. The development of a robust defence industrial base can stimulate economic growth by creating high-skilled jobs and fostering innovation as well as investments in defence R&D can lead to technological advancements.

The Indian government's initiative of 'Make in India' and '*Atmanirbhar Bharat*,' underscore the importance of indigenous manufacturing not only for defence but for overall economic resilience. These initiatives aim to transform India into a global manufacturing hub, enhancing its economic security and reducing its trade deficits. Developing a strong defence industrial base involves enhancing the capabilities of PSUs like HAL and BEL, while also fostering the growth of private sector participation. Collaborations and joint ventures with foreign defence firms play a crucial role in this process by facilitating technology transfer and skill development. However, building a self-reliant defence industrial base is not without challenges. Issues such as bureaucratic inefficiencies, regulatory hurdles, and the need for continuous innovation must be addressed. Streamlining procurement processes, enhancing transparency, and investing in R&D are essential steps to overcome these challenges.

The path forward for achieving self-reliance in defence manufacturing involves a multi-faceted approach. Firstly, continued policy reforms are necessary to create a conducive environment for defence manufacturing. Simplifying regulatory processes, providing financial incentives, and fostering public-private partnerships are crucial measures. Secondly, significant investment in defence R&D is essential to develop cutting-edge technologies and reduce dependency on foreign technology. This includes enhancing the capabilities of research institutions like the DRDO and promoting innovation through start-ups and small enterprises. Thirdly, developing a skilled workforce is critical for sustaining and advancing indigenous manufacturing capabilities. This requires targeted education and training programs to equip individuals with the necessary technical skills. And fourthly, while the focus is on self-reliance, strategic international collaborations remain important. These collaborations can provide access to advanced technologies and best practices, which can be adapted and further developed domestically. India's journey towards self-reliance in defence manufacturing is a strategic imperative that aligns with its broader objectives of ensuring national security, achieving economic growth, and enhancing technological capabilities. The success of this endeavour will not only strengthen India's defence preparedness but also contribute to its stature as a major global power. By fostering a robust defence industrial base, India can ensure that it remains well-equipped to protect itself from any threat from within the neighbourhood or from within.

Chapter Three

Defence Exports: A Strategic Pathway to Self-Reliance

Introduction

India's defence export landscape has undergone significant transformation in recent years, reflecting the country's evolving strategic priorities and economic ambitions. Historically, India's defence sector was predominantly import-oriented, relying heavily on foreign suppliers to meet its defence requirements. However, in recent years, there has been a concerted effort to shift from being a major importer of defence equipment to becoming a significant exporter. This shift is crucial for various reasons. Firstly, defence exports are seen as a means to enhance India's strategic autonomy and reduce dependency on foreign suppliers. Secondly, they contribute to the national economy by generating revenue and creating jobs. Thirdly, they serve as a tool of diplomacy, strengthening bilateral ties with importing countries and enhancing India's global standing. The push for increasing defence exports is intrinsically linked to India's broader goal of achieving self-reliance in defence manufacturing, encapsulated in the 'Atmanirbhar Bharat' initiative launched by Prime Minister Narendra Modi. This initiative aims to transform India into a global manufacturing hub by boosting indigenous production capabilities, fostering innovation, and reducing the reliance on imports. In the defence sector, self-reliance is not merely about meeting domestic needs but also about positioning India as a key player in the global defence market. By exporting indigenously developed defence equipment, India aims to showcase its technological prowess and manufacturing capabilities, thereby attracting further investments and collaborations.

This chapter aims to provide a comprehensive analysis of India's defence export landscape by exploring its historical context, current trends, and future prospects. This chapter forms a critical component of the book, which examines the broader theme of India's strategic autonomy and economic growth through defence manufacturing and exports. By delving into the defence export landscape, this chapter highlights how India is leveraging its defence capabilities to achieve strategic and economic objectives. It also provides insights into the challenges and opportunities that lie ahead, offering a nuanced understanding of India's journey towards self-reliance in defence. The current trends and future prospects are analyzed using a mixed-methods approach, by analysing the primary and secondary sources thoroughly. India's journey towards becoming a defence exporter has been a gradual and evolving process. In the early years post-independence, India's defence sector was primarily focused on establishing a robust defence industrial base to meet domestic needs. The emphasis was on self-reliance through indigenous production, driven by the geopolitical imperatives of the Cold War era and the need to secure national borders. However, the limited technological capabilities and the lack of a comprehensive industrial policy meant that India remained heavily dependent on foreign suppliers.

The turning point came in the 1990s with the liberalisation of the Indian economy. The opening up of the economy and the subsequent integration into the global market provided new opportunities for the Indian defence sector. The establishment of the Defence Procurement Procedure (DPP) in 2002 marked the beginning of a structured approach towards defence procurement and exports. The DPP aimed to streamline procurement processes, encourage indigenous production, and promote exports. Further, the subsequent revisions of the DPP and the introduction of the Defence Production Policy in 2011 emphasised the importance of exports as a key component of India's defence strategy. In recent years, India's defence exports have witnessed significant growth. According to data from the Directorate-General for Foreign Trade (DGFT), defence exports have increased from approximately $ 213 million in 2015-16 to over $ 1.5 billion in 2020-21.[87] This growth has been driven by several factors, including policy reforms, the emergence of private sector players, and increased international collaborations.

The 'Make in India' initiative has played a pivotal role in promoting defence manufacturing and exports. India's defence exports go to 84 countries and regions around the world. Major export items include helicopters, radars, patrol vessels, and various types of ammunition and firearms components.[88] The export of advanced systems like the BrahMos supersonic cruise missile and the Akash surface-to-air missile system has further underscored India's growing capabilities in defence manufacturing.

The Indian government has undertaken several policy initiatives to boost defence exports. The Defence Export Strategy, unveiled in 2014, set an ambitious target of achieving almost $ 5 billion in annual defence exports by 2025.[89] The strategy outlined various measures to enhance export capabilities, including the establishment of a defence export steering committee, streamlining export procedures, and providing financial incentives for exporters.

The introduction of the Defence Production and Export Promotion Policy (DPEPP) in 2020 further reinforced the government's commitment to promoting defence exports. The DPEPP aimed to create an ecosystem conducive to defence production and exports by fostering innovation, enhancing production capabilities, and encouraging private sector participation. The policy also emphasises the importance of research and development, technology transfer, and international collaborations. Looking ahead, the future of India's defence exports appears promising.[90] However, several challenges need to be addressed to sustain and enhance this growth. These include the need for greater technological advancements, addressing regulatory bottlenecks, and enhancing marketing and promotion efforts. The government and industry need to work collaboratively to overcome these challenges and capitalise on emerging opportunities. India's defence export landscape is undergoing a dynamic transformation. The shift from being a major importer to an emerging exporter reflects the country's strategic and economic aspirations. By promoting defence exports, India aims to enhance its strategic autonomy, boost its economy, and strengthen its global standing. The journey towards self-reliance in defence manufacturing is fraught with challenges, but with the right policies, strategies, and collaborations, India is well-positioned to achieve its goals and emerge as a key player in the global defence market.

Historical Context of India's Defence Exports

In the years following independence in 1947, India's defence policy was primarily focused on self-reliance and building a robust defence industrial base.[91] However, India's technological capabilities were limited, and the defence sector was heavily reliant on foreign imports to meet its requirements. During this period, defence exports were minimal and largely incidental. The initial foray into defence exports can be traced back to the 1960s and 1970s when India began exporting small arms and ammunition to friendly countries.[92] The exports were modest and aimed at fostering diplomatic relationships rather than achieving significant economic gains. The key policy framework during this time was the establishment of state-owned defence enterprises such as Hindustan Aeronautics Limited (HAL) and Bharat Electronics Limited (BEL), which played a crucial role in developing indigenous capabilities.

Significant milestones in India's defence export history (Table 3.1) include the export of the *INS Vikrant* aircraft carrier's systems to Sri Lanka in the 1970s and the sale of indigenously developed equipment such as the Dornier Do 228 aircraft and various naval vessels in the subsequent decades.[93] The 1990s saw the formulation of more structured export policies, culminating in the Defence Procurement Procedure (DPP) in 2002, which laid the groundwork for a more comprehensive approach to defence exports.

Table 3.1: Key Milestones in India's Defence Exports

Year	*Milestone*	*Description*
1960s	Initial Exports	Small arms and ammunition to friendly countries
1970s	*INS Vikrant* Systems to Sri Lanka	Export of aircraft carrier systems
1980s	Dornier Do 228 Aircraft	Export of indigenously developed aircraft
2002	Introduction of Defence Procurement Procedure	Formalised approach to defence exports

During the Cold War era, India's defence exports remained relatively limited due to several factors, including its focus on self-reliance and the geopolitical complexities of those times. India's defence industry was in its nascent stages, and the emphasis was largely on meeting domestic needs rather than exporting arms. Nonetheless, there were instances of defence exports, primarily to friendly nations within the Non-Aligned Movement (NAM).

Exports during this period included small arms, ammunition, and basic military equipment, often intended as gestures of solidarity and support rather than for significant economic benefit. India's non-alignment policy played a critical role in shaping its defence export strategy during the Cold War. As a founding member of the NAM, India sought to maintain autonomy and avoid entanglement in the US-Soviet rivalry. This stance influenced its defence export activities, focusing on fostering diplomatic ties with other non-aligned and developing countries. Despite its non-aligned status, India did forge strategic alliances that impacted its defence sector. For instance, substantial military cooperation with the Soviet Union facilitated the transfer of technology and the development of indigenous defence capabilities, indirectly aiding its limited export activities.

The end of the Cold War marked a significant shift in India's defence export policies. With the disintegration of the Soviet Union and the consequent reduction in military aid, India was compelled to re-evaluate its defence strategies. This period saw the liberalisation of the Indian economy, which included reforms in the defence sector aimed at boosting self-reliance and promoting exports. The 1991 economic reforms under Prime Minister P.V. Narasimha Rao and Finance Minister Manmohan Singh played a pivotal role in opening up the defence sector to private players and foreign investments.[94] The establishment of the DPP in 2002 formalised the approach to defence procurement and exports, emphasising transparency, efficiency, and self-reliance.

In the post-Cold War period, India's strategic priorities shifted towards integrating with the global economy and enhancing its defence capabilities through indigenous production.[95] The global market dynamics also evolved, with increasing demand for advanced defence technologies. India recognised the potential of defence exports as a means to strengthen strategic ties and economic interests. Major initiatives such as the Defence Production Policy (DPrP) of 2011 and the 'Make in India' campaign launched in 2014 aimed to transform India into a global manufacturing hub and boost defence exports. The focus areas included developing advanced systems like missiles, aircraft, and naval vessels, with strategic partnerships and joint ventures playing a crucial role in this transformation.

Evolution of Policy Framework

India's journey towards becoming a significant player in the global defence export market has been marked by several key policy reforms and initiatives. The early years post-independence saw a focus on self-reliance, but it wasn't until the late 20th and early 21st centuries that substantial efforts were made to develop a structured defence export strategy. The Defence Export Strategy of 2002[96] marked a pivotal moment in India's defence policy. This strategy was introduced as part of the broader DPP 2002, which aimed to streamline defence procurement processes and promote indigenous production. The strategy emphasised the need for India to shift from being a major importer of defence equipment to an exporter. Important elements of this strategy included the identification of potential markets, the development of exportable products, and the establishment of a supportive institutional framework. The strategy highlighted the significance of leveraging India's technological advancements and production capabilities to penetrate global markets. It also called for enhanced coordination between various stakeholders, including government agencies, defence public sector undertakings (DPSUs), and private industry players. The goal was to create a favourable environment for defence exports by addressing policy, regulatory, and logistical challenges.[97]

The DPrP was first introduced in 2011 to provide a clear roadmap for enhancing indigenous defence production capabilities. It aimed to achieve substantive self-reliance in the design, development, and production of defence equipment. One of the key objectives was to promote exports by developing a competitive and export-oriented defence industrial base. Subsequent updates to the DPrP have further refined and expanded its scope. For instance, the Defence Production and Export Promotion Policy (DPEPP) 2020 was introduced to give a renewed push to defence exports. The DPEPP 2020 set an ambitious target of achieving \$ 5 billion in annual defence exports by 2025.[98] It outlined specific measures to boost exports, including simplifying export procedures, providing financial incentives, and establishing a dedicated export promotion body.

In recent years, the Indian government has undertaken several policy reforms to enhance defence exports. These reforms are part of the broader 'Make in India' initiative, which aims to transform India into a global manufacturing hub. Mentioned below are the major reforms introduced by the Government of India:

1. **Simplification of Export Procedures**: The government has streamlined export procedures to reduce bureaucratic hurdles and facilitate quicker approvals. This includes the introduction of an online portal for export applications and approvals.
2. **Financial Incentives**: Various financial incentives have been introduced to encourage defence exports. These include tax exemptions, subsidies, and export credit facilities.
3. **Strategic Partnerships**: The government has promoted strategic partnerships and joint ventures with foreign companies to enhance technological capabilities and market access. This includes initiatives such as the Strategic Partnership (SP) model, which encourages collaboration between Indian and foreign defence companies.
4. **Focus on MSMEs**: The government has recognised the potential of micro, small, and medium enterprises (MSMEs) in the defence sector. Various schemes and programs have been launched to support MSMEs in developing exportable products and accessing global markets.

India's early export policies and subsequent reforms have laid a strong foundation for the country's emergence as a significant player in the global defence export market. Major policy initiatives such as the Defence Export Strategy of 2002, the DPrP, and the recent DPEPP of 2020 have provided strategic direction and support for defence exports. Institutional mechanisms, including the Ministry of Defence (MoD), DRDO, and export promotion bodies, play a crucial role in facilitating and promoting defence exports. With continued focus on innovation, technology transfer, and strategic partnerships, India is well-positioned to achieve its defence export targets and strengthen its position in the global defence market.[99]

Current Trends in India's Defence Ammunition Exports

India has significantly enhanced its defence manufacturing capabilities, resulting in the export of a diverse range of ammunition products. The country's defence exports now encompass small arms ammunition, artillery shells, rockets, and other ordnance, which have found buyers across different regions globally. India exports various calibres of small arms ammunition, which are widely used by military and law enforcement agencies worldwide.[100] The Ordnance Factory Board (OFB), now under the newly corporatised entities, is a major producer of small arms ammunition.

1. **Artillery Shells and Rockets**: India's export portfolio includes artillery shells of different calibres, such as 105-mm, 155-mm, and other types. The export of Pinaka multi-barrel rocket launcher systems to countries like Armenia has marked a significant achievement in the artillery segment. In 2020, India secured a deal to export the Pinaka multi-barrel rocket launcher system to Armenia. This deal, valued at approximately $ 40 million, includes not just the rockets but also associated systems, highlighting India's capability in producing and exporting advanced artillery systems.
2. **Ammunition Exports to UAE**: The export of ammunition to the United Arab Emirates (UAE), including various types of small arms and artillery ammunition, underscores India's expanding footprint in the Middle Eastern defence market. These exports are part of broader defence cooperation agreements aimed at strengthening bilateral ties.

India's defence exports have found a market in various regions, with significant sales in Southeast Asia, Africa, and West Asia. The strategic and geopolitical dynamics of these regions make them important destinations for Indian defence products. Southeast Asia is a key region for India's defence exports. Countries such as Vietnam, Myanmar, and the Philippines have procured Indian defence products, driven by their need to modernise their military capabilities and enhance regional security.[101] India and Vietnam have strengthened their defence cooperation, with Vietnam procuring various defence systems, including naval vessels and missile systems.[102] This cooperation is part of India's Act East Policy, which aims to enhance ties with Southeast Asian nations. The Philippines' purchase of BrahMos missiles in 2022 is a landmark deal, underscoring the deepening defence ties between the two countries. This deal, valued at around $ 375 million, marks India's entry into the Southeast Asian defence market.[103] African nations have been significant recipients of Indian defence exports. India's defence cooperation with Africa is often part of broader diplomatic and economic engagement strategies.[104] Mauritius[105] and Seychelles have procured patrol vessels and other defence equipment from India,[106] enhancing their maritime security capabilities. These exports are part of India's broader strategy to secure the Indian Ocean region. India has exported various military supplies to Mozambique to support its internal security operations and strengthen bilateral ties.[107] West Asia presents a lucrative market for Indian defence exports. The region's demand for advanced military technology and India's growing capabilities creates opportunities for substantial export growth. The UAE has been a major buyer of Indian defence products, including small arms ammunition and artillery shells.[108] These exports are part of broader defence cooperation agreements aimed at enhancing strategic ties between the two countries. Saudi Arabia has shown interest in procuring Indian defence equipment, including surveillance systems and ammunition, as part of its efforts to diversify its defence suppliers and strengthen its military capabilities.[109] The strategic partnerships and defence agreements are crucial for bolstering India's defence exports. These partnerships often involve technology transfer, joint ventures, and collaborative research and development.

- **India-Russia Defence Cooperation**: The longstanding defence cooperation between India and Russia has facilitated the development and export of advanced systems like the BrahMos missile. This partnership exemplifies successful technology transfer and joint production efforts.[110]
- **Indo-French Collaboration**: India's collaboration with France, particularly with Dassault Aviation for the Rafale fighter jets, has potential spill-over benefits for defence exports. The transfer of technology and expertise through such partnerships enhances India's capabilities to produce exportable defence products.[111]
- **Quad Cooperation**: The Quadrilateral Security Dialogue (Quad) comprising India, the USA, Japan, and Australia, fosters defence cooperation in the Indo-Pacific region. While not directly focused on exports, the enhanced defence collaboration within the Quad framework strengthens India's strategic position and indirectly supports its export ambitions.[112]

India's defence exports have shown a notable increase from 2020 to 2024, driven by strategic initiatives and enhanced production capabilities. According to data from the Directorate-General of Foreign Trade (DGFT), India's defence exports grew from $ 1.2 billion in 2020 to approximately $ 2.63 billion in FY 2023-24. The growth of 32.5 per cent from the past year in defence exports has a significant economic push for India.[113] Firstly, defence exports contribute to the diversification of India's export portfolio, reducing reliance on traditional sectors like IT services and textiles. Secondly, defence exports generate substantial revenue, contributing to the national GDP. For instance, the increase from $ 1.2 billion in 2020 to $ 2.5 billion in 2024 represents a substantial inflow of foreign exchange, bolstering the country's economic stability.[114] Furthermore, defence exports drive industrial growth and create high-skill job opportunities. The development and production of advanced defence systems require a skilled workforce, promoting job creation in sectors like engineering, research and development, and manufacturing. Additionally, defence exports stimulate technological advancements and innovation, as companies invest in R&D to meet global standards and customer requirements. Moreover, defence exports strengthen India's geopolitical influence and strategic partnerships. By exporting defence equipment to various countries, India enhances its diplomatic relations and builds strategic alliances. This, in turn, supports India's broader foreign policy objectives and strengthens its position on the global stage.

India's defence export landscape has evolved significantly over the past few years, driven by strategic initiatives, technological advancements, and robust policy support. The export of key defence products such as missiles, aircraft, naval vessels, and ammunition has opened new markets and strengthened India's position in the global defence arena. The country's defence exports have found buyers in Southeast Asia, Africa, and the Middle East, with strategic partnerships and defence agreements playing a crucial role in facilitating these exports. The analytical data from 2020 to 2024 (Table 3.2) underscores the impressive growth in India's defence exports, which have doubled in value over this period. This growth has had a substantial economic impact, contributing to national GDP, creating high-skill jobs, and promoting technological innovation. Furthermore, defence exports have bolstered India's geopolitical influence and strategic alliances, supporting its broader foreign policy objectives. As India continues to enhance its defence manufacturing capabilities and pursue strategic partnerships, the future of its defence exports looks promising. Continued focus on innovation, quality, and strategic engagement will be key to sustaining and further accelerating this growth.

Table 3.2: India's Defence Exports

FY	*Value of Defence Exports (Rs in crores)*	*Year on Year (YOY) Increase*
2016-17	1,521	—
2017-18	4,682	208%
2018-19	10,745	129%
2019-20	9,115	–15%
2020-21	8,434	–7%
2021-22	12,814	52%
2022-23	15,920	24%
2023-24	21,083	32.5%

Source: Author's Collated Data.

The highest defence exports have so far been achieved in FY 2023-24, with a YOY increase of 32.5 per cent. Looking at the trends, India's total defence exports during the period 2014-15 to 2023-24 amount to Rs. 88,319 crore as compared to Rs. 4,312 crore over the previous decade.[115] This is a 21-times increase between two successive decades, suggesting an accelerated positive trend. The resolve to further build on this trend is evident from the goal of defence production now set at Rs. 3,00,000 crore and defence exports pitched at Rs. 50,000 crore annually, by 2028-29.[116]

Policy Framework for Promoting Defence Resilience

India's pursuit of self-reliance in defence has been shaped by the experiences of wars it has encountered since independence. Following the Chinese aggression in 1962, the Department of Defence Production (DDP) was established to cultivate a self-reliant and self-sufficient indigenous defence production base. This department focuses on matters related to defence production and the indigenisation of imported stores, equipment, and spares. However, it was the Kargil conflict in 1999 that brought to light the Indian Army's inadequacy in conventional warfare in high altitude and extreme climate conditions. In response, a committee of 'Group of Ministers on National Security' was formed shortly after the war. This committee, in its report submitted to the Prime Minister on 26 February 2001, recommended the establishment of a separate and dedicated institutional structure to handle the complete spectrum of procurement functions. The objective was to inject a higher level of professionalism and reduce delays in the acquisition process. Consequently, following the acceptance of the report, a new acquisition set-up was instituted within the Ministry of Defence (MoD) in October 2001.[117]

In the pursuit of achieving self-reliance in defence, the government established a committee in 2004 under Mr. Vijay Kelkar's leadership. One of its main objectives was to examine and recommend strategies for integrating the user, Ministry of Defence (MoD), and Indian industry (both private and public) in the acquisition process and defence production.[118] This committee submitted its report in two parts, the first part in April 2005, which primarily focused on defence procurement procedures and proposed various measures to promote indigenous production. While certain recommendations from the Kelkar committee, such as the creation of a 15-year equipment acquisition plan and the introduction of offsets in defence purchases, were accepted, many others were not. Notably, the crucial recommendation for accrediting and nurturing Raksha Udyog Ratnas, or industrial 'jewels', in the private sector to undertake significant defence manufacturing projects and joint ventures, was shelved. The second part of the report, submitted later in the same year, advocated greater autonomy for India's nine defence public sector undertakings (DPSUs) to form joint ventures and consortiums with overseas original equipment manufacturers, aimed at enhancing their efficiency.[119] Additionally, the committee recommended the corporatisation of the Ordnance Factory Board, a proposal that had previously been suggested by the T.K.A. Nair committee in 2000. This recommendation was reiterated by subsequent committees, including the Vice Admiral Raman Puri (retd.) committee in 2015 and the Lieutenant General D.B. Shekatkar (retd.) committee. However, it wasn't until 2021 that this recommendation was finally implemented.[120]

The Kelkar Committee made a significant recommendation concerning projects involving indigenous development under the 'Make' procedure, which was subsequently incorporated into the Defence Procurement Procedure (DPP) of 2006. This recommendation aimed to focus the Defence Research and Development Organisation (DRDO) solely on projects requiring sophisticated technology of strategic, complex, and security-sensitive nature. However, it wasn't until 2014 with the launch of the 'Make in India' initiative that the government aimed to incentivise both indigenous and foreign companies to invest in manufacturing in India, making it an attractive destination for capital and technological investments.

To align the Defence Procurement Procedure (DPP) with the objectives of 'Make in India,' the Ministry of Defence (MoD) constituted an expert committee under Dhirendra Singh in May 2015. This committee emphasised the integration of the private sector, advocating for two well-defined partnership models depending on strategic needs, quality criticality, and cost competitiveness. One such model suggested was the 'Strategic Partnership' to create capacity in the private sector for platforms of strategic importance, supplementing the capacity and infrastructure existing in the public sector. The recommendations of the expert committee led to the promulgation of DPP-2016, effective from 1 April 2016. This procedure adopted a three-pronged approach to support the 'Make in India' initiative, including institutionalisation, streamlining, and simplification of the procedure to promote indigenous design, development, and manufacturing of defence equipment. Notably, it introduced a new category called 'Buy (Indian-IDDM)' with overriding preference, followed by 'Buy (Indian)' and 'Buy & Make (Indian)' categories. Furthermore, DPP-2016 streamlined the 'Make' procedure, aiming at developing long-term indigenous defence capabilities. Under the revised 'Make' procedure, projects are categorised into 'Make-I' and 'Make-II,' with government funding of 90 per cent for 'Make-I' projects and no government funding for 'Make-II' projects. Additionally, to support Micro, Small, and Medium Enterprises (MSMEs), preference is given to them for 'Make-1' and 'Make-2' projects costing less than Rs. 10 crore and Rs. 3 crore, respectively, for prototype development.[121]

In the face of evolving security threats, geopolitical uncertainties, and economic vulnerabilities, establishing a robust policy framework is imperative to promote defence resilience and cultivate self-reliance in ammunition manufacturing. This framework should encompass a comprehensive array of policies and initiatives aimed at bolstering indigenous capabilities, enhancing competitiveness, and safeguarding national security interests. Central to this framework is the need for a clear strategic vision and national security objectives that take into account the changing threat landscape, geopolitical dynamics, and technological advancements. A cohesive and forward-looking strategy forms the bedrock upon which specific policies and initiatives can be devised and executed. One crucial aspect of this framework is investment in research and development (R&D) to drive innovation and technological progress. Governments should allocate resources towards R&D endeavours focused on developing cutting-edge technologies, refining manufacturing processes, and addressing technological gaps in ammunition production. Public-private partnerships, along with collaboration with academia and research institutions, can further harness expertise and resources to accelerate innovation in the defence sector. Promoting the growth of indigenous manufacturing capabilities is paramount for reducing reliance on foreign suppliers and bolstering defence resilience. Policymakers can incentivise domestic production through measures such as tax incentives, subsidies, and preferential procurement policies. Moreover, fostering collaboration between defence industries and small and medium-sized enterprises (SMEs) can spur innovation, generate employment opportunities, and fortify the domestic defence industrial base. By embracing these strategies, nations can strengthen their defence posture and enhance their ability to address emerging security challenges effectively.

Export promotion is instrumental in bolstering defence resilience through market diversification, revenue generation, and technological exchange. Governments can facilitate defence exports by leveraging trade agreements, export financing mechanisms, and diplomatic efforts to ease market access and overcome trade barriers. International cooperation and collaboration with strategic partners further enhance interoperability, knowledge sharing, and technology transfer, thereby strengthening defence capabilities. Efficient regulatory frameworks and procurement processes are essential for promoting transparency and accountability in defence acquisitions. Policy reforms aimed at simplifying bureaucratic procedures, reducing red tape, and accelerating decision-making can improve efficiency and effectiveness. Embracing best practices like competitive bidding and performance-based contracting fosters innovation and ensures value for money in defence acquisitions. Investing in human capital development is crucial for building a skilled workforce to support defence resilience efforts. Policymakers can promote education and training programs tailored to the defence industry's needs, including specialised training in manufacturing, quality assurance, and cyber security. Creating incentives for talent retention and career advancement within the defence sector addresses skill shortages and strengthens workforce resilience. In an increasingly digitised world, cyber security and protection of critical infrastructure are paramount for defence resilience. Governments must prioritise cyber security initiatives to safeguard defence networks, systems, and data from cyber threats. Additionally, investing in resilience measures for critical infrastructure, such as manufacturing facilities and supply chains, ensures continuity of operations in the face of cyber attacks or other disruptions. By implementing a coherent and proactive policy framework addressing these areas, governments can enhance defence resilience, promote self-reliance in ammunition manufacturing, and safeguard national security interests in a complex and uncertain global landscape.

Analysis of Defence Equipment Export Trends

Understanding the dynamics of defence equipment export and import trends is crucial for devising effective policies and strategies to promote self-reliance and resilience in ammunition manufacturing. Analysing data on export and import volumes, trends, and patterns offers valuable insights into market dynamics, competitive landscapes, and growth opportunities. In this section, we conduct a comprehensive analysis of defence equipment export and import trends, supported by statistics and tables. To grasp the export-import trends in arms and ammunition, it is imperative to examine the leading exporters and importers of major arms, as well as their primary recipients during the period 2019-2023.[122]

Table 3.3: Leading exporters and importers of major arms, as well as their primary recipients during the period 2019-2023

Exporter	*Share of global arms exports (%)*		*Main recipients and their share of exporter's total exports (%) 2019-2023*					
	2019-23	*2014-18*	*1st*		*2nd*		*3rd*	
USA	42	34	Saudi Arabia	15	Japan	9.5	Qatar	8.2
France	11	7.2	India	29	Qatar	17	Egypt	6.4
Russia	11	21	India	34	China	21	Egypt	7.5
China	5.8	5.9	Pakistan	61	Bangladesh	11	Thailand	6.0
Germany	5.6	6.3	Egypt	20	Ukraine	12	Israel	12

Source: SIPRI Fact Sheet 2024. Compiled by the Author[123]

In Table 3.3 India does not find a place in the top 25 largest exporters of major arms. The table highlights the dominance of the USA in the global arms exports market, with a share ranging from 34 per cent in the 2014-2018 period to 42 per cent in the 2019-2023 period. Russia also maintains a significant share, although it experienced a decline from 21 per cent to 11 per cent between the two periods which can be attributed to its active involvement with Ukraine. Furthermore, the table identifies the main recipients of arms exports from each major exporting country and their respective shares of the exporter's total exports. Notably, Saudi Arabia emerges as a primary recipient of arms exports from the USA, accounting for 15 per cent of its total exports between 2019 and 2023. India appears as a significant recipient for both France and Russia, with shares of 29 per cent and 34 per cent, respectively, in the same period. Pakistan is highlighted as a major recipient of arms exports from China, constituting a substantial 61 per cent of its total exports. Additionally, Egypt, Qatar, and Israel feature prominently as recipients of arms exports from multiple exporting countries, indicating their significance in the global arms trade network. Comparing the two periods, there are notable shifts in the main recipients of arms exports for some exporting countries. For instance, while Saudi Arabia remains a primary recipient of US arms exports, India's share of French arms exports increased significantly from 7.2 per cent in 2014-2018 to 29 per cent in 2019-2023. Similarly, China's arms exports to Pakistan saw a substantial increase from 5.9 per cent to 61 per cent between the two periods, indicating evolving dynamics in arms trade relationships. India's increasing imports from Russia and France signify efforts to diversify defence procurement and enhance military capabilities. However, the concentration of arms exports to regions characterised by conflict and instability raises concerns about arms proliferation and exacerbating regional tensions.

Table 3.4: Comparing the leading exporters and importers of major arms, as well as their primary recipients during the period 2019-2023

Importer	*Share of global arms imports (%)*		*Main recipients and their share of importer's total imports (%) 2019-2023*					
	2019-23	*2014-18*	*1st*		*2nd*		*3rd*	
India	9.8	9.1	Russia	36	France	33	USA	13
Saudi Arabia	8.4	11	USA	75	France	7.6	Spain	7.0
Qatar	7.6	1.5	USA	45	France	25	Italy	15
Ukraine	4.9	0.1	USA	39	Germany	14	Poland	13
Pakistan	4.3	2.9	China	82	Sweden	4.0	Türkiye	3.8

Source: SIPRI Fact Sheet 2024. Compiled by the Author[124]

The provided data presents an analysis of trends in global arms imports, focusing on the share of global arms imports by various countries and their main suppliers. India has consistently ranked among the top importers of arms globally, with a share of around 9.8 per cent during 2019-2023, showing a slight increase from the previous period (2014-2018). Despite efforts towards indigenous defence production and self-reliance, India's dependence on imports for its defence requirements remains substantial. Russia emerges as India's primary arms supplier, accounting for a significant portion (36 per cent) of India's total arms imports during 2019-2023. This dependency on Russia has historical roots dating back to the Cold War era and continues due to ongoing defence contracts and technology partnerships. France and the USA also play crucial roles in supplying arms to India, with France being the second-largest supplier (33 per cent) and the USA ranking third (13 per cent). This diversification in suppliers is strategic, providing India with options and leveraging different technological strengths.

Other notable importers of arms include Saudi Arabia, Qatar, Ukraine, and Pakistan each with varying degrees of dependence on foreign arms. Saudi Arabia's arms imports have shown a slight decrease during 2019-2023 compared to the previous period, but it remains a significant importer, relying heavily on the USA for its defence needs (75%). Qatar has witnessed a substantial increase in arms imports during 2019-2023, with the USA being its primary supplier (45%). This trend could be attributed to Qatar's efforts to modernise its military capabilities. Ukraine has experienced a remarkable surge in arms imports during the specified period, which can be attributed to its conflict with Russia. The USA and Germany are key suppliers to Ukraine. Pakistan's arms imports have slightly decreased, with China being its dominant supplier (82%), followed by Sweden and Turkey.

India's heavy reliance on arms imports poses several challenges and considerations, including vulnerabilities in the supply chain, geopolitical dependencies, and limitations on technology transfer and customisation. Diversifying suppliers is a strategic move by India to mitigate risks associated with over-reliance on a single country. However, achieving complete self-sufficiency in defence production remains a long-term goal. For other importers like Saudi Arabia, Qatar, Ukraine, and Pakistan, the choice of suppliers reflects geopolitical alliances, technological requirements, and economic factors. The dominance of the USA and Western European countries as major arms exporters underscores their strategic influence in global defence markets and international relations.

India's dependence on defence imports has been a longstanding reality, yet recent years have witnessed a noteworthy increase in its defence exports, despite not ranking among the top 25 largest arms exporters globally. Over the past five years, India has demonstrated its capabilities by exporting a range of defence equipment, including weapon simulators, tear gas launchers, torpedo loading mechanisms, alarm monitoring and control systems, night vision devices, lightweight torpedoes, armoured protection vehicles, weapon locating radars, HF radios, and coastal surveillance radars.[125] These exports underscore India's growing prowess in defence manufacturing and technological expertise. By diversifying its defence portfolio and tapping into international markets, India not only bolsters its economic growth but also strengthens bilateral defence ties with partner nations. Moreover, India's defence exports highlight its commitment to self-reliance in defence production and its willingness to engage in global defence cooperation, marking a significant step forward in its defence industrial capabilities.

Table 3.5: Export Performance

Years	*Export Value (Rs. in crores)*
2014-2015	1,941
2015-2016	2,059
2016-2017	1,522
2017-2018	4,682
2018-2019	10,746
2019-2020	9,116
2020-2021	8,435
2021-2022	12,815
2022-23 (till 21 Feb, 2023)	11,085

Source: Ministry of Defence, India, Annual Report 2022-23. Compiled by the Author[126]

Figure 3.1: Graphical Representation of Export Performance

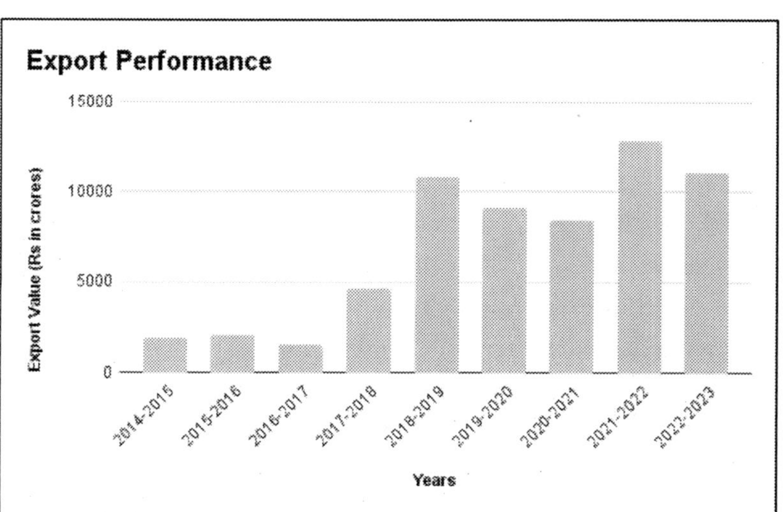

The details of export performance from 2014 onwards are tabulated according to the data provided by the Ministry of Defence in its Annual Report 2022-2023. The table delineating the export-import profile of the Indian defence industry spanning from 2014-2015 to 2022-2023 reveals a discernible upward trend in defence exports over the specified period, with notable fluctuations observed from year to year. Total exports have demonstrated more than a twofold increase from the initial recorded figures in 2014-2015 to the latest data available in 2022-2023. While certain years exhibit substantial growth in exports, such as the periods from 2016-2017 to 2017-2018 and from 2019-2020 to 2020-2021, there are also instances of decline, notably from 2018-2019 to 2019-2020. This observed fluctuation in export figures underscores the influence of the pandemic which led to fluctuations in international demand for Indian defence products, geopolitical dynamics, and shifts in domestic industry capabilities and competitiveness. The significant growth witnessed in recent years, particularly from 2019-2020 onwards, suggests the potential successful implementation of policies or initiatives aimed at bolstering defence exports during this period. Nonetheless, sustained monitoring and strategic planning are imperative to navigate the nuances of the defence export landscape and foster continued growth and resilience in the Indian defence industry.

Role of Defence Exports in Fostering Self-Reliance

Defence exports play a vital role in fostering self-reliance in defence capabilities, as evidenced by several key factors. Firstly, exporting defence equipment allows a nation to showcase its indigenous manufacturing capabilities and technological expertise, which are essential for bolstering domestic defence industries. According to a report by the Stockholm International Peace Research Institute (SIPRI) in 2020, countries like India have increasingly diversified their defence exports, demonstrating their competence in producing a wide range of defence products.[127] This diversification not only showcases the country's capabilities but also helps in building confidence in the domestic defence industry.

Secondly, defence exports contribute to economies of scale, leading to cost efficiencies and increased competitiveness in the global market. The *Defence News* Top 100 list for 2020 highlights how defence exports enable countries to benefit from larger production runs, leading to reduced unit costs per item. This reduction in production costs makes domestically manufactured defence equipment more attractive, both domestically and internationally, thereby further strengthening the country's defence industrial base.

Furthermore, revenue generated from defence exports can be reinvested into domestic defence research, development, and procurement programs. A study published in the *Journal of Strategic Studies* in 2018 underscores how defence exports can contribute to the funding of domestic defence initiatives, thereby reducing dependency on external sources.[128] This reinvestment not only enhances technological innovation and capability development but also ensures a more sustainable defence industrial base over the long term.

In conclusion, defence exports serve as a critical component of a comprehensive strategy towards achieving self-reliance in defence capabilities. By showcasing indigenous manufacturing prowess, driving cost efficiencies, and generating revenue for domestic defence programs, defence exports contribute significantly to strengthening a country's national security and reducing dependency on imports. Singh[129] delineates three pivotal factors propelling the expansion and diversification of India's defence exports. Firstly, the bolstering of domestic defence manufacturing, notably through initiatives like the Defence Acquisition Procedure 2020[130] and positive indigenisation lists, emerges as a cornerstone. These frameworks prioritise indigenous defence industry development, thereby enhancing domestic manufacturing capabilities and subsequently fuelling export growth. Secondly, the adoption of liberalised licensing and certification procedures marks a significant shift. This shift empowers both private and public manufacturers to select export markets independently, moving away from previous government-directed approaches. Nonetheless, government clearances remain imperative to ensure adherence to regulatory standards. Lastly, the adoption of a whole-of-government approach stands out as another critical enabler. By integrating the Ministry of External Affairs (MEA), India has expanded its defence export framework, fostered diplomatic efforts and facilitated initiatives such as providing lines of credit to African nations seeking military procurement from India. This integrated strategy underscores India's commitment to leveraging its domestic manufacturing prowess and diplomatic channels to realise its defence export ambitions.[131]

Furthermore, it is essential to address the challenges faced by the public sector, which has been the primary beneficiary of India's drive for self-sufficiency in arms production and research. Despite its extensive infrastructure and workforce, the public sector has not performed up to expectations, contributing to India's continuing arms import dependency. Inefficiencies, such as poor indigenisation, inadequate innovation, and suboptimal management of human resources, underscore the need for improvement. The entry of the private sector, particularly into research and development, is gradually challenging the public sector's monopoly, demonstrating competence in obtaining orders and advancing technology. While the government must demand strict accountability from the public sector, given its size, experience, and expertise, India must ensure that it plays a more meaningful role. Ultimately, by fostering collaboration between the public and private sectors, India can navigate towards a more self-reliant and resilient defence industry, safeguarding national interests and reducing import dependency.

Technological Innovations and Investments

One of the first aims of India as a nation since Independence has been to achieve self-reliance in the field of defence and defence production. Technological innovations and investments are critical drivers of self-reliance and competitiveness in the defence manufacturing sector. By investing in R&D, fostering innovation, and harnessing cutting-edge technologies, nations can enhance their indigenous manufacturing capabilities, develop high-quality defence products, and compete effectively in the global defence market.

Deep tech in defence is of paramount importance today, as militaries recognise its potential to revolutionise strategic and tactical capabilities. Technologies such as automated logistics using robotics and drone swarms, AI-assisted projection and planning, and augmented soldiers via brain-machine interfaces have the power to transform operations both on and off the battlefield. This aligns seamlessly with the goal of 'Atmanirbharta' (self-reliance) highlighted in the defence budget, aiming to reduce dependency on imports. Encouraging emerging start-ups to develop solutions in areas like AI-powered satellite analytics, automated logistics drones, and secure quantum communications systems can address specific military challenges and problem statements, driving innovation and self-sufficiency in defence technology.

A recent example of this is the launch of the Acing Development of Innovative Technologies with iDEX (ADITI) scheme at DefConnect 2024 and the corpus fund of Rs. 750 crore for three years beginning from FY 2023-

24 to develop about 30 deep-tech critical and strategic technologies in a proposed timeframe for capability enhancement of the tri-services and the Defence Space Agency. The Ministry has also enhanced the funding from Rs. 10 crore to Rs. 25 crore for start-ups for research, innovation and development of defence technologies. The aim of ADITI under iDEX is to create a 'technology watch tool' to bridge the gap between the expectations and requirements of the modern armed forces and the capabilities of the defence innovation ecosystem. To motivate young innovators, iDEX was expanded to iDEX Prime, with the assistance increasing from Rs. 1.5 crore to Rs. 10 crore. The 11th edition of the Defence India Start-up Challenge (DISC) was also launched at the event, rolling out a new chapter in the collaboration between the defence establishment and the start-up ecosystem. The DISC 11 introduces 22 problem statements—Indian Army (4), Indian Navy (5), Indian Air Force (5), Armoured Vehicles Nigam Ltd. (7) and Hindustan Shipyard Ltd. (1)—aimed at addressing critical defence challenges, inviting innovators to propose innovative solutions that can enhance the country's defence capabilities and contribute to national security.[132]

Investing in defence technology in India presents lucrative opportunities for both domestic and international investors. With a steady rise in defence spending, reaching approximately $ 73.65 billion for the 2021-22 budget, the government's commitment to modernise its armed forces and enhance defence capabilities is evident. The 'Make in India' initiative further stimulates domestic defence production, fostering innovation and self-reliance while providing access to a vast market. India's strategic geographical location amid volatile regions underscores its significance in maintaining regional stability and safeguarding national interests, contributing to its crucial role in the Indian Ocean region and beyond. Investing in Indian defence technology enables investors to tap into a dynamic ecosystem, leveraging the country's technological expertise to develop innovative solutions with applications across civilian and military domains. Moreover, the stability of defence spending amidst economic uncertainties makes it an attractive investment avenue, bolstered by India's substantial consumer base for defence technologies, including surveillance systems, communication equipment, and cyber security solutions.[133]

Challenges and Opportunities

Indian defence companies have made notable strides in the global market, driven by several competitive advantages. One of the primary advantages Indian defence companies have over their global counterparts is cost-effectiveness. The relatively lower cost of labour and manufacturing in India allows companies to produce high-quality defence equipment at competitive prices. This cost advantage makes Indian defence products attractive to developing countries and nations with limited defence budgets. India's emphasis on self-reliance has led to significant investments in research and development (R&D). Organisations like the Defence Research and Development Organisation (DRDO) and state-owned enterprises have developed indigenous technologies such as the BrahMos missile, Tejas fighter jet, and Pinaka rocket system. These home-grown innovations not only reduce dependency on foreign technology but also position Indian products as unique offerings in the global market. India's strategic location and its role as a key player in the Indo-Pacific region enhance its attractiveness as a defence partner. Countries seeking to balance regional power dynamics often turn to India for defence collaborations, thus boosting Indian exports.

Despite these advantages, Indian defence companies face several challenges that hinder their competitiveness. While India has made significant progress in defence technology, it still lags behind global leaders like the USA, Russia, and Western European countries in terms of advanced technology and capabilities. High-end technology areas such as stealth, artificial intelligence, and advanced avionics are sectors where Indian companies need to catch up. India's export infrastructure, including logistics and supply chain management, is still developing.[134] Compared to established exporters like the USA and Europe, Indian defence companies face challenges in ensuring timely delivery and support services for their products abroad. Indian defence products often suffer from limited international visibility and marketing. Established exporters have strong branding and marketing networks that help them secure large contracts. Indian companies, on the other hand, need to invest more in global marketing efforts and building brand recognition.

One of the significant hurdles faced by Indian defence exporters is the complex and time-consuming approval process. Multiple clearances are required from various ministries and regulatory bodies, which can delay the export of defence products. India has stringent export control regulations to ensure that defence products do not fall into the wrong hands. While these regulations are crucial for national security, they can also act as barriers to legitimate exports, requiring extensive documentation and compliance. Furthermore, the coordination between different government agencies involved in the defence export process is often lacking. This can lead to inefficiencies and delays, impacting the overall export performance of Indian defence companies. The Indian government has taken steps to simplify export procedures. The introduction of an online portal for export applications has streamlined the process, reducing the time required for approvals and enhancing transparency. The establishment of the Defence Export Promotion Council (DEPC) and the Export Promotion Cell within the Department of Defence Production has provided a single point of contact for exporters. These bodies facilitate smoother interactions between the industry and government, addressing export-related issues promptly. To encourage exports, the government has introduced various financial incentives, including tax exemptions, subsidies, and export credit facilities. These measures help reduce the financial burden on exporters and make Indian defence products more competitive globally.

As mentioned in the above sections, Southeast Asia remains a crucial market for Indian defence exports due to its geopolitical importance and the increasing defence needs of countries in the region. Nations like Vietnam, the Philippines, and Indonesia are looking to modernise their military capabilities, presenting significant opportunities for Indian defence products. Africa is another promising market for Indian defence exports. The demand for military equipment in Africa is driven by the need for internal security and counter-terrorism operations. Indian products, known for their cost-effectiveness and reliability, are well-suited to the requirements of African nations. West Asia with its high defence spending, offers substantial opportunities for Indian defence exports. Countries like the UAE, Saudi Arabia, and Oman have shown interest in Indian defence products, especially in the areas of small arms, ammunition, and naval systems. With the increasing importance of cyber security and electronic warfare in modern military operations, Indian companies can leverage their expertise in IT and software development to offer advanced solutions in these areas. Developing and exporting cyber security products and electronic warfare systems can open new avenues for growth. The global demand for UAVs is on the rise, and Indian companies are investing in the development of indigenous drones. By focusing on this sector, India can cater to both military and civilian markets worldwide, enhancing its export portfolio. The integration of artificial intelligence (AI) and robotics in defence applications is a growing trend. Indian companies can capitalise on their strong IT sector to develop AI-driven defence solutions, positioning themselves as leaders in this emerging field. Innovation and technology are critical to maintaining and enhancing export competitiveness. Indian defence companies are increasingly investing in R&D to develop cutting-edge technologies and products that meet international standards. For instance, the DRDO's efforts in developing advanced missile systems and HAL's work on next-generation fighter jets demonstrate the focus on innovation.[135]

Strategic collaborations and joint ventures with global defence giants can significantly enhance India's technological capabilities. Partnerships with countries like Israel, the USA, and France have facilitated technology transfer and co-development of advanced systems, boosting the competitiveness of Indian products in the global market. The adoption of emerging technologies such as AI, machine learning, and Big Data analytics in defence applications can provide Indian companies with a competitive edge. By integrating these technologies into their products, Indian defence manufacturers can offer sophisticated solutions that address the evolving needs of modern militaries. Ensuring high quality and adherence to international standards is essential for export success. Indian defence companies are increasingly focusing on quality control and certification processes to meet the stringent requirements of global markets. This focus on quality enhances the credibility and reliability of Indian defence products. The Indian government's support through various policies and incentives plays a crucial role in fostering innovation and technology development. Initiatives like the 'Make in India' campaign and the Defence Production and Export Promotion Policy (DPEPP) 2020 provide a conducive environment for innovation, encouraging companies to invest in advanced technologies.

While Indian defence companies benefit from cost-effectiveness, indigenous innovation, and strategic geopolitical positioning, they face hurdles related to technological gaps, export infrastructure, and limited marketing. The Indian government has taken significant steps to streamline export processes and support defence exporters through financial incentives, simplification of procedures, and establishment of export promotion bodies. Emerging markets and potential areas for expansion, such as cyber security, UAVs, and AI-driven solutions, offer substantial opportunities for Indian defence companies. Innovation and technology will continue to play a crucial role in enhancing export competitiveness, with a focus on R&D, strategic collaborations, and adoption of emerging technologies. As India continues to enhance its defence manufacturing capabilities and pursue strategic partnerships, the future of its defence exports looks promising. Continued focus on innovation, quality, and strategic engagement will be key to sustaining and further accelerating this growth.

Strategic Implications for Self-Reliance

Becoming a significant defence exporter brings numerous strategic benefits to India, influencing its defence diplomacy and geopolitical standing. Defence exports are a powerful tool for strengthening diplomatic relations. Countries importing defence equipment from India are likely to develop closer strategic and military ties with it. These relationships can lead to enhanced cooperation in areas such as intelligence-sharing, joint exercises, and coordinated responses to regional security challenges. For instance, the export of BrahMos missiles to the Philippines not only marks a commercial success but also signifies a deepening defence partnership between the two countries, which could have broader implications for regional security dynamics in Southeast Asia. As a significant defence exporter, India can leverage its defence products to enhance its geopolitical influence. By supplying advanced defence equipment to various countries, India positions itself as a key player in global security architecture. This influence can be particularly crucial in strategically important regions such as the Indian Ocean Region (IOR) and Southeast Asia, where India aims to counterbalance the growing influence of other major powers like China. Defence exports can also help India counter regional threats by strengthening the military capabilities of friendly countries. For instance, supplying advanced defence systems to countries facing security challenges from adversaries aligned against Indian interests can indirectly enhance India's security. This strategy of building a network of well-equipped allies serves as a force multiplier for India's defence posture.

In addition to strategic and diplomatic benefits, defence exports provide economic leverage. Countries dependent on Indian defence supplies may be more inclined to support India's positions in international forums or trade negotiations. This economic leverage can be a valuable tool in pursuing broader national interests beyond the defence sector. By becoming a prominent defence exporter, India reinforces its position as a regional leader. The ability to produce and supply advanced military equipment showcases India's technological capabilities and its commitment to regional security. This leadership role is crucial in the context of India's aspirations to be a net security provider in the IOR and beyond. Successful defence exports enhance India's credibility and reliability as a defence partner, thereby consolidating its leadership position. Defence exports contribute to India's strategic autonomy by reducing dependence on foreign defence suppliers. A robust export-oriented defence industry ensures that India can meet its defence needs internally while also supporting allied nations. This autonomy is vital for maintaining independent foreign and defence policies, free from external pressures and influences.

India's growing stature as a defence exporter facilitates its engagement in multilateral defence forums and initiatives. Participation in international defence exhibitions, such as Defence Expo and Aero India, not only boosts exports but also enhances India's visibility and influence in global defence circles. Additionally, India's role in initiatives like the Quadrilateral Security Dialogue (Quad) is bolstered by its capability to contribute to the defence needs of member-countries through exports. Supplying defence equipment to countries involved in or affected by conflicts can also increase India's influence in those regions. By providing necessary defence support, India can shape the outcome of conflicts in a manner that aligns with its strategic interests. This influence can extend to post-conflict reconstruction efforts, in which India can play a crucial role in rebuilding defence infrastructure and capabilities. Defence exports facilitate the formation of strategic partnerships with other countries. These partnerships often involve joint research and development, co-production, and technology transfer agreements, which can significantly enhance India's defence capabilities. For example, the collaboration with Russia on the BrahMos missile project has not only resulted in a successful export product but has also strengthened the strategic partnership between the two nations.

Enhancing domestic manufacturing capabilities in India's defence sector and achieving success in defence exports are mutually reinforcing goals. The synergy between these objectives lies in building a robust industrial base, fostering innovation, and reaping economic benefits, all of which contribute to India's strategic autonomy and economic growth. As a significant defence exporter, India gains numerous strategic benefits, including strengthened diplomatic ties, enhanced geopolitical influence, and increased economic leverage. These benefits play a crucial role in India's defence diplomacy and its aspirations to be a regional leader and a net security provider. The implications for India's defence diplomacy and geopolitical influence are profound. Successful defence exports reinforce India's regional leadership, contribute to its strategic autonomy, facilitate multilateral engagements, and enhance its influence in conflict zones. Moreover, the strategic partnerships formed through defence exports further bolster India's defence capabilities and its standing on the global stage. The integration of self-reliance initiatives with export success strategies is pivotal for India's defence sector. By continuing to invest in domestic manufacturing, fostering innovation, and leveraging defence exports, India can achieve its goals of strategic autonomy, economic growth, and enhanced global influence.

Conclusion

India's defence export landscape has evolved significantly over the decades, reflecting changes in domestic policies, technological advancements, and shifting geopolitical dynamics. The historical context reveals a journey from heavy dependence on imports to a concerted push towards self-reliance and export-oriented growth. The current trends indicate a more structured and ambitious approach to becoming a significant player in the global defence market. In the early years post independence, India's defence sector was primarily focused on achieving self-reliance through the establishment of state-owned enterprises and the development of indigenous production capabilities. Despite these efforts, technological limitations and a lack of comprehensive policies hindered significant progress in defence exports. The Cold War era saw minimal export activities, primarily as diplomatic gestures to friendly nations, influenced by India's non-alignment policy which aimed to maintain strategic autonomy amidst superpower rivalry. The post-Cold War period marked a shift with economic liberalisation in the 1990s, which opened new avenues for defence exports. Policy reforms such as the Defence Procurement Procedure (DPP) 2002, and later the Defence Production Policy (DPrP) 2011, laid the groundwork for a more focused approach towards defence manufacturing and exports. The Defence Production and Export Promotion Policy (DPEPP) 2020 further reinforced these efforts with clear targets and supportive measures.

India's enhanced defence export capabilities align with its broader strategic objectives of achieving strategic autonomy and asserting its geopolitical influence. By reducing dependency on foreign suppliers and building a robust domestic defence industrial base, India strengthens its strategic autonomy. The ability to export advanced defence equipment not only generates economic benefits but also bolsters India's diplomatic and military standing. Defence exports serve as a powerful tool for strengthening diplomatic relations and enhancing regional leadership. By supplying defence equipment to various countries, India can forge stronger military and strategic ties. These relationships are crucial for collaborative security efforts, intelligence sharing, and coordinated responses to regional threats. For instance, defence exports to Southeast Asian countries support India's Act East Policy, aimed at countering China's influence in the region.

The economic implications of a thriving defence export sector are substantial. Defence exports contribute to national revenue, support job creation, and stimulate technological innovation. A vibrant defence industrial base also attracts foreign investments and encourages the development of ancillary industries. The focus on high-tech defence manufacturing can lead to spill-over benefits for other sectors, driving overall industrial growth and economic development. For sustained growth in defence exports, continued policy support and reforms are essential. The government needs to ensure that the regulatory framework remains conducive for exports, with streamlined procedures and robust support mechanisms. Financial incentives, export credit facilities, and marketing support should be enhanced to make Indian defence products more competitive globally. Investment in R&D and the adoption of emerging technologies are critical for maintaining a competitive edge. Indian defence companies must focus on developing cutting-edge technologies such as artificial intelligence, cyber security, and unmanned systems. Strategic partnerships and joint ventures with global defence giants can facilitate technology transfer and co-development of advanced systems, further boosting India's export capabilities.

Identifying and penetrating new markets is vital for the growth of defence exports. India should leverage its diplomatic channels and participate actively in international defence exhibitions to showcase its capabilities. Focused efforts on regions like Latin America, Eastern Europe, and Africa, where there is potential demand for cost-effective and reliable defence equipment, can open new avenues for exports. Improving export infrastructure, including logistics and supply chain management, is essential for timely delivery and after-sales support. Establishing dedicated export hubs and leveraging digital technologies for efficient supply chain management can enhance the overall export experience and build trust with international customers. Maintaining high quality items and adherence to international standards is crucial for establishing credibility in the global market. Indian defence companies should focus on quality assurance, certification processes, and customer satisfaction to ensure that their products meet the stringent requirements of international buyers.

India's defence export landscape has come a long way from its early years of post-independence to becoming a significant player in the global defence market. The synergy between self-reliance initiatives and export success is evident, with policy reforms, technological advancements, and strategic partnerships driving this transformation. The economic, strategic, and diplomatic benefits of being a significant defence exporter are substantial, enhancing India's global standing and contributing to its broader strategic objectives. As India continues on this path, the focus should be on sustaining policy support, fostering innovation, expanding market reach, and maintaining high-quality standards. By doing so, India can not only achieve its goals of self-reliance and economic growth but also reinforce its position as a key player in the global defence landscape, contributing to regional and global security.

Chapter Four

Advancing Ammunition Tech: Pathways to Self-Reliance in Indian Defence Production

Introduction

The ammunition sector in India has undergone significant transformation over the past decade, driven by the country's strategic push towards self-reliance and indigenisation in defence manufacturing. India's defence manufacturing market, including ammunition, is poised for growth due to increasing defence budgets, government initiatives, and geopolitical tensions. At present, the ammunition manufacturing market in India was valued at INR 883.06 billion in FY 2022, which is higher than the INR 788.20 billion in FY 2018. It reflects a compound annual growth rate (CAGR) of approximately 2.88 per cent.[136] This growth is attributed to increased defence spending due to ongoing disputes with China and Pakistan which necessitates robust defence preparedness. This chapter aims to understand the feasibility of self-reliance in terms of the Indian defence sector including the ammunition industry.

The Indian government has launched several initiatives to boost domestic production under its 'Make in India' initiative to encourage domestic manufacturing with the aim of reducing dependency on foreign imports. It includes policies such as increasing the foreign direct investment (FDI) limit in the defence sector and establishing defence corridors in various parts of India.[137] Furthermore, the involvement of the private sector is crucial for the defence sector's development. Companies like Adani Defence & Aerospace have set up large-scale ammunition and missile manufacturing complexes. All of these efforts align with India's ambition to become a global defence manufacturing hub.[138] It is pertinent to mention here that technological innovation is a cornerstone of India's ammunition sector growth. Collaborations between public sector undertakings (PSUs) and academic institutions are developing advanced technologies like smart ammunition. As, for instance, the development of the 155-mm smart ammunition is a significant step towards enhancing the precision and lethality of India's artillery capabilities.[139]

To indigenise production and technological development in the defence sector, DRDO and other PSUs remain at the frontline for developing indigenous capabilities focussing on producing a wide range of ammunition domestically such as small arms, large calibre artillery shells, etc., to achieve self-reliance and sustainability in defence supplies.[140] At the same time, it should be noted that despite these advancements, India remains one of the largest importers of military equipment globally. According to SIPRI, India was the world's second-largest importer of major weapons between 2016 and 2020. This heavy reliance on imports underscores the need for accelerated indigenisation and capacity building within the domestic industry.[141] Added to this are the geopolitical tensions with China and Pakistan that drive New Delhi's demand for advanced ammunition and defence technologies. The need for a technologically advanced arsenal has never been greater, and this has led to increased government and private sector investments in the ammunition sector also.[142]

India's public defence sector, marked by its complex history and strategic importance, plays a pivotal role in the nation's security and technological advancement. The development of India's defence sector can be traced back to the post-independence era and has undergone significant transformations over the decades. Historically, in the post-independence period, India inherited a defence infrastructure primarily designed for policing and internal security. The geopolitical realities of the region, marked by partition and subsequent conflicts with neighbouring countries, necessitated the development of a robust defence manufacturing capability. The India-China war of 1962 and the India-Pakistan wars of 1947, 1965, and 1971 further exposed the vulnerabilities in India's defence preparedness, emphasising the need for self-reliance in defence production.

In response to the above-mentioned security challenges, the Indian government established several defence public sector undertakings (DPSUs) under the aegis of the Ministry of Defence. These included giants like Hindustan Aeronautics Limited (HAL), established in 1940; Bharat Electronics Limited (BEL), set up in 1954; and Bharat Dynamics Limited (BDL), founded in 1970. These DPSUs were tasked with the production of a wide range of defence equipment, from aircraft and electronics to missiles and naval ships. In correspondence to DPSUs, the network of Indian ordnance factories, some of which date back to the 18th century, was expanded and modernised. This network was administered by the Ordnance Factory Board and played a crucial role in providing the armed forces with diverse products including firearms, ammunition, and protective gear. Another important aspect of India's defence production is the ordnance factories. In this respect, Behera[143] has studied the performance of the Indian ordnance factories and found that they had their roots in the pre-colonial period when these factories were engaged in minimal low-end defence production. The management of these ordnance factories in India is categorised in three parts. The first level is the apex level, managed by the Department of Defence Production, which comes under the Ministry of Defence. The secondary level is controlled by the Ordnance Factory Board, headed by a chairman and nine other board members. The manager or the assistant manager runs the third level. The government has set up multiple committees to provide solutions for the deficiencies that existed in the operation of these ordnance factories with restricted growth. Regarding pricing, since these factories work on a 'no-profit, no loss' basis, the prices are based on the actual cost incurred, and the army claims that these products are overpriced.

The government has also accepted in Parliament that the ordnance factories produce low-quality products with certain deficiencies. The export performance of these factories is also minimal, with only 0.6 per cent of the total sales value being exported. The problem with the ordnance factories is that their autonomy is limited, preventing them from becoming an independent, efficient production centre. Though the factories produce numerous products for the armed forces, these products are insufficient, and thus, the government needs to spend endlessly on the import of arms and weapons. As explained by Neihsial,[144] the culture of outsourcing and vendor development in the ordnance factories has found that these factories are not efficient. The outsourcing process has many barriers like government intervention and lack of independence in deciding the production process. Similarly, the vendor development process, though given to the ordnance factories and the DPSUs in 2005, still follows the traditional method of vendor development. The ordnance factories are still capable of increasing capacity utilisation and reducing their costs, thus reducing prices that are very high due to inefficient production methods.

However, the policy of indigenisation has been the cornerstone of India's defence strategy since the 1960s. The aim was to reduce dependence on imports and build domestic capabilities in terms of defence production. This policy was given a structured framework in the 1990s through the Defence Procurement Procedure (DPP), which prioritised domestic manufacturing under various categories. There are significant programs that were initiated under this framework which include the Tejas Light Combat Aircraft (LCA) and the Arihant-class nuclear submarines. This also helped in showcasing India's growing proficiency in developing sophisticated technology for its armed forces. At the same time, these advancements in the Indian defence sector faced several challenges which included bureaucratic delays, budget constraints, and issues with quality control and technological obsolescence. Furthermore, the issues related to corruption and inefficiency in DPSUs have also been points of concern, leading to calls for greater transparency and efficiency.

To overcome technological gaps and modernise its forces, India has also engaged in strategic partnerships and collaborations with foreign countries. This includes significant deals such as the purchase of Rafale jets from France and the S-400 missile defence system from Russia. Such acquisitions are complemented by technology transfer agreements to boost domestic production capabilities. The Defence Research and Development Organisation (DRDO) plays a crucial role in the R&D of defence technologies. Established in 1958, DRDO has been involved in major projects including the development of the Agni and Prithvi missiles, and more recently, the Advanced Towed Artillery Gun System (ATAGS). The defence sector significantly impacts the Indian economy, contributing to job creation, technological advancements, and infrastructure development. It also fosters a wide range of ancillary industries, from materials and electronics to software and services.

The sections below discuss in detail India's public defence sector highlighting its rich history and strategic imperatives. It remains central to the country's national security objectives. While it has achieved substantial growth and technological advancement, continuous efforts in reform, innovation, and strategic alignment with global technologies are essential to maintain and enhance its defence capabilities. This overview draws upon the rich tapestry of India's defence sector's development, highlighting key historical milestones, challenges, and the ongoing efforts to achieve self-reliance and technological prowess in defence production.

Role of DRDO in India's Defence Production Scenario

The Defence Research and Development Organisation (DRDO) plays a pivotal role in India's defence manufacturing landscape, supporting the nation's aim for self-reliance in defence capabilities. Established in 1958, the DRDO's mission has been to provide the Indian military with cutting-edge technologies and solutions, reducing dependence on foreign imports and enhancing national security. This literature review explores the multifaceted contributions of DRDO to India's defence manufacturing sector, assessing its impact on technology development, collaborations, and economic implications.

The DRDO was created by amalgamating the Technical Development Establishment and the Defence Science Organisation, with the primary goal of developing indigenous defence technologies. Since its inception, it has grown into a network of more than 50 laboratories, which specialise in varied domains of defence technology including aeronautics, armaments, electronics, combat vehicles, engineering systems, and naval systems. DRDO's contributions to India's defence are most evident in its success with missile technologies and the Integrated Guided Missile Development Programme (IGMDP). Launched in 1983, the IGMDP led to the development of several key missile systems including Agni, Prithvi, Akash, Nag, and the BrahMos, the latter being a joint venture with Russia. These missile systems represent significant advancements in propulsion technologies, guidance systems, and payload delivery mechanisms, significantly boosting India's strategic deterrence capabilities.[145]

Another notable contribution is the development of the Light Combat Aircraft (LCA)-Tejas. Designed to replace the aging fleet of Indian Air Force fighter jets, Tejas showcases DRDO's capabilities in aerospace engineering and avionics. Despite facing criticism for delays and cost overruns, Tejas has marked a milestone in India's pursuit of developing an indigenous advanced fighter jet.[146] DRDO's role extends beyond mere technology development; it has substantial economic implications. By focusing on indigenous development, DRDO supports the Indian government's 'Make in India' initiative, which aims to boost the domestic manufacturing sector. This not only reduces the heavy reliance on imported military hardware but also stimulates domestic industries, creating employment and building technical expertise within the country.[147] Collaborations have been a cornerstone of the DRDO's strategy. Its partnerships with academic institutions, private sector entities, and international defence organisations enhance its technological capabilities and innovation. For instance, the collaboration with Russia on the BrahMos missile and with Israel on various defence technologies underscores the importance of international partnerships in achieving advanced technological capabilities.

Moreover, DRDO actively engages with the Indian private sector and academia to foster innovation. Initiatives like the Technology Development Fund aim to fund research and development in defence technologies, encouraging start-ups and small enterprises to contribute to defence technology advancements.[148] Despite its successes, DRDO has faced its share of challenges and criticisms. Issues such as project delays, budget overruns, and management inefficiencies have been major concerns. Critics argue that for DRDO to be more effective, there must be greater accountability and transparency in project management. Moreover, some projects have faced technical hurdles that delayed their deployment, affecting the overall strategic preparedness of the armed forces.[149]

The future of the DRDO looks towards embracing new technologies such as artificial intelligence (AI), robotics, and cyber warfare. With the global defence landscape rapidly evolving, DRDO's strategic focus is also shifting towards developing technologies that can provide a competitive edge in modern warfare. Additionally, DRDO aims to improve its efficiency by adopting better project management practices and enhancing collaborations with other global defence technology leaders. DRDO remains a key player in India's defence sector, crucial for the country's aim to achieve self-reliance in defence manufacturing. Its contributions have not only enhanced military capabilities but also stimulated economic growth and technological advancement within the country. However, continuous improvement in efficiency and adaptability to new technological trends is essential for maintaining its relevance and effectiveness. Future research could explore the potential impacts of emerging technologies on DRDO's strategic direction and operational capabilities, providing insights into how it can continue to support India's defence imperatives in an increasingly complex global environment. This literature review synthesises various sources and research studies, highlighting DRDO's integral role in shaping India's defence manufacturing capabilities, the challenges it faces, and the path forward in leveraging technology for national security.

Academic Contributions to Technological Advancements in India's Defence Sector

The role of academia is becoming instrumental in terms of technological advancements in defence sectors regarding pioneering developments in the domains of artificial intelligence, drone technology, cyber security, and advanced materials. By collaborating with defence agencies and industries, academic researchers translate theoretical knowledge into practical solutions that address specific challenges faced by the military and defence forces. Furthermore, academic contributions often extend to policy advisory roles, where research findings and expert analyses appraise government decisions on defence spending, technology adoption, and strategic initiatives. This symbiotic relationship between academia and the defence sector can catalyse continuous innovation and technological progression, crucial for maintaining and enhancing national defence capabilities.

The role of academia in the technology development of the defence industry in India is pivotal, not only in fostering innovation but also in bridging the gap between theoretical research and practical, combat-ready technologies. The strategic significance of the defence sector in India, underpinned by its geopolitical context, stresses on advanced technological capabilities that academia is uniquely positioned to provide. In the past, India's defence sector has traditionally been contingent on foreign technology and partnerships. However, recent initiatives by the Indian government aim to promote self-reliance or '*Atmanirbhar Bharat*' or 'Make in India', particularly in defence production. Universities, technical institutes, and research organisations are increasingly collaborating with defence public sector undertakings (DPSUs) and private enterprises to develop a range of defence applications, from advanced materials to new systems.

Academic institutions like the Indian Institutes of Technology (IITs), Indian Institute of Science (IISc), and the Defence Institute of Advanced Technology (DIAT) across India are at the forefront of research being conducted in the domains of materials science, aerospace engineering, and electronic warfare. Research projects from these institutions often focus on innovating cheaper, more efficient solutions that are tailor-made to India's specific defence requirements. For example, developments in lightweight composite materials from these institutions have led to enhanced armour protection and mobility for military vehicles. Besides technological innovations, academia can play an important role in training and equipping a skilled workforce. It is to be noted that specialised courses and dedicated defence studies programs help prepare a new generation of engineers and scientists who are well-versed in the unique challenges of defence technology. Various programmes designed by these institutes across India help to align academic curricula with the specific needs of the defence sector, thus ensuring a steady pipeline of qualified professionals who can contribute to various projects. Furthermore, strategic partnerships between academic institutions and industry are crucial for the practical application of research. For instance, the 'Technology Development Fund' initiated by DRDO aims to harness R&D capabilities of academia and channel them into viable defence products. Such initiatives not only foster innovation but also encourage the commercialisation of technology developed within university labs. In terms of policy-making and advisory roles, academia also plays a significant role in advising the government on developing policies related to defence technology. Think tanks and university departments provide valuable insights into global trends and strategic imperatives that can influence India's defence technology policies.

While the contribution of academia is significant, it is still fraught with challenges. Issues such as funding constraints, bureaucratic hurdles, and the need for a more dynamic interface between academia and industry are persistent. It is necessary to address these challenges that require policy interventions to not only provide adequate funding but also ensure that intellectual property rights are protected to encourage innovation.

Therefore, it can be said that academia's role in the technology development of India's defence industry is multifaceted and vital. As India is moving towards greater self-reliance in terms of defence capabilities, the symbiotic relationship between academia and the defence industry will undoubtedly play a crucial role in shaping the future of India's defence landscape. This partnership not only helps to boost technological advancements but also strengthens national security. Furthermore, it also helps to position India's role as a significant player in the global defence markets in terms of technological developments and advancements.

Role of Private Sector in India's Defence Production before 1991

Before the liberalisation of the Indian economy in 1991, the private sector's involvement in India's defence production was highly restricted. This period, characterised by a state-dominated industry with public sector enterprises (PSEs) playing a pivotal role, saw limited participation from private entities. This essay explores the status of the private sector in India's defence production prior to economic liberalisation, detailing the historical context, regulatory environment, and the roles and limitations faced by private companies. Post-independence, India's defence policy was influenced by its non-aligned status and the goal of achieving self-reliance in defence production. The government established a number of public sector undertakings (PSUs) like Hindustan Aeronautics Limited (HAL), Bharat Electronics Limited (BEL), and Bharat Dynamics Limited (BDL), which became the backbone of India's defence manufacturing capability. These PSUs were tasked with the development and production of a wide range of defence equipment, from aircraft to missiles and electronic systems. The involvement of the private sector in defence production before 1991 was minimal and highly regulated. The Industrial Policy Resolutions of 1956 and subsequent policies categorised industries into three schedules, with defence manufacturing reserved exclusively for the state under Schedule A. This policy placed severe restrictions on private sector participation, confining it to non-critical components and sub-systems under strict licensing conditions.[150]

Prior to liberalisation, the role of the private sector in defence production was primarily limited to supplying raw materials, semi-finished products, and components. Private companies were engaged as subcontractors to the DPSUs. These firms provided basic inputs and non-strategic parts, which were then assembled or further processed by the DPSUs. The involvement was under stringent government control, with little scope for independent product development or innovation in defence technologies. Some notable private companies, such as Tata Group, Mahindra, and Larsen & Toubro, were involved in minor capacities, mainly in the fabrication and supply of specialised materials and parts. Their participation was restricted by extensive bureaucracy and licensing requirements, which stifled potential growth and innovation in private defence manufacturing.[151]

The regulatory environment before 1991 imposed significant challenges on the private sector's involvement in defence production. The Defence Procurement Procedures (DPP) were heavily biased towards PSUs, which led to inefficiencies and a lack of competition. The monopoly of PSUs often resulted in delays, cost overruns, and technology obsolescence, which affected the overall effectiveness and modernisation of India's defence capabilities. The private sector also faced challenges in terms of technology transfer and development. With stringent controls on defence-related foreign collaborations and investments, private companies had limited access to advanced technologies, which hindered their ability to contribute effectively to defence production (Kumar, 1989). The minimal role of the private sector in defence production before liberalisation had significant economic and strategic implications. Economically, it limited the growth potential of an indigenous defence industry and constrained the development of a broader industrial base capable of innovative defence technology production. Strategically, it resulted in dependency on foreign technology and equipment, as PSUs were often unable to meet the sophisticated technology requirements of the Indian Armed Forces.[152] Before the economic liberalisation of 1991, India's defence production was predominantly a government domain with minimal private sector engagement. The strict regulatory framework and the monopoly of PSUs resulted in several inefficiencies and a lack of innovation within the sector. The economic reforms of the 1990s marked a significant shift, gradually opening up the defence industry to greater private sector involvement and competition, which aimed to overcome the limitations of the pre-liberalisation era. This historical overview highlights the constraints faced by the private sector in contributing to India's defence production before liberalisation and underscores the transformative impact of the post-1991 economic policies on this vital sector.

Challenges of Private Sector in India's Defence Sector Post 1991

Behera[153] has explained the private sector participation in the defence industry, saying that the public sector industries, though having objectives of growth for the defence sector, cannot attain self-sufficiency in their sector with a self-reliance index of just 30 to 35 per cent. This condition has led to extensive dependence on external firms for defence and reduced technology development costs for local firms. The May 2001 policy change allowed the private sector to make 100 per cent investments in the sector and 26 per cent Foreign Direct Investment.[154] Despite vast private and public sector enterprises in the country, there is an extensive list of weapons and ammunition that are still being imported by India.

The constraints faced by the private sector mostly relate to the secrecy and heavy research and development requirements. A press release by the Ministry of Defence[155] stated that 333 companies have been provided with 539 production licences, of which 110 companies have started production. Despite getting licences, less than 33 per cent of companies have started production, showing the inefficiency of the private players in working in this sector. Maheshwari[156] has also underlined the limited private defence sector growth in the Indian scenario because of the far from satisfactory profits and resource utilisation in the private industries. Khan and Shaikh[157] have also identified the problems associated with the Indian private defence industry with regard to the licensing requirements that haunt the industry, which causes the Indian defence industry to become less competitive internationally. They have also identified problems with the research and development scenario in the Indian context, whereby the difference in the time between research and production often leads to escalated prices in the private sector in the defence domain.

Position of India's Defence Exports in the Past Decade

Since the launch of the 'Make in India' initiative in 2014, India's defence export landscape has undergone significant changes, reflecting a strategic shift towards enhancing domestic manufacturing capabilities and boosting exports. This section explores the evolution of India's defence exports since 2014, examining key policies, growth trends, and the implications of these changes on India's position in the global defence market.

The growth in India's defence exports can be largely attributed to a series of government policies aimed at promoting the defence manufacturing sector. The 'Make in India' initiative has been a critical driver, encouraging both the public and private sectors to boost manufacturing and export indigenous military products. The Defence Procurement Procedure (DPP) was revised several times since 2014 to simplify the rules and increase participation from private entities. The introduction of the Strategic Partnership Model in the DPP 2016 further aimed to foster collaboration between Indian and foreign companies, enhancing the export capabilities of Indian enterprises.[158] According to the data from the Department of Defence Production (DDP), India's defence exports have witnessed a substantial increase. From a modest $ 111 million in exports in 2014-15, India saw a rise to approximately $ 1.5 billion by 2019-20. This growth has been propelled by exporting items like offshore patrol vessels, helicopters, sonar systems, and radars, mainly to countries in Southeast Asia, West Asia, and Africa (DDP Annual Reports). India's defence exports include a variety of products ranging from personal protective items to sophisticated defence equipment. Among the major items, India has successfully exported Dhruv advanced light helicopters, Tejas light combat aircraft, and various missiles. The primary importers of Indian defence goods include countries like Sri Lanka, Mauritius, Bangladesh, Myanmar, and the United Arab Emirates. Notably, the export of the BrahMos missile system, developed jointly with Russia, to the Philippines marked a significant milestone, showcasing India's capabilities in exporting large weapon systems.[159] Despite the growth, the Indian defence sector faces several challenges that hinder its potential in the international arms market. One of the primary challenges is the perception of the reliability and quality of Indian defence products. Issues such as delays in delivery schedules and the operational performance of some exported items have impacted India's reputation as a reliable supplier.[160] Moreover, stringent export control regulations and the lack of international lobbying compared to countries like the USA, Russia, and Israel also pose significant obstacles.

The increase in defence exports has strategic and economic implications for India. Economically, the growth in exports is creating jobs, developing technological capabilities, and generating foreign exchange. Strategically, it allows India to strengthen ties with key countries, especially in its neighbourhood and with other strategic partners globally. By exporting defence equipment, India also projects its power and enhances its stature as a regional security provider.[161] Mishra[162] has also analysed India's defence exports and has explained the connection and mutual efforts of the Ministry of Defence (MoD) and the Ministry of External Affairs (MEA) to send out delegations to foreign nations to promote India's defence exports and imports. Defence reforms by the government and the 2+2 dialogue initiated by the government have led to an increase in defence exports by India (Reforms in Defence Sector, DDP, 2014-2021). Defence exports also seem to impact India's domestic production capacity significantly, increasing investment for India's domestic producers. In 2021-22, defence exports were at the highest ever amount of Rs. 13,000 crore which was a 54.1 per cent rise since the previous year, 2020-21.[163] Looking ahead, India aims to expand its defence exports further. The government has set an ambitious target to achieve USD 5 billion in defence exports by 2025. To realise this, it plans to leverage agreements like the Indo-US Defence Technology and Trade Initiative (DTTI) and to participate actively in international defence expos and trade shows. Additionally, there is a focus on innovation and research and development to create more competitive and advanced defence products that meet international standards.

Exploring the Viability of Joint Defence Production in India

Joint production in defence manufacturing has become a strategic approach to enhance defence capabilities and manage costs efficiently. This generally occurs in forms of collaboration either between nations or between government and private sector entities. It is presumed that this kind of model, if implemented in India, could significantly reinforce India's defence sector, leveraging international expertise and resources. However, the feasibility and success of joint production in India's defence sector hinge on several factors, including policy frameworks, strategic alignment, and the capability to manage complex relationships between nations globally. One of the primary advantages of joint production is the potential for cost reduction. Defence projects often require substantial investment, and by sharing these costs, nations can allocate resources more efficiently. In India's context, joint production can mitigate the financial burdens of developing advanced technology from scratch. For example, collaborations like the BrahMos missile project between India and Russia demonstrate how joint ventures can lead to successful outcomes in critical defence technologies.

Moreover, joint production can significantly accelerate technological advancements. By collaborating with technologically advanced nations, India can bypass the extensively tedious research and development phases with the possibility of swiftly acquiring sophisticated ammunition capabilities. This is crucial for maintaining a strategic edge, especially given the rapid pace of global military technology evolution.[164] Additionally, joint production also helps in enhancing interoperability which is also a critical factor for multinational defence operations or humanitarian missions. With joint development of equipment and technologies developed through international cooperation, armed forces can operate more cohesively in coalition settings. This is also emerging as a common scenario in global defence strategies. There are also significant challenges that are associated with joint production such as concerning sovereignty and security. Partnerships in defence manufacturing often require sharing sensitive technologies, which can lead to security concerns. India must carefully negotiate technology transfer terms to protect its national interests while gaining the technological benefits of joint ventures.

Intellectual property rights (IPR) are another critical issue. The negotiation of IPR terms can be complex, with potential conflicts arising from the co-development of technologies. India's ability to secure favourable terms that protect its innovations and provide room for domestic industries to grow is crucial.[165] Not only that, the differences in geopolitical interests can cause difficulties in joint ventures. For instance, partnerships with countries having conflicting interests might strain regional relationships and affect ongoing and future collaborations. For India, establishing robust legal and regulatory frameworks that facilitate joint production while protecting national interests is essential. It is necessary for the policies to be clearly defined in terms of the level of engagement, including technology transfer, IPR, and the extent of foreign involvement in strategic sectors.[166] Furthermore, enhancing the capabilities of India's defence sector to engage in high-tech manufacturing and R&D through increased investment in education and infrastructure is vital. This will not only prepare the ground for fruitful collaborations but also ensure that the benefits of joint production are maximally retained within the country. While joint production in defence manufacturing presents a promising avenue for India to enhance its military capabilities and manage costs, it requires careful strategic planning and robust policy support. The success of such ventures will depend on India's ability to navigate complex geopolitical landscapes, negotiate equitable terms, and build a conducive domestic environment for technology assimilation and innovation.

Self-Reliance in the Indian Defence Industry: Is It Possible?

India's quest for self-reliance in its defence industry through the 'Atmanirbhar Bharat' or 'Make in India' initiative, has garnered significant attention. The aim of this initiative is to reduce dependence on foreign arms and build a robust indigenous defence manufacturing network. However, it involves numerous challenges requiring sustained effort across multiple dimensions. In order to boost self-reliance, the Indian government has implemented several policy measures in the defence sector. One such initiative is the Defence Procurement Procedure (DPP) 2020, renamed as the Defence Acquisition Procedure (DAP) 2020. It prioritises indigenous design and manufacturing in the defence sector. The DAP includes provisions for the indigenisation of imported spares and mandates higher indigenous content in defence procurement contracts. Additionally, the Strategic Partnership Model aims to enhance private sector participation by collaborating with foreign original equipment manufacturers (OEMs) for technology transfer and joint production.[167]

Furthermore, the Defence Production and Export Promotion Policy (DPEPP) 2020 charts out a clear roadmap for enhancing indigenous defence production and exports. The policy positions targets, including a turnover of $ 25 billion in defence manufacturing and exports worth $ 5 billion by 2025.[168] These policy measures will help in creating a favourable environment for indigenous defence manufacturing and reduce dependency on foreign imports.

With substantial contributions from both the public and private sectors, India's defence industrial base is expanding, with significant contributions from both the public and private sectors. DPSUs and organisations like Hindustan Aeronautics Limited (HAL), Bharat Electronics Limited (BEL), and Bharat Dynamics Limited (BDL) play a crucial role in domestic defence production.[169] Moreover, private sector companies such as Larsen & Toubro, Tata Advanced Systems, and Mahindra Defence Systems are increasingly participating in defence projects, bringing in innovation and efficiency.

Technological advancements are essential for achieving self-reliance. India's indigenous defence programs, such as the light combat aircraft (LCA) Tejas, Arjun main battle tank, and the Akash missile system, demonstrate significant progress. The Defence Research and Development Organisation (DRDO) spearheads numerous R&D initiatives, developing technologies in areas like missile systems, electronic warfare, and unmanned aerial vehicles. However, despite these positive developments, several challenges impede India's path to self-reliance in the defence sector. Firstly, India still lags in critical technologies such as jet engines, advanced electronics, and cyber warfare capabilities. Developing these technologies requires substantial investment, skilled manpower, and sustained R&D efforts.[170] Secondly, while India aims to reduce import dependency, it remains one of the largest importers of arms globally. High-value platforms like fighter jets, submarines, and advanced artillery systems are still primarily sourced from foreign manufacturers (Pradhan, n.d.). Transitioning from import-prone to indigenous production is a steady process that requires strategic planning and execution. Thirdly, the indigenous defence industrial base needs to be more robust and diversified. There are gaps in the supply chain, particularly in the production of critical components and materials. Strengthening the supply chain involves enhancing manufacturing capabilities, establishing quality standards, and ensuring timely delivery of components (Press Information Bureau, 2024). Fourthly, efficient policy implementation is crucial for achieving self-reliance. Bureaucratic delays, procedural inefficiencies, and lack of coordination among various stakeholders can hinder progress. Furthermore, streamlining the procurement processes and ensuring the effective execution of policies will help ensure the success of self-reliance initiatives.

However, to overcome these challenges there are some steps that need to be taken. First, it is necessary to enhance investment in research and development which is vital for technological advancements. Encouraging collaboration between DRDO, DPSUs, the private sector, and academia can foster innovation and accelerate the development of indigenous technologies. Second, developing a skilled workforce is crucial for the defence industry to maintain technological superiority, enhance innovation, and ensure operational readiness. Advanced skills in engineering, cyber security, and systems integration are essential to meet evolving security threats and sustain competitive advantage. Third, building a robust industrial ecosystem involves enhancing manufacturing capabilities, promoting small and medium enterprises (SMEs), and ensuring a reliable supply chain. Incentives for domestic production and procurement preferences for indigenous products can stimulate growth. Fourth, strategic partnerships with global defence manufacturers can facilitate technology transfer and joint ventures. Collaborative projects and co-development initiatives can help bridge technological gaps and enhance India's defence capabilities. Fifth, continuous policy reforms and efficient governance are essential for achieving self-reliance. Streamlining procurement processes, reducing bureaucratic red tape, and ensuring transparency in defence contracts can foster a conducive environment for indigenous manufacturing.

India's pursuit of self-reliance in the defence industry is a challenging yet achievable goal. The government's policy initiatives, coupled with technological advancements and industrial growth, have laid a strong foundation for reducing dependency on imports. However, addressing technological gaps, strengthening the industrial base, and ensuring efficient policy implementation are critical for sustaining progress. With strategic investments, skill development, and international collaboration, India can achieve its vision of becoming a self-reliant defence manufacturing hub. The journey towards self-reliance is gradual and requires a concerted effort from all stakeholders, but the potential benefits for national security and economic growth make it a worthy endeavour.

Conclusion

The future of India's ammunition sector shows potential, with continued government support and increasing private-sector involvement. The establishment of defence corridors, increased FDI, and strategic collaborations help in boosting this growth. The ammunition sector in India is at a pivotal juncture, with significant growth prospects driven by strategic initiatives, technological advancements, and geopolitical imperatives. While challenges such as dependence on imports and bureaucratic hurdles remain, the concerted efforts towards indigenisation and innovation promise a robust and self-reliant future for India's defence manufacturing industry. Achieving self-reliance in Indian defence production, particularly in the crucial area of ammunition technology for the Indian Army, represents a multifaceted challenge that involves strategic planning, robust policy support, and effective implementation. The pursuit of self-reliance is not merely about reducing dependency on foreign sources but also about enhancing the quality, reliability, and effectiveness of the ammunition used by the Indian Army, thus ensuring operational readiness and national security. India's journey towards self-reliance in defence production has been shaped by several key policies and initiatives, including the 'Make in India' program and the more recent 'Atmanirbhar Bharat' campaign. These initiatives aim to foster an ecosystem that encourages innovation, development, and production within the country. For ammunition technology, this means developing capacities that can not only meet the demands of the Indian Armed Forces but also adhere to the highest standards of safety and precision. In all this, the role of the DRDO and other DPSUs has been pivotal. By prioritising the development of indigenous technologies in ammunition, such as guided munitions, extended-range artillery shells, and advanced fusing systems, these organisations lay the groundwork for technological sovereignty. Moreover, DRDO's partnerships with academic institutions and private sector involvement have been crucial in bridging the gap between research and production.

The opening up of the defence manufacturing sector and the establishment of a more conducive policy environment for FDIs in that sector have led to increased participation from private entities. This shift not only drives competition but also promotes higher efficiency and innovation. However, significant challenges remain, such as the need for a clear regulatory framework, assurance of order continuity, and intellectual property rights protection, which are essential to sustain and encourage private investment and involvement in defence technology. Furthermore, the establishment of defence corridors in various Indian states offers a structured approach to create clusters of manufacturing and innovation hubs. These corridors are expected to synergise the efforts of various stakeholders, including MSMEs, large corporations, and research institutions, to create a comprehensive ecosystem capable of sustaining the entire lifecycle of defence manufacturing. The technological sophistication required in modern ammunition production necessitates a highly skilled workforce. Initiatives to enhance skill sets through specialised courses in military engineering colleges and partnerships with technical institutes are steps in the right direction. However, achieving self-reliance in ammunition technology also requires addressing the challenges of quality control and standardisation. The operational needs of the Indian Armed Forces demand ammunition that performs consistently in terms of quality across different batches and production cycles. Establishing stringent quality assurance mechanisms and continuous monitoring at all stages of the production process is essential to maintain the trust and confidence of the armed forces in indigenously produced ammunition. In conclusion, while significant progress has been made towards self-reliance in Indian defence production, the path forward requires a cohesive and integrated approach. Strengthening collaborations among government organisations, the private sector, and academic institutions is crucial. Moreover, a clear policy direction, consistent government support, and an emphasis on research and development are vital to overcome existing hurdles and ensure that the advancements in ammunition technology not only meet the current demands but also anticipate future needs. With strategic focus and sustained efforts, India can achieve its goal of self-reliance in defence production, thereby securing its defence capabilities and supporting its long-term strategic interests.

Chapter Five

Synergies and Stumbling Blocks: The Role of Public and Private Sectors in Ammunition Production

Introduction

The production of ammunition, an essential component of a nation's defence capabilities, involves intricate interactions between the public and private sectors. These interactions, characterised by both synergies and stumbling blocks, play a crucial role in determining the effectiveness and efficiency of ammunition production. In the context of India, a country striving for strategic autonomy and self-reliance in defence production, understanding the dynamics between these sectors is particularly important. This chapter explores the role of the public and private sectors in ammunition production in India, highlighting the collaborative efforts and challenges that shape this critical industry. Ammunition production is a vital element of national security, providing the armed forces with the necessary tools to defend the country against various threats. The ability to produce advanced and reliable ammunition domestically reduces dependency on foreign suppliers, enhances national security, and ensures a steady supply during times of conflict or geopolitical tension. For India, a country with significant regional security challenges and aspirations for greater strategic autonomy, developing a robust and self-sufficient ammunition production capability is a strategic imperative. Historically, ammunition production in India has been dominated by state-owned enterprises (SOEs), such as the Ordnance Factory Board (OFB), now restructured into various defence public sector undertakings (DPSUs).

The government's control over ammunition production was driven by the need to maintain strict oversight and ensure the quality, reliability, and security of the defence supply chain. The public sector's involvement provided a stable and controlled environment for ammunition production, benefiting from direct government funding, access to resources, and policy support. However, the traditional dominance of the public sector has also been associated with certain inefficiencies. Issues such as bureaucratic red tape, slow decision-making processes, lack of innovation, and outdated technology have often plagued public sector enterprises, leading to delays and suboptimal performances. These challenges have necessitated a re-evaluation of the role of the public sector and the exploration of opportunities for private sector involvement. This chapter aims to provide a comprehensive analysis of the role of public and private sectors in ammunition production in India, offering insights for enhancing collaboration and achieving strategic autonomy in defence production.

In recent years, the Indian government has recognised the need to involve the private sector more actively in defence production, including ammunition manufacturing. The private sector brings several advantages to the table, including agility, innovation potential, and efficiency. Private companies, driven by competitive pressures and market dynamics, are often more inclined to adopt cutting-edge technologies, streamline production processes, and focus on quality and cost-effectiveness. The government's policy initiatives, such as the Make in India campaign, the Defence Procurement Procedure (DPP), and the Strategic Partnership Model, have aimed to create an enabling environment for private sector participation. These initiatives seek to leverage the strengths of both the public and private sectors, fostering collaboration and creating a more dynamic and responsive defence industrial base. The collaboration between the public and private sectors in ammunition production can yield significant synergies. Public sector entities, with their established infrastructure, experience, and regulatory support, can provide a solid foundation for production activities. Meanwhile, private companies can contribute innovation, efficiency, and advanced technologies. This complementary relationship can enhance the overall capabilities of the ammunition production industry.

Joint ventures and public-private partnerships (PPPs) are potential models for leveraging these synergies. Such collaborations can facilitate technology transfer, improve production processes, and accelerate the development of new and advanced ammunition systems. By combining the strengths of both sectors, India can enhance its indigenous production capabilities and reduce its reliance on imports. Despite the potential benefits of public-private collaboration, several stumbling blocks and challenges need to be addressed. One major issue is the regulatory and bureaucratic environment, which can pose significant hurdles for private sector participation. Complex approval processes, inconsistent policy implementation, and lack of clarity in regulations can deter private companies from entering the defence sector.

Additionally, there are concerns related to intellectual property rights (IPR) and technology transfer. Private companies are often wary of sharing their proprietary technologies and innovations due to fears of inadequate protection and potential misuse. Ensuring robust IPR protection and fostering a culture of trust and transparency are crucial for successful collaboration. Another challenge is the cultural and operational differences between the public and private sectors. Public sector entities may be more risk-averse and bureaucratic, while private companies tend to be more dynamic and profit-driven. Bridging these differences and fostering effective communication and collaboration requires concerted efforts and mutual understanding.

To overcome these challenges and maximise the synergies between the public and private sectors, robust policy and institutional support are essential. The government needs to streamline regulations, simplify approval processes, and provide clear guidelines to facilitate private sector participation. Creating a conducive business environment, with incentives for investment and innovation, can attract more private companies to the defence sector. Institutional mechanisms, such as dedicated defence industrial corridors and innovation hubs, can provide platforms for collaboration and knowledge sharing. These mechanisms can bring together public sector entities, private companies, academic institutions, and research organisations, fostering a collaborative ecosystem for defence production. To illustrate the potential and challenges of public-private collaboration in ammunition production, this chapter will present case studies and examples from India and other countries.

These case studies will highlight successful collaborations, identify best practices, and draw lessons that can inform India's approach to enhancing its ammunition production capabilities.

For instance, the collaboration between Bharat Forge, a leading private sector company, and the Defence Research and Development Organisation (DRDO) in developing advanced artillery systems showcases the benefits of public-private partnerships. Similarly, international examples, such as the US defence industry's collaboration between the Department of Defence (DoD) and private defence contractors, can provide valuable insights. The role of the public and private sectors in ammunition production in India is characterised by a complex interplay of synergies and stumbling blocks. While the public sector provides a stable foundation and regulatory support, the private sector brings innovation, efficiency, and advanced technologies. Harnessing the strengths of both sectors through effective collaboration is essential for developing a robust and self-reliant ammunition production capability. By addressing regulatory and bureaucratic challenges, ensuring robust IPR protection, and fostering a culture of trust and transparency, India can create an enabling environment for public-private collaboration. Robust policy and institutional support, coupled with successful case studies and best practices, can guide the country in leveraging the synergies and overcoming the stumbling blocks in ammunition production.

Historical Development of Ammunition Production in India

Ammunition production in India has a rich and complex history, marked by numerous challenges and significant milestones. The development of this crucial sector has been pivotal for the country's defence capabilities, strategic autonomy, and national security. This section provides an in-depth exploration of the historical development of ammunition production in India, tracing its evolution from the early years of British colonial rule to the contemporary era, and highlighting key challenges and achievements along the way.

The origins of ammunition production in India can be traced back to the British colonial period. The British established the first ordnance factories in the mid-18th century to supply the East India Company's forces with weapons and ammunition. The first notable establishment was the Gun and Shell

Factory in Cossipore, Kolkata, which began operations in 1801.[171] This marked the beginning of a structured approach to defence manufacturing in India. The colonial era saw the establishment of several other ordnance factories, such as the Ammunition Factory Khadki in Pune (1869) and the Metal and Steel Factory in Ishapore (1872). These factories were primarily designed to meet the needs of the British Indian Army, producing a range of ammunition and artillery shells. Despite these developments, the focus was largely on fulfilling immediate military needs, with little emphasis on indigenous technological advancement or self-reliance. With India's independence in 1947, the nascent nation inherited a modest but operational defence manufacturing infrastructure. The newly-independent government recognised the strategic importance of self-reliance in defence production and sought to build on the existing colonial framework. However, this period was fraught with significant challenges.

One of the primary challenges was the lack of indigenous technological expertise. The existing ordnance factories were heavily reliant on outdated British technology, and there was a significant gap in local research and development capabilities. Additionally, the nascent Indian government faced the monumental task of addressing widespread poverty and underdevelopment, which meant that defence manufacturing was not always prioritised.[172] In the immediate post-independence years, the focus was on maintaining and slightly expanding the existing infrastructure. The government established new ordnance factories to enhance the country's ammunition production capacity. The Ordnance Factory Board (OFB), set up in 1979, became the umbrella organisation overseeing these factories. Despite these efforts, progress was slow, and the sector remained heavily dependent on foreign technology and imports.[173]

The 1960s and 1970s were transformative decades for India's defence sector, driven by geopolitical developments and conflicts such as the Sino-Indian War (1962) and the Indo-Pakistani wars (1965 and 1971). These conflicts underscored the critical need for self-reliance in defence production, particularly in ammunition. During this period, the Indian government initiated several measures to modernise and expand its ammunition production capabilities. One significant development was the establishment of the DRDO in 1958, tasked with fostering indigenous research and development in defence technologies. The DRDO played a crucial role in advancing India's capabilities in various defence sectors, including ammunition.[174]

In the 1980s and 1990s, the focus shifted towards achieving greater technological self-sufficiency. The Indian government invested in modernising the ordnance factories, incorporating advanced manufacturing technologies and improving quality control measures. The erstwhile OFB expanded its product range to include more sophisticated ammunition types such as anti-tank ammunition, high-explosive shells, and specialised small arms ammunition. One of the key milestones during this period was the development and production of the Pinaka multi-barrel rocket launcher system, which entered service in the early 2000s. This system, developed by DRDO and manufactured by the Ordnance factories represented a significant leap in India's artillery capabilities and demonstrated the growing competence of the country's defence production sector.[175]

The economic liberalisation of the 1990s brought about significant changes in India's industrial landscape, including the defence sector. Recognising the limitations of a purely state-controlled defence manufacturing set up, the Indian government began to encourage private sector participation in defence production. This shift was formalised with the introduction of the Defence Procurement Procedure (DPP) in 2002, which laid out guidelines for involving private players in defence manufacturing. The private sector's involvement has been pivotal in addressing some of the longstanding challenges faced by the public sector, such as inefficiencies, bureaucratic inertia, and a lack of innovation. Companies like Bharat Forge, Larsen & Toubro, and Tata Advanced Systems have emerged as key players in the defence sector, bringing in advanced technologies, efficient manufacturing processes, and a culture of innovation.[176] One notable example of successful public-private collaboration is the development of the Dhanush artillery gun, an upgraded version of the Bofors FH77, jointly produced by the Ordnance factories and private sector companies. This collaboration has not only enhanced India's artillery capabilities but also demonstrated the potential of leveraging private sector strengths to augment public sector efforts.[177]

In recent years, India's ammunition production sector has achieved several key milestones, reflecting its growing maturity and capability. In 2018, the Indian government announced the creation of two defence industrial corridors in Uttar Pradesh and Tamil Nadu. These corridors aim to create a robust defence manufacturing ecosystem, fostering collaboration between the public and private sectors, and attracting investment in defence production, including ammunition.[178] India has significantly increased its defence exports in recent years, with ammunition being a major component. The government's focus on promoting defence exports has led to the establishment of new markets for Indian-made ammunition, contributing to the sector's growth and sustainability.[179] The DRDO and Ordnance factories have developed a range of advanced ammunition types, including precision-guided munitions, cluster bombs, and specialised anti-tank ammunition. These developments have enhanced the operational capabilities of the Indian armed forces and reduced dependence on imports.[180] The Make in India (2014) initiative has provided a significant boost to indigenous defence production. The initiative emphasises the importance of self-reliance and aims to transform India into a global manufacturing hub. In the context of ammunition production, this has led to increased investment, technology transfers, and the establishment of joint ventures with foreign companies.[181]

Despite these achievements, several challenges remain in India's quest for self-reliance in ammunition production. One of the primary challenges is the need for continuous technological innovation to keep pace with evolving threats and warfare technologies. The defence sector's heavy reliance on imports for critical components and raw materials also poses a significant challenge. Moreover, the bureaucratic and regulatory environment can sometimes stifle private sector participation and innovation. Streamlining approval processes, enhancing transparency, and providing clear guidelines can help create a more conducive environment for collaboration and growth. To address these challenges, the Indian government has outlined several policy measures and initiatives. The Defence Production Policy 2018 aims to achieve a turnover of INR 1,70,000 crore (US$ 26 billion) in defence goods and services by 2025, with significant contributions from the ammunition sector.[182] Additionally, the establishment of innovation hubs and incubation centres can foster a culture of research and development, ensuring that India remains at the cutting edge of ammunition technology. The historical development of ammunition production in India is a testament to the country's resilience, strategic foresight, and commitment to self-reliance in defence. From its colonial roots to the modern era of public-private collaboration, the sector has evolved significantly, overcoming numerous challenges and achieving key milestones. As India continues to strengthen its defence manufacturing capabilities, the role of both the public and private sectors will be crucial in ensuring that the country remains well equipped to meet future security challenges. By fostering innovation, enhancing collaboration, and addressing regulatory hurdles, India can build a robust and self-sufficient ammunition production capability. This not only enhances national security but also positions India as a key player in the global defence industry.

The future of ammunition production is likely to be shaped by several emerging technologies and trends. Also known as 3D printing, additive manufacturing allows for the production of complex ammunition components with reduced material waste and shorter lead times. This technology is being explored for both small-arms ammunition and larger munitions.[183] The development of smart ammunition, which incorporates sensors and electronics to enhance accuracy and effectiveness, is an area of active research. These advancements could revolutionise the capabilities of ammunition in both conventional and unconventional warfare.[184] The push towards environmentally sustainable practices is influencing ammunition production. Lead-free primers, biodegradable casings, and green propellants are being developed to reduce the environmental impact of ammunition.[185] AI and IoT technologies are being integrated into ammunition production to improve quality control, predictive maintenance, and supply chain management. These technologies can enhance efficiency and reduce costs while ensuring high standards of quality.[186]

Technological Base for Ammunition Production

Ammunition production is a complex and technologically advanced field that requires a combination of precision engineering, material science, and sophisticated manufacturing processes. The current technologies employed in manufacturing various types of ammunition range from traditional methods to cutting-edge innovations. This section examines the current technologies used in ammunition production, highlighting the manufacturing techniques for different types of ammunition and comparing them with global standards and practices. Ammunition encompasses a broad spectrum of products, each with specific manufacturing requirements. The primary categories include small arms ammunition, artillery shells, rockets, and missiles. Each category employs distinct technologies and processes to meet the stringent requirements of performance, reliability, and safety.

Small arms ammunition includes bullets used in handguns, rifles, and machine guns. The production of small-arms ammunition involves several critical steps. For cartridge case manufacturing the process begins with drawing brass or steel into the shape of a cartridge case using multi-stage drawing and forming presses. Modern technologies employ computer numerical control (CNC) machines to ensure precision and consistency.[187] In the case of primer production, they are manufactured using a combination of mechanical and chemical processes. The sensitivity and reliability of primers are crucial, requiring precision engineering and stringent quality control measures. The bullets are typically made from lead or a lead core with a copper jacket. The swaging process forms the bullet to precise dimensions, and CNC machines ensure uniformity in mass production. The components (cartridge case, primer, powder, and bullet) are then assembled using automated machinery that precisely measures and inserts each element. Automated inspection systems check for defects and ensure quality control.[188]

Artillery shells are large-calibre ammunition used in tanks, howitzers, and other heavy artillery. The shell bodies are typically forged from high-strength steel and then machined to exact specifications. Advanced CNC machines and robotic machining centres are used to achieve the required precision. The shells are then filled with high-explosive material using automated filling machines. This process must adhere to strict safety protocols to prevent accidental detonation. The final steps involve assembling the fuse and other components, followed by rigorous testing to ensure the shell's performance and reliability.[189] Rockets and missiles represent the most technologically advanced category of ammunition, incorporating complex guidance systems and propulsion technologies. Solid and liquid propellant technologies are used in rocket and missile propulsion. Solid propellants are manufactured using casting and curing processes, while liquid propellants require precise mixing and handling of highly reactive chemicals.[190] Advanced electronics and software are used to develop guidance systems. These systems include inertial navigation, GPS, and radar-based technologies to ensure accuracy and effectiveness. Composite materials and advanced manufacturing techniques such as 3D printing are increasingly used to produce lightweight and strong structural components for rockets and missiles. The final assembly integrates all components, followed by extensive testing in simulated conditions to validate performance and reliability.

Comparison with Global Standards and Practices

The technologies and practices used in ammunition production vary significantly across different countries, influenced by factors such as technological capabilities, regulatory environments, and industrial infrastructure. Here, we compare the practices in leading ammunition-producing countries with global standards. Ammunition production is a critical aspect of national defence capabilities. Leading global producers, such as the USA, Russia, and China, set high standards in terms of technology, production capacity, and quality control. This section benchmarks the Indian ammunition production sector against these global leaders, highlighting key areas of comparison.

The USA

The USA is a global leader in ammunition production, with a strong emphasis on innovation and quality. American manufacturers employ advanced CNC machines, automated assembly lines, and rigorous quality control measures. The use of smart manufacturing technologies, such as the Internet of Things (IoT) and artificial intelligence (AI), enhances efficiency and traceability.[191] The US Department of Defence sets stringent standards for ammunition production, including detailed specifications for materials, dimensions, and performance. The National Institute of Standards and Technology (NIST) also plays a role in developing and maintaining these standards. The USA leads the world in advanced ammunition technology. Companies like Lockheed Martin, Raytheon, and Northrop Grumman are at the forefront of innovation, producing precision-guided munitions (PGMs), smart bombs, and advanced artillery shells.[192] It employs cutting-edge technologies such as additive manufacturing (3D printing), artificial intelligence (AI), and the Internet of Things (IoT) in its production processes. These technologies enhance efficiency, precision, and quality control.[193] In terms of production capacity and quality control, the USA maintains a vast production capacity supported by a robust industrial base and government contracts. The Department of Defence (DoD) ensures stringent quality control measures, adhering to rigorous standards set by the National Institute of Standards and Technology (NIST).[194]

European Union (EU)

The EU has a significant and well-established ammunition production and export industry, driven by several key member-states with advanced defence manufacturing capabilities. Major producers within the EU include Germany, France, Italy, and Sweden, each contributing to the robust defence industrial base that supports both domestic needs and international markets. European manufacturers are known for their precision engineering and high-quality standards. European ammunition production emphasises environmentally friendly practices, such as the use of lead-free primers and green propellants. Advanced CNC machines, automated inspection systems, and digital twins for simulation and testing are widely used.[195] The European Defence Agency (EDA) sets harmonised standards for ammunition production across EU member-states, ensuring interoperability and quality.

Germany is a leading producer of ammunition in the EU, with companies like Rheinmetall AG and Diehl Defence playing pivotal roles. These firms produce a wide range of ammunition types, including small arms, medium-calibre rounds, and advanced artillery shells. Rheinmetall, for instance, is renowned for its innovative artillery and tank ammunition.[196] France also has a strong ammunition production sector, with companies like Nexter Munitions and Thales Group at the forefront. Nexter Munitions, part of the KNDS Group, produces ammunition for various platforms, including land, air, and naval systems.[197] Italy's ammunition industry is represented by companies such as Leonardo S.p.A. and Fiocchi Munizioni. These firms are known for their production of high-quality small arms ammunition and specialised military rounds.[198] Sweden, with companies like Saab Bofors Dynamics, contributes significantly to the EU's ammunition production, particularly in the development of advanced artillery and missile systems.[199]

The EU is a major exporter of ammunition, benefiting from a well-regulated and integrated market. The European Defence Agency (EDA) coordinates defence-related activities among member-states, promoting standardisation and interoperability. This coordination enhances the competitiveness of EU-made ammunition in global markets.[200] The export of ammunition from the EU is governed by stringent regulations to ensure compliance with international arms control agreements. The EU's Common Position on Arms Exports sets criteria for export licences, ensuring that exports do not contribute to human rights abuses or regional instability (Council of the European Union, 2008). In recent years, the EU has seen substantial growth in defence exports. According to the Stockholm International Peace Research Institute (SIPRI), EU member-states are among the top global exporters of military equipment, including ammunition.[201]

Russia

Russia has a long history of ammunition production, with a focus on robustness and mass production. Russian manufacturers utilise a mix of traditional and modern technologies, with an emphasis on high-volume output. While Russia employs advanced CNC machines and automated assembly lines, there is also significant use of manual labour in certain processes. Russian ammunition is known for its durability and reliability under harsh conditions.[202] The Russian Ministry of Defence sets comprehensive standards for ammunition production, covering all aspects from material selection to final testing. Russia's state-owned enterprises like *Rostec* and *Rosoboronexport* lead the industry. Despite economic challenges, Russia continues to innovate, focusing on durability and reliability under harsh conditions.[203] Modernisation efforts have introduced advanced CNC machines and automated assembly lines, though the industry still relies significantly on traditional methods.[204] The Russian Ministry of Defence sets comprehensive standards for ammunition production. Quality control remains stringent, though occasional lapses highlight the challenges of maintaining consistency across a vast production network.[205]

China

China has rapidly advanced its ammunition production capabilities in recent decades, leveraging its large industrial base and state-driven innovation programs. Chinese manufacturers employ modern CNC machines, automated assembly lines, and advanced testing facilities. There is a strong emphasis on adopting new materials and technologies to enhance performance and reduce costs.[206] The Chinese government sets stringent standards for ammunition production, with a focus on achieving parity with global leaders in terms of quality and performance. China has rapidly expanded its ammunition production capabilities, driven by state-led initiatives and substantial investments. Companies like *Norinco* (China North Industries Group Corporation) are pivotal to this growth.[207] Chinese manufacturers utilise advanced technologies, including automation, robotics, and digital quality control systems. The integration of these technologies has enabled China to achieve high production volumes with improved quality standards.[208] The Chinese government has implemented strict standards and regulatory frameworks to ensure the quality of its ammunition. China's emphasis on exports has also driven the need to meet international quality standards, enhancing its competitiveness in global markets.[209]

Comparison with India

While India has made significant strides in modernising its ammunition production facilities, it still lags behind the USA and China in adopting the latest technologies. Efforts to integrate AI, IoT, and additive manufacturing are ongoing but not yet widespread.[210] The DRDO and private companies like Bharat Forge and Larsen & Toubro are key players in driving technological advancements. However, the pace of innovation needs to accelerate to match global leaders. India's production capacity has increased with the involvement of the private sector, but it remains constrained by bureaucratic inefficiencies and regulatory hurdles.[211] The Ordnance factories have faced criticism for outdated infrastructure and inconsistent quality control. Benchmarking against global standards reveals that India must enhance its quality control mechanisms to avoid incidents of ammunition failure and improve overall reliability.[212] To bridge the gap with leading global producers, India needs to make strategic investments in R&D, infrastructure modernisation, and workforce training. Collaborations with international defence companies can facilitate technology transfers and best practice adoption.[213]

Technological Challenges

The challenges to the Indian ammunition industry stem from a combination of factors including legacy technologies, limited Research and Development (R&D) capabilities, and bureaucratic inefficiencies. This section examines some of the key technical challenges encountered by the industry and presents case studies that highlight specific technological hurdles. One of the primary challenges facing the Indian ammunition industry is the reliance on outdated technologies inherited from the colonial era. Many of the ordnance factories still operate with machinery and processes that are decades old. This reliance on legacy technologies hampers efficiency and quality, making it difficult for the industry to meet modern standards and demands. The Ordnance factories, responsible for a significant portion of India's ammunition production, have struggled with modernisation. Despite efforts to upgrade facilities, many Ordnance factories continue to use antiquated equipment, resulting in frequent production delays and quality issues.[214] The government's attempts to modernise these factories have been slow due to bureaucratic hurdles and funding constraints, leading to persistent challenges in meeting both domestic and export demands.

Limited Research and Development Capabilities

Another significant challenge is the limited R&D capabilities within the Indian ammunition industry. While organisations like the Defence Research and Development Organisation (DRDO) play a crucial role, their focus is often spread across a broad range of defence technologies, limiting the specific advancements in ammunition technology. The development of advanced artillery shells has been a particular area where R&D limitations are evident. For instance, the indigenous development of the Pinaka multi-barrel rocket launcher system showcased the capabilities of the DRDO and Ordnance factories. However, the program faced several delays and setbacks due to technological challenges and the need for multiple iterations to achieve the desired performance standards.[215] These challenges highlight the gaps in R&D and the need for more focused efforts to innovate and improve ammunition technologies.

Quality Control and Standardisation Issues

Quality control and standardisation are critical aspects of ammunition production, ensuring reliability and safety. The Indian ammunition industry has faced significant issues in maintaining consistent quality standards, leading to incidents of ammunition failure and accidents. There have been several incidents of ammunition-related accidents in recent years, underscoring the importance of stringent quality control. For example, in 2016, a series of explosions at the Pulgaon Central Ammunition Depot were attributed to defective ammunition, leading to loss of life and substantial property damage.[216] Investigations revealed lapses in quality control during the manufacturing process, highlighting the urgent need for improved quality assurance mechanisms and adherence to international standards.

Supply Chain and Logistics Challenges

The supply chain and logistics involved in ammunition production and distribution are complex, involving multiple stakeholders and processes. Inefficiencies and delays in the supply chain can significantly impact production schedules and operational readiness. The procurement of raw materials and components is often delayed due to bureaucratic processes and regulatory hurdles. For instance, delays in procuring key materials for the manufacture of high-explosive shells have disrupted production timelines, affecting the readiness of the armed forces.[217] Streamlining procurement processes and improving coordination among various stakeholders are essential to mitigate these challenges.

Technological Hurdles in Modern Ammunition Systems

The development of modern ammunition systems, such as precision-guided munitions (PGMs) and smart artillery shells, presents specific technological challenges. These systems require advanced materials, sophisticated guidance technologies, and integration with existing platforms. The development and production of PGMs have been a significant challenge for the Indian ammunition industry. Efforts to indigenise these advanced systems have faced obstacles related to the miniaturisation of guidance components, integration with existing delivery systems, and achieving the required accuracy.[218] These challenges underscore the need for sustained investment in advanced R&D and collaboration with global technology leaders.

The Indian ammunition industry faces a myriad of technical challenges that hinder its ability to fully meet the demands of modern warfare. From legacy technologies and limited R&D capabilities to quality control issues and supply chain inefficiencies, these challenges require comprehensive and sustained efforts to address. Case studies such as the modernisation struggles of the erstwhile OFB, the development of advanced artillery shells, and the hurdles in producing PGMs highlight specific technological barriers that need to be overcome. To surmount these challenges, the Indian ammunition industry must invest in modernising its infrastructure, enhancing R&D capabilities, and adopting international best practices in quality control and standardisation. Furthermore, improving supply chain logistics and fostering greater collaboration between public and private sectors will be crucial in building a more robust and resilient ammunition production capability. Addressing these issues will not only enhance India's defence preparedness but also position it as a significant player in the global defence industry.

Industrial Base for Ammunition Production

The Indian ammunition production sector is predominantly driven by key public sector undertakings, with the erstwhile Ordnance Factory Board (OFB) being the most prominent. Established in 1775, the OFB (now DPSUs) operates under the Ministry of Defence and is one of the oldest and largest defence production organisations in India. It comprises 41 factories, 13 development centres, and nine institutes of learning spread across the country.[219]

The erstwhile OFB was responsible for the production of a wide range of defence equipment, including small arms, ammunition, explosives, and artillery systems. Its extensive network of factories specialises in different types of ammunition, such as the Ammunition Factory Khadki (AFK), which focuses on small arms ammunition, and the Heavy Vehicles Factory (HVF) in Avadi, which produces armoured vehicles and their ammunition.[220] Despite its historical significance, the erstwhile OFB has faced criticism for inefficiencies and outdated technology. Recent modernisation efforts aim to upgrade production facilities with advanced machinery and improve quality control processes to meet contemporary defence needs.[221]

The DRDO plays a crucial role in the research and development of advanced ammunition technologies. It collaborates with Ordnance factories and private sector companies to develop new types of ammunition and enhance existing systems. Key DRDO laboratories involved in ammunition development include the Armament Research and Development Establishment (ARDE) and the High Energy Materials Research Laboratory (HEMRL).[222]

Key Private Sector Players

In recent years, the Indian government has encouraged private sector participation in defence production, recognising the need for innovation, efficiency, and technological advancement. Several private companies have emerged as significant players in the ammunition production sector. The private sector's involvement in defence production is subject to the government's approval through a process of industrial licensing. As of April 2023, the government has issued 606 licences to 369 companies. Most large Indian private conglomerates, such as Tata Group, Larsen & Toubro (L&T), Mahindra, and Bharat Forge, are involved in some form of defence production. Some of the big-ticket items being manufactured (or contracts won) by the private sector include transport aircraft (Tata), artillery guns (L&T, Tata, and Bharat Forge) and Pinaka Rocket launchers (Tata and L&T), among others. In significant orders won by the private sector recently, L&T signed two contracts—for high-powered radar and close-in-weapon system—with the MoD in a combined deal worth INR 133.69 billion (approximately US$ 1.6 billion). As of January 2023, 14,000 MSMEs and 329 start-ups are engaged in defence production in India.[223]

Bharat Forge, part of the Kalyani Group, is a leading engineering and manufacturing company with significant involvement in defence production. It produces a range of ammunition and artillery systems, including the ATAGS (Advanced Towed Artillery Gun System) developed in collaboration with DRDO.[224] Bharat Forge boasts state-of-the-art manufacturing facilities equipped with advanced CNC machines, robotic automation, and comprehensive quality control systems.

Larsen & Toubro (L&T) is a major Indian multinational conglomerate with a dedicated defence division. It manufactures a variety of defence equipment, including artillery systems, armoured vehicles, and precision-guided munitions.[225] L&T's defence facilities are equipped with cutting-edge technologies for precision engineering and assembly. The company's focus on R&D and innovation has positioned it as a key player in modernising India's defence capabilities.

Tata Advanced Systems Limited (TASL), a subsidiary of Tata Sons, is involved in the production of advanced defence systems, including missiles, rocket launchers, and small arms ammunition. TASL collaborates with global defence companies to bring advanced technologies to India.[226] TASL's facilities are designed to meet international standards, with advanced production lines, automated assembly, and stringent quality assurance protocols.

Kalyani Group – Kalyani Strategic Systems Ltd. Kalyani Group has been a traditional supplier over the last 35 years of components and subsystems to Indian defence forces, including a wide range of safety and critical components like ammunition and shells, aluminium road wheels, track shoe assembly for MBTs, Grad BM 21 rocket tubes, T-72 crankshafts, front axle beams, steering knuckles, transmission parts, etc. However, all these supplies were restricted to only component and sub-system levels.[227]

India's ammunition production infrastructure includes a mix of legacy facilities and modern manufacturing plants. Public sector factories, primarily the Ordnance factories, are undergoing modernisation to enhance production capacity and quality. These facilities are spread across various locations, each specialising in different types of ammunition and defence equipment. The private sector's entry has introduced state-of-the-art facilities with advanced manufacturing technologies, such as CNC machining, robotic automation, and digital quality control systems. These facilities are often located in industrial hubs with access to logistical support and skilled labour. While the Ordnance factories have historically been the backbone of ammunition production, the private sector's involvement is driving modernisation and innovation. The combined efforts of the public and private sectors, supported by robust manufacturing facilities and infrastructure, are crucial for enhancing India's defence capabilities and achieving self-reliance in ammunition production.

Supply Chain and Logistics

The supply chain and logistics involved in ammunition production are crucial for ensuring timely and efficient delivery of high-quality ammunition to meet the demands of national defence. The ammunition supply chain consists of several key components, including raw material procurement, manufacturing processes, quality control, storage, and distribution.

The production of ammunition requires various raw materials such as metals (brass, copper, and steel), propellants, explosives, and chemicals for primers and casings.[228] Securing a consistent supply of these materials can be challenging due to factors such as market fluctuations, geopolitical tensions, and regulatory restrictions. For example, the procurement of explosives and propellants is tightly regulated to prevent misuse, adding complexity to the supply chain.[229] Ammunition manufacturing involves precision engineering processes such as casting, machining, assembling, and testing. Advanced technologies like computer numerical control (CNC) machining and automated assembly lines are employed to ensure high quality and consistency.[230] Effective coordination with suppliers is essential to ensure the timely delivery of components and materials. Delays or disruptions at any stage can impact the entire production schedule. Quality control is a critical aspect of ammunition production, given the safety and performance requirements. Each batch of ammunition undergoes rigorous testing for reliability, accuracy, and safety. Standards are set by national defence organisations and international bodies.[231] Automated inspection systems and advanced testing facilities are employed to detect defects and ensure that the ammunition meets the required specifications. The logistics and distribution mechanisms in ammunition production involve the storage, transportation, and delivery of finished products to military units and other end-users. Ammunition must be stored in secure facilities with stringent access controls to prevent theft, sabotage, or accidents.

These storage facilities are designed to handle hazardous materials safely and are equipped with fire suppression systems and environmental controls.[232] Effective inventory management practices are crucial to ensure that stock levels are maintained, and that ammunition is rotated to prevent degradation over time. Advanced software systems are used to track inventory and manage stockpile levels. The transportation of ammunition is subject to strict regulations to ensure safety and security. This includes specialised vehicles, secure packaging, and adherence to legal requirements for transporting hazardous materials. Coordinating transportation involves multiple stakeholders, including manufacturers, logistics providers, and military units. Efficient logistical planning is essential to avoid delays and ensure timely delivery. Distribution mechanisms for military supply chains are complex and involve multiple layers, from central depots to forward operating bases. The logistics network must be resilient and adaptable to varying operational requirements. Distribution challenges can include infrastructure limitations, environmental conditions, and geopolitical risks. For example, delivering ammunition to remote or conflict-prone areas requires careful planning and coordination. The supply chain and logistics involved in ammunition production are complex and require meticulous planning and coordination. From raw material procurement to manufacturing, quality control, storage, transportation, and distribution, each component plays a vital role in ensuring the availability and reliability of ammunition for national defence. Effective management of these processes is essential to address challenges and ensure the efficient delivery of high-quality ammunition. Continuous improvement and adoption of advanced technologies can enhance the resilience and efficiency of the supply chain, contributing to national security and operational readiness.

Production Capacity and Output

The Indian ammunition industry, a critical pillar of the nation's defence sector, has seen significant developments in its production capacities and output in recent years. This section provides an overview of the current production capacities and output statistics, highlighting trends and patterns that have emerged in the industry. The erstwhile Ordnance Factory Board (OFB) is the primary entity responsible for ammunition production in India. It operates 41 factories that collectively have a substantial production capacity. According to the Ministry of Defence,[233] these factories produce a wide range of ammunition types, including small arms ammunition, artillery shells, rockets, and explosives. The annual production capacity of the Ordnance factories is estimated to be over 1 million units of small arms ammunition and thousands of units of larger munitions such as artillery shells and rockets. Recent policy shifts have allowed increased participation of private sector companies in ammunition production. Companies such as Bharat Forge, Larsen & Toubro, and Tata Advanced Systems have established significant production capabilities. Bharat Forge, for instance, has expanded its facilities to include advanced manufacturing technologies capable of producing precision-guided munitions and artillery systems.[234] These companies contribute to diversifying and enhancing the overall production capacity of the Indian ammunition industry.

The output of the Indian ammunition industry has shown an upward trend in recent years, driven by increased defence spending and modernisation efforts. The Ministry of Defence[235] reports that the annual production of small arms ammunition by the Ordnance factories and private sector entities combined has exceeded 1.2 million units in recent years. For larger munitions such as artillery shells and rockets, the combined output is estimated to be in tens of thousands. The implementation of modernisation programs has improved production efficiency and output quality. For example, the introduction of advanced CNC machines, automated assembly lines, and digital quality control systems has streamlined production processes, reducing lead times and enhancing output consistency.[236] India's focus on becoming a net exporter of defence equipment has also impacted ammunition production. The Federation of Indian Chambers of Commerce and Industry (FICCI) reported a significant increase in defence exports, with ammunition being a major component. In 2020, defence exports, including ammunition, were valued at approximately US$ 1.5 billion, reflecting a growing trend towards increasing production not just for domestic needs but also for international markets.[237]

Trends and Patterns

The role of private sector companies in ammunition production has been expanding. government initiatives such as the Defence Procurement Procedure (DPP) and the Strategic Partnership Model have encouraged private companies to invest in defence manufacturing. This shift has led to increased competition, innovation, and efficiency in the industry.[238] There is a noticeable trend towards the development and production of advanced ammunition types, such as precision-guided munitions and smart artillery shells. These advanced systems are being developed through collaborations between DRDO, (now MIL), and private sector companies, aiming to enhance the operational capabilities of the Indian armed forces. Modernisation of existing infrastructure has been a key focus area. The Ordnance factories, along with private sector players, have been upgrading manufacturing facilities to incorporate state-of-the-art technologies. This modernisation is aimed at improving production capacities, quality, and overall efficiency.[239]

The Indian ammunition industry has witnessed significant growth in its production capacities and output in recent years. The increased involvement of the private sector, modernisation of manufacturing facilities, and a focus on advanced ammunition types are key trends shaping the industry. These developments are expected to continue driving the growth of ammunition production in India, enhancing both domestic defence capabilities and export potential.

SWOT Analysis of India's Technological and Industrial Base

The ammunition production sector in India is a critical component of the country's defence industry, contributing significantly to national security and defence capabilities. This SWOT analysis provides an in-depth examination of the strengths, weaknesses, opportunities, and threats facing the sector.

Strengths

The erstwhile Ordnance Factory Board (now Munitions India Limited), with its extensive network of factories and multiple development centres, provides a robust foundation for ammunition production in India. This established infrastructure allows for large-scale production across a variety of ammunition types. Significant government support through policies and initiatives such as the Defence Procurement Procedure (DPP) and the Strategic Partnership Model has bolstered the sector. These policies aim to enhance self-reliance and boost private sector participation.[240] Continuous modernisation efforts, including the integration of advanced manufacturing technologies like CNC machines, automation, and digital quality control systems, have improved production efficiency and quality.[241] Companies such as Bharat Forge, Larsen & Toubro, and Tata Advanced Systems have established significant capabilities, contributing to innovation and diversification in the sector.[242] MIL, with its extensive network of factories, provides a solid foundation for ammunition production.

These factories have long been the backbone of India's defence manufacturing, capable of producing a wide range of ammunition types, from small arms to artillery shells. The Indian government has launched several initiatives to bolster the defence manufacturing sector, including the Defence Procurement Procedure (DPP) and the Strategic Partnership Model. These policies aim to enhance self-reliance, encourage private sector participation, and promote exports.[243] Major private-sector players like Bharat Forge, Larsen & Toubro, and Tata Advanced Systems have entered the defence manufacturing space, bringing innovation, efficiency, and advanced technologies. These companies have established modern production facilities with state-of-the-art equipment, contributing to the sector's growth.[244] India has made significant strides in adopting advanced manufacturing technologies. The integration of computer numerical control (CNC) machines, automation, and digital quality control systems has improved production efficiency and product quality.[245] The Defence Research and Development Organisation (DRDO) plays a crucial role in advancing ammunition technology. DRDO's collaborations with public and private sectors have led to the development of advanced systems like the Pinaka multi-barrel rocket launcher and the Dhanush artillery gun. With a strategic focus on becoming a net exporter of defence equipment, India has identified significant potential in the global market. The Federation of Indian Chambers of Commerce and Industry (FICCI) reported an increase in defence exports, with ammunition being a major component.[246]

Weaknesses

A significant weakness in India's ammunition production sector is the dependence on imported raw materials and components. This reliance creates vulnerabilities in the supply chain, potentially leading to disruptions and delays.[247] The Indian ammunition industry remains dependent on imported raw materials and components, which can lead to supply chain vulnerabilities and disruptions.[248] Bureaucratic red tape and regulatory hurdles often slow down decision-making processes and impede timely production and procurement activities, affecting overall efficiency.[249] Despite the presence of the DRDO and other research institutions, the sector's R&D capabilities are spread thin across various projects, limiting focused advancements in ammunition technology.

There have been instances of ammunition failures and accidents, indicating persistent quality control challenges. Ensuring consistent quality and reliability remains an ongoing issue.[250] The sector is often hampered by bureaucratic red tape and regulatory hurdles, which slow down decision-making processes and impede timely production and procurement activities. These inefficiencies can affect the overall performance and competitiveness of the industry.[251] Despite improvements, quality control remains a persistent challenge. There have been instances of ammunition failures and accidents, highlighting the need for more stringent quality assurance measures.[252] While the DRDO and other institutions contribute significantly to R&D, the focus on ammunition technology can sometimes be diluted by the broad range of projects they undertake. This can limit the depth and pace of advancements in specific ammunition technologies. Although there have been efforts to modernise infrastructure, many Ordnance factories still operate with outdated equipment and processes. This lack of comprehensive modernisation can hinder the sector's ability to meet contemporary standards and demands. Competing in the global market poses challenges, including meeting international standards and certifications, navigating complex export regulations, and establishing a presence in highly competitive markets.[253]

Opportunities

The ongoing modernisation of India's armed forces presents opportunities for the ammunition sector to develop and supply advanced ammunition types, including precision-guided munitions and smart artillery shells. With the government's emphasis on boosting defence exports, there is significant potential for Indian-made ammunition to capture international markets. The Federation of Indian Chambers of Commerce and Industry (FICCI) has highlighted growing defence exports as a strategic goal.[254] Enhanced collaboration between public and private sectors can lead to improved technology transfer, innovation, and production capabilities. Such partnerships can leverage the strengths of both sectors to drive growth.[255] The integration of emerging technologies such as additive manufacturing (3D printing), artificial intelligence (AI), and the Internet of Things (IoT) can revolutionise ammunition production, making it more efficient and adaptable to changing defence needs.[256]

Threats

Geopolitical tensions and conflicts can disrupt supply chains, impact the availability of raw materials, and lead to increased volatility in production and procurement processes.[257] Rapid advancements in global defence technology pose a threat if the Indian ammunition sector fails to keep pace. Falling behind in technology can undermine the competitiveness and effectiveness of Indian-made ammunition.[258]

Stringent regulatory requirements and compliance issues can hamper the sector's growth. Navigating these regulations requires significant resources and can slow down innovation and production.[259] The production of ammunition involves hazardous materials and processes that pose environmental and safety risks. Addressing these concerns requires stringent measures and investments in safer and more sustainable practices.[260]

India's ammunition production sector boasts several strengths, including established infrastructure, government support, and technological advancements. However, it also faces significant weaknesses such as dependence on imports, bureaucratic inefficiencies, and quality control issues. Opportunities lie in defence modernisation, export potential, and the adoption of emerging technologies. Meanwhile, threats from geopolitical risks, technological lag, regulatory challenges, and environmental concerns must be effectively managed to ensure the sector's growth and sustainability.

Conclusion

Ammunition production is a technologically advanced and highly specialised field that has evolved significantly over the years. The integration of modern technologies, such as CNC machining, automated assembly lines, and advanced testing facilities, has improved the efficiency, precision, and reliability of ammunition production. Comparing the practices of leading ammunition-producing countries reveals a range of approaches and standards, influenced by technological capabilities and regulatory environments.

As the field continues to evolve, emerging technologies like additive manufacturing, smart ammunition, and AI-driven processes promise to further revolutionise ammunition production. By adopting these innovations and maintaining high standards, manufacturers can ensure that ammunition production meets the rigorous demands of modern defence requirements while adhering to global best practices.

Benchmarking against leading global ammunition producers highlights the strengths and areas for improvement in India's ammunition production sector. While India has made commendable progress, especially with increased private sector involvement, it must accelerate technological adoption and enhance quality control to compete with the USA, Russia, and China. Strategic investments and international collaborations will be crucial for India to achieve and sustain a competitive edge in ammunition production.

India's ammunition production sector boasts significant strengths, including a robust public sector infrastructure, increasing private sector involvement, and government support. However, it also faces notable weaknesses, such as dependence on imports, bureaucratic inefficiencies, and quality control issues. Addressing these challenges through strategic investments, policy reforms, and enhanced collaboration between public and private sectors will be crucial for maximising the sector's potential, both domestically and internationally. The EU's ammunition production and export industry is characterised by advanced technological capabilities, significant production capacity, and a strong regulatory framework. Leading producers in Germany, France, Italy, and Sweden contribute to a diverse and competitive market, ensuring that the EU remains a key player in the global defence industry.

Chapter Six

Securing Ammunition Supply Chains: Reliable Sourcing of Raw Materials and Components

"A soldier can survive forever without mail; for thirty days without food; for three days without water; for three minutes without air; and not one second without ammunition."[261]

Introduction

The current global ammunition supply chain faces significant pressures which are driven by rapidly evolving geopolitical tensions, revealing critical vulnerabilities in production, sourcing and distribution networks leading to stress on the need for securing the ammunition supply chains. This chapter examines the complexities of ammunition manufacturing, supply chain vulnerabilities, limited domestic resource availability and technological-logistical challenges. It also explores the strategic approaches with which it highlights the importance of indigenous resource development, raw material sourcing, public-private partnerships, international collaborations and the diversification of supply chains. The intricate interplay of economic, technological and geopolitical dynamic emphasises the critical need to minimise import dependency, harness more indigenous resources and cultivate strategic partnerships for the nations. The proposed recommendations include a policy on defence supply chain security, incentivising domestic production and strengthening the defence procurement policies. The chapter emphasises the need for securing ammunition supply chains from the end of policy makers, defence organisations and stakeholders of the industry.

The defence supply chains are strategically significant in safeguarding national security of a nation as they represent the foundation of any military operation by providing necessary materials, technologies, and components. Modern defence systems are complex especially, with the emergence of advanced technologies. Therefore, there is a need for robust and resilient supply chains to counter or preferably avoid any critical vulnerability. The primary challenge in this aspect is reliance on global networks for procuring raw materials and advanced technologies as in some cases regions are unstable economically or politically. Additionally, these logistics and supply chains are also hampered by pandemics, natural disasters or cyber-attacks. These failures result in cost overruns, delays and also compromises military readiness. Therefore, it is extremely important to secure a resilient and diversified supply chain with reduced dependence on foreign imports and global disruptions.

This chapter aims to put forth strategic solutions for secure ammunition supply chains by evaluating existing vulnerabilities. The study stresses on reducing the dependency on imports and working on a self-sufficient defence ecosystem or 'Atmanirbhar Bharat'. It comprehensively analyses the structure of the supply chain from raw materials to manufacturing process to logistics. It also examines the challenges constituting limited raw materials domestically, technological gaps and global trade dynamics. Furthermore, the chapter explores the impact of strategic approaches like public-private partnerships, alliances and technological advancements for a robust defence ecosystem. It seeks to contribute to the discourse on national security by providing actionable recommendations to address complexities in ammunition supply chains for policy makers and industry stakeholders.

Ammunition Supply Chain: An Overview

The ammunition supply chain process is a complex operation that constitutes multiple stages in order to ensure efficaciousness of the final product. The stages include procurement of raw material which forms the foundation of ammunition, for instance, brass, steel, propellants, etc., followed by manufacturing individual components such as casings, primers, etc., and assembling it to form a complete cartridge. According to Hancock Jr.,[262] the ammunition chain begins at the factory and ends when it reaches the end-user of the product. The entire process can be understood across three 'levels of war' vis-à-vis strategic, operational and tactical and the ammunition system can be divided into the wholesale distribution system and retail distribution system.[263] The wholesale distribution system acts as a support base for all forces and therefore this part is associated with the strategic level of operations wherein ammunition demand rates are determined and forecasted. This stage includes 'manufacturing, the storage of ammunition in depots, and transportation' which is based on factors such as ammunition tiering, strategic considerations, and configured loads. On the other hand, the retail ammunition distribution system constitutes 'operational and tactical levels of war'.[264] The operational level connects both the strategic and the tactical level of war as it is the stage where the ammunition leaves the country and is transported to the theatre of operations wherein moving ammunition in containers is the preferred method. Finally, the ammunition supply chain ends with the tactical level which ensures the availability of the product with the end-user. The process of an Ammunition Supply Chain can be depicted as below.[265]

Compiled by the Author[266]

While the management systems include the wholesale systems, retail systems, and future systems, the transportation capabilities include depot capability, port throughput capability, in-transit visibility and lift and in-theatre capability.

Broadly the components of the ammunition supply chain can be divided into procurement of raw materials, manufacturing processes and quality control standards. The procurement of raw materials is the first step. Ammunition are projectiles that are used in 'small arms, artillery and other guns and weapons.' Its key components include cartridge case, primer, propellant, and projectile.[267] Therefore, the raw materials would include procuring brass, steel or aluminium for casings and lead or tungsten for projectiles. In addition to this, raw materials also constitute chemicals for propellants but the availability and quality of these materials are dependent on various factors such as extraction capacities or geopolitical stability of the region. This step is critical as the suppliers are evaluated on rigorous standards especially on the ability to consistently deliver high quality raw material and strict compliance with defence standards as well. Recently, many nations have begun exploring environment-friendly material so that there are minimum ecological impacts as a result of the ammunition supply chain.[268] In the stage of production and procurement, a major challenge that arises is dependency on external suppliers for critical raw materials and geopolitical tensions or restrictions with respect to trade from that nation hence, leading to significant bottlenecks in the supply chain.[269]

The next step is the manufacturing process which includes stages such as designing ammunition according to the needs of an operation, sourcing raw materials for production, assembling all the components with precision to come up with an end product and, lastly, followed by quality control tests. Once the product is approved, it is then packaged and distributed through defence supply chains to military depots and operational theatres all over the world. It is important to note that all these stages are interdependent on each other and seamless integration within the supply chain is key. Any small disruption in any one aspect of the process might result in cascading effects on the operational readiness of the defence forces.

Figure 6.1: Army Supply Chain Management

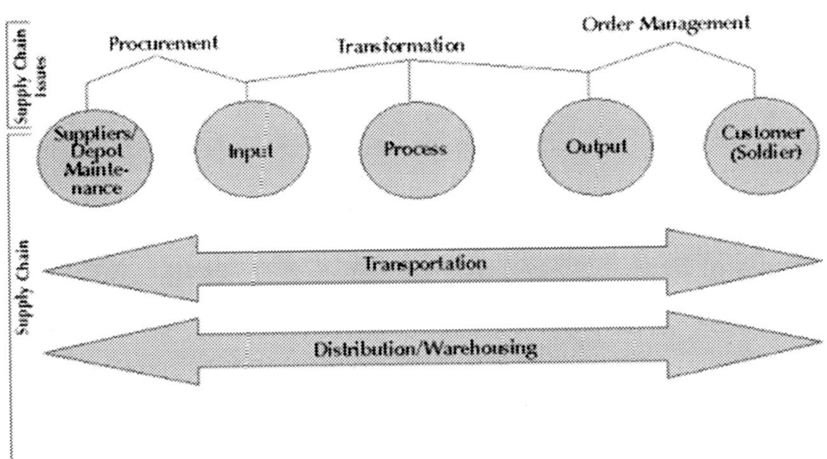

The ammunition supply chain is susceptible to much vulnerability, primarily logistical challenges. For instance, delays in transportation, customs delays or any mismanagement can result in delay in critical supplies which, in the defence sector, might alter the outcome of a conflict. Many raw materials such as rare earth metals are mostly sourced from limited countries and in some cases sourced from politically volatile or conflictual regions which might result in bottlenecks during international issues. Furthermore, the world of today is technologically advanced; therefore, dependence on technology for ammunition supply chains might pose additional risks such as cyber-security threats, intellectual property risks, etc. There has been an increase in compliance costs and a reduced number of suppliers that deal with extraction of raw materials like lead and explosives, primarily due to stringent environment regulations throughout the world. Lastly, over-reliance on a single supplier for any critical component is a risk in itself as any natural disaster or economic instability might have cascading effects on the entire supply chain. In order to address these vulnerabilities, a multi-pronged approach is imperative which should consider diversifying suppliers, investment in domestic production and maintaining strategic reserves to avoid any spontaneous supply disruption.

Lastly, the stage of ammunition storage and disposal are critical components in defence sector. The managing of explosive materials and ensuring safety of workforce and population as a whole, requires specialised facilities which are equipped to handle volatile materials passing through supply chains. Therefore, a vulnerable situation arises if any catastrophic accident occurs due to lapse in procedure or a slight oversight. Concurrently, the disposal of expired and obsolete ammunition or non-functional materials presents significant environmental challenges. The interconnected nature of all the stages amplifies the risks and vulnerabilities in the ammunition supply chain.

Challenges in Sourcing Raw Materials and Components

Ammunition supply chains are highly dependent on the availability of critical raw materials. With respect to raw materials firstly, metals like brass and steel for making casings, shells and projectiles, secondly, propellants which comprise nitro-glycerine, nitrocellulose and stabilisers for generating the thrust to fire projectiles and, lastly, the explosives. The critical components made from the raw materials mentioned above are casings, primers, fuzes, electronic modules and so on. They provide structural integrity, reliable performance, precision targeting and guided programmes to defence ammunition equipment. The interconnected nature of sourcing of raw materials and manufacturing of components leads to several challenges.

One of the major challenges most nations face is not having sufficient reserves of the essential materials that are required for producing ammunition components and the countries that do have limited extraction capacities.[270] For instance, the European defence industry relies on the USA for beryllium, Brazil for niobium, South Africa for platinum and China for rare earth metals, antimony, magnesium, etc.[271] In fact, in order to ensure a 'sustainable and secure supply of critical raw materials' and at the same time reduce dependency on single country suppliers it came up with the European Raw Materials Act which came into force in May 2024.[272] While relying on domestic resources is imperative, it might also face challenges because of heightened demand due to any conflict.

According to AmmoIndia 2024, a report by KPMG Ltd., the Indian ammunition industry is faced with three major challenges, vis-à-vis technological hurdles, supply-side constraints and regulatory barriers. Ammunition can be broadly divided into Small Calibre (<14.7 mm), Medium Calibre (20mm – 60 mm), Heavy Calibre (>60 mm), 'mortars, mines, grenades' and Loitering Ammunition. Challenges vary for each category of ammunition. For instance, the raw material cost for grenades, mortars and mines is high as it has to 'withstand extreme conditions without degrading'.[273] Input material availability is another significant challenge. For instance, India does not produce antimony which is used for making small arms and bullets. India does not have sufficient production of iron and copper ores which are crucial for manufacturing bullet cartridges. Even toluene, which is an essential material in TNT production, is limited in India. Therefore, this calls for huge financial investment from the government and policy support too.

Dependence on imported materials is another significant challenge that needs to be examined. For instance, rare earth metals are used in defence. Although they are not rare, its supply chain is dominated by China which accounts for 70 per cent of rare earth ore extraction and 90 per cent of its processing. Its dominance in this sphere has been a result of early investment in the field but this dominance has alerted the nations and therefore has pushed other nations to invest in rare earth metal extraction. For example, the US

Department of Defence recommended stockpiling of rare earth metals as early as in 2013.[274] Lastly, technological gaps and insufficient infrastructure also impact the domestic production of ammunition or even the robustness of the supply chain. For instance, with respect to heavy calibre, lack of technical know-how and absence of technology transfer is the main challenge. For loitering ammunition, integration of AI has become important which would allow for 'autonomous navigation, target identification, and mission planning'.[275]

The Indian ammunition industry ecosystem can therefore be categorised as a strictly regulated industry with stringent licensing and oversight. The suppliers are highly concentrated and the market has few major players who dominate the markets. While the developed nations use advanced ammunition systems, India is constrained by limited technology transfer agreements and shortage of skilled personnel in this sector. India's defence sector is a monopsony market wherein the government and defence organisations are the major buyers. There has been a minimal investment in R&D and India has not yet reached its potential of adopting technological advancements like precision-guided munitions. Therefore, to tackle this, ammunition stockpiles are imperative as they affect the outcome of conflicts. Atmanirbharta in ammunition production is key as it would help India to better position itself in times of conflicts and would help India avoid any potential disruption in its ammunition supply chains.[276] Furthermore, the gaps in digitisation of supply chains and integrated digital system often result in delays particularly when coordinating a complex logistics system. Hence, the need for technological, infrastructural and workforce development.

In addition, other supply chain vulnerabilities include threats to cyber security as they might target either production lines or logistics operations. It is pertinent to note that these interconnected ammunition supply chains are extremely fragile as any minute delay in either shipping or container shortages might heavily impact the delivery of the end product. Therefore, robust supply chains should be characterised by, first, strategic stockpiling of ammunition, and second, diversified suppliers and continued collaboration so as to avoid any effect of geopolitical volatility. For geopolitical risk mitigation, it requires a multi-pronged approach which involves coordinated efforts from the government, major private stakeholders and international collaborators in the form of regional alliances.

Strategic Approaches to Secure the Ammunition Supply Chain

Domestic production of raw materials is one of the best strategies to reduce dependency on imports and enhance the robustness of ammunition supply chains. Countries around the work have focused on promoting domestic manufacturing in the defence sector. For instance, India's initiative of 'Atmanirbhar Bharat' has resulted in significant growth in its exports which has increased thirty times in the last decade and domestic production has hit almost 1.27 lakh crore, that is, even defence production has increased approximately 174 per cent in the last decade. With this initiative, India aims to transform itself from a major arms importer and position itself as a defence exporter in the coming years. This is the result of consistent efforts by the government through its initiatives like liberalising its FDI policy, increased budget allocation for defence, releasing positive indigenisation lists, and launching of schemes like iDEX, SRIJAN portal, Defence Industrial Corridors, etc.[277] Additionally, under the 'Make in India' initiative and the Defence Production and Export Promotion Policy (DPEPP), a major effort is given to production of critical materials such as propellants, primers and explosives, simultaneously to create an ecosystem for sustainable production hence emphasising indigenous resource development. Similarly, in order to reduce China's dominance in the extraction and processing of rare earth elements, the USA has started opening new mines and stockpiling the output as well. The USA is collaborating with its allies to counter Chinese dominance in this sector; for instance, the Elk Creek mine in Nebraska, Canada, or the Mount Weld Mine in Western Australia.[278] Additionally, recycling and re-using materials also seems to be an innovative approach that can be explored; for instance, extracting metals from scrap military hardware.[279]

Furthermore, public-private partnership (PPP) has emerged as a cornerstone to promote domestic production of ammunition components as it allows the government to collaborate with private firms which further help to share risks and mobilise resources efficaciously. For instance, the growth of India's defence sector can be seen through the development of Dhanush artillery gun system, Tejas, submarines, main battle tank, corvettes, etc.[280] One of the important approaches for capacity building is adopting cutting-edge technologies such as additive technologies such as 3D-printing that would help in cost reduction and decreasing the logistic footprints of an operation.[281] Additionally, R&D is imperative to further the technological capabilities of a nation, especially in artificial intelligence, machine learning, etc., as predictive analysis can help in optimising ammunition supply chain flows and enhancing quality assurance. It can result in significant cost savings and integrating user feedback can help enhance the applicability of new technologies which are tailored to specific requirements.[282] Lastly, diversified suppliers can result in robust pathways for logistics and single-source dependencies result in exposing the supply chains to vulnerabilities. Additionally, nations should reduce their reliance on distant suppliers and develop shorter supply chains which are dependent on localised production and minimise transportation costs and, at the same time are comparatively easy to manage and control. Moreover, adopting block chain technology can help promote transparency and security in ammunition supply chain management but this requires massive investment and overhauling on the part of the government as it would then have to focus its efforts on cyber security measures.

Policy Recommendations for Strengthening Ammunition Supply Chains

In order to secure ammunition supply chains, the following recommendations can be considered.

1. A comprehensive policy framework is imperative for the ammunition supply chain to be resilient as it would ensure protection from global disruptions and geopolitical volatility. Defence supply chains are extremely crucial for the security of any nation; therefore, its robustness should be made a strategic priority. For instance, a National Policy on Defence Supply Chain Security can be formed into a Comprehensive National Policy wherein the key focus should be Supply Chain Security Framework, Monitoring & Risk Assessment, and Tri-Sectoral Strategic Framework. The government should encour-age such initiatives to mitigate the vulnerabilities in production, procurement, and logistics. Furthermore, regular assessment of geopolitical threats and market fluctuations due to which supply chain risks occur should be monitored. Lastly, the tri-sectoral

framework should include formalised partnerships between government agencies, stakeholders of the industry and international partners to bolster supply chain resilience. The government should roll out such initiatives and policy measures that reduce dependency on imports and technology gaps. It should focus on diversified imports and ensure that the supply chains are secure from any external threat. India should focus on establishing national reserves of critical raw materials and also encourage supplier diversification.

2. Supply chain risks can be mitigated if ammunition components are domestically produced as that would help the government keep an oversight on the entire supply chain. In fact, in times of need, one can even provide incentives to bolster domestic manufacturing capabilities such as subsidies, access to low-interest loans or tax breaks. Favourable policies can help private manufacturers to focus their efforts on R&D and develop technologies that are tailored to our needs. Also, a targeted financial and infrastructural aid should be provided to MSMEs and SMEs which specialise in niche manufacturing. Furthermore, to promote innovation, a defence ecosystem can be established which would contain defence-focused clusters or corridors so as to facilitate collaboration between academic, industry and government agencies. Lastly, the government can also simplify the regulatory process or probably have a single window to reduce bureaucratic hurdles for defence manufacturers and start-ups.
3. Traditional procurement practices in defence sector were by and large focused on minimising the expense but the government can now look into reforming the procurement policies and base it on factors such as supply chain, resilience, quality and reliability. Transparency in contracts can help foster trust and accountability between the suppliers and government and it would further help in streamlining decision making. It is pertinent that the strategy involves implementing of local sourcing mandates and with long-term contracts with suppliers for stability and capacity building. Furthermore, performance-based metrics can help to ensure better quality standards.
4. India can incorporate sustainable practices by rewarding suppliers that adopt green technologies so as to reduce any operational footprint. For instance, the initiatives should focus on a recycling and re-use system to

recover valuable material like brass and steel from ammunition that has been used and reduced to waste and thus conserve resources. Additionally, green manufacturing standards can be adopted across production processes and investments can be prioritised to create biodegradable alternatives so that the carbon footprint of military equipment can be minimised.

5. To address the emerging challenges in the present world dynamic, forming regional alliances with neighbouring and resource-rich nations can assure access to critical materials. This strategic partnership will help in seamless working of R&D that is simply access to new technology, scholarly works, and research for advanced materials used in ammunition such as nano-composites. Moreover, it will create new opportunities within the academic field as specialised training modules would be formed for the workforce.

Therefore, a coordinated approach which focuses on prioritising domestic production, innovation, and transparency is the need of the hour as it would not only enhance national security but result in growth and make India self-reliant or 'Atmanirhbhar'.

Conclusion

The security of ammunition supply chains is critical for national security. It is important to note that the supply chains are complex and vulnerable and a strategic approach to raw material and component sourcing is pivotal. This multi-pronged approach should include diverse suppliers, reducing single-country dependence, and collaborating with nations across the globe to counter geopolitical instability or resource scarcity. Above all, the primary way to start is by investing in R&D and promoting domestic production. The supply chains can further be enhanced by adopting innovative technologies like adoption of block chain technology, additive technologies like 3D printing, predictive analysis and pushing for transparency in order to minimise the risks.

Chapter Seven

Modernising Ammunition Acquisitions: Transition from Qualitative Requirement Based to Technology-Based Model for Procurement

Introduction

The contemporary world is characterised by technological advancements, and this has an impact on defence procurement model as well, especially ammunition. The existing Qualitative Requirement (GSQR) model negatively impacts agility and innovation which result in outdated capabilities of the defence forces. This chapter examines the shift from a QR-based procurement method to technology-based procurement (TBP) model and highlights the importance of adaptability, flexibility and continuous integration of advanced technologies in real time. This chapter highlights the challenges faced by the QR model and what makes the TBP model more advantageous. It delineates an implementation framework and outlines a phased approach and essential policy reforms. It also looks into the challenges and proposes risk mitigation strategies such as a change in management strategy, integration of cyber security and training programs in modular contracts, and digital tools for all personnel involved in the procurement process. The chapter concludes with tangible recommendations, illustrating how TBP may improve operational preparedness, reduce costs, and foster continuous innovation within defence procurement which is the need of the hour.

In order to ensure national security, the role of defence procurement is crucial as it provides the armed forces with adequate resources but for the longest time, ammunition procurement has been based on the 'Qualitative Requirements' process. General Staff QR-based process constitutes predefined specifications which have rigid standards of compliance. While this model ensures a high standard of quality, it often hinders innovation and adaptability in procurements. The security landscape today is rapidly evolving; therefore, dynamic procurement frameworks are the need of the hour to meet the strategically evolving demands of modern warfare. It is notable that under the QR-based model, the procurement processes often face delays and might result in exorbitant prices. Although this model might inhibit innovative solutions, it surely does offer strategic advantages. This model is comprehensive and lays stress on quality defence equipment but is unable to incorporate cutting-edge technology during its production process and this is where the Technology-based Procurement Model comes to the fore. Even in the US Department of Defence, procurement often encounters delays and this has led to them adopting the TBP model which lays emphasis on adapting updated technologies in defence acquisitions (Ali et al., 2018). Therefore, this chapter explores the feasibility of the TBP model by analysing the limitations of the QR-based procurement model. The aim is to outline a resilient framework for a procurement system which incorporates advancing technologies in real-time and explores the pathway to transition from a QR-based model to a TBP model steadily.

Analysis of QR-Based Procurement Process

The QR-based procurement process in defence is characterised by a detailed criteria for military acquisitions which ensures that the procured equipment meets stringent standards and maintains uniformity across products. The primary stakeholders in this process include government bodies, procurement agencies, and all these agencies collaborate with each other to ensure that all the acquired products adhere to adequate standards and comprehensive specifications for defence acquisitions.[283] The primary focus of the QR-based model is to reduce risk and as a result it prioritises risk mitigation over flexibility. Therefore, this model constitutes rigid processes where any change in the initial specification is discouraged or in some cases even penalised.[284] The procurement process can be comprehended as illustrated in Figure 7.1. This type of framework includes detailed documentation, rigorous testing and stringent standards so as to exclude and minimise any uncertainties that might occur.

Figure 7.1: Procurement Process

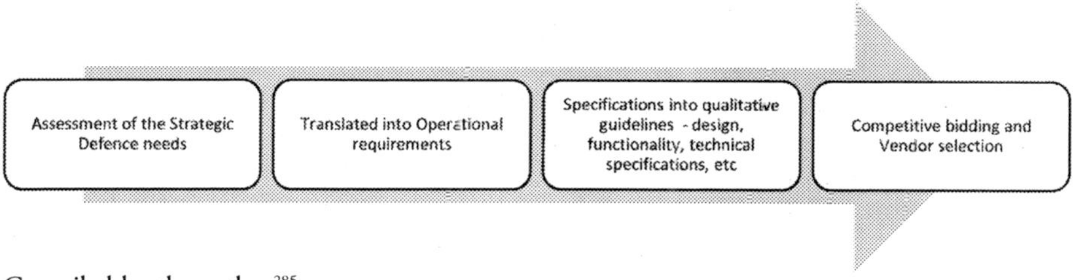

Assessment of the Strategic Defence needs

Translated into Operational requirements

Specifications into qualitative guidelines - design, functionality, technical specifications, etc

Competitive bidding and Vendor selection

Compiled by the author[285]

While this model takes into consideration quality-control and accountability, it has several limitations. First is rigidity as the entire process of the QR-based model requires strict adherence to criteria and pre-defined specifications but because of the increased technological advancements, the initial requirements soon fall out of scope as new technologies come into the picture. For instance, by the time a company fulfils the initial specification of the products, those products already become outdated with the emerging of fields such as artificial intelligence, Big Data computing, machine learning, certain types of new generation ammunition and so on and so forth. The second limitation of the QR-based model is bureaucratic delays as the procurement of any equipment requires extensive approvals.[286] Each phase forms the requirement assessment for vendor selection to quality assurance multiple levels of authorisation and checks are involved to minimise the risks but this in turn prolongs the procurement process. For instance, even the US Department of Defence faces such problems which results in lengthy procurement timelines and delays in critical equipment deployment. However, these delays are not purely administrative in nature and might also result in impacting the operational readiness of the armed forces. As already stated, in the QR-based model, it is not feasible to adjust additional requirements and incorporate any new changes mid-process; therefore, its lack of adaptability is the third limitation of this model. It affects the agility of the armed forces by not coping with the changing operational landscapes and emerging dynamic threats. Even if the stakeholders agree to any minor change mid process, this sole decision again needs to go through a process of revaluations and assessments which again prolongs the procurement timeline. Lastly, innovation in any form is discouraged in the QR-based procurement primarily because the process as a whole requires strict adherence to established criteria and uniformity. This tends to push the defence industry to comply with the standards rather than innovate as the QR process does not accommodate cutting-edge technologies readily.[287] It is important to note that the Service QRs are specific to that service. Any formulation of QRs should be based on factors such as 'core operational requirements; the technology potential within and outside the country; comprehensive, structured and concrete SQRs which represent the requirements of the users clearly; and finally, they should be broad and practical so that multiple vendors can bid for the production of the product'.[288, 289] More importantly, the armed forces have to be able to assess their requirements for 10-15 years down the line after analysing the emerging challenges and threats in the form of technological advancement. In addition, it is important to realise that resources are limited; therefore all countries should strive for Cost-efficient Qualitative requirements.

Many developed nations follow different procedures in order to evolve QRs. For instance, the USA came up with the concept of Advanced Concept Technology Demonstration (ACTD) wherein stabilised technologies are offered to the defence forces and then it is left to the military commander to determine their suitability for operational readiness of the nation. This method helps the military to take advantage of the nation's well developed scientific base and its technological prowess.[290] The Russians, on the other hand, have a large variety of military equipment based on 'baseline standards' which are grouped together into basic profiles. These act like building blocks which during the further course of action are converted into functional standards wherein a particular equipment has specific and distinct requirements. This type of arrangement is generally considered effective for a nation which relies heavily on indigenously building its military hardware in order to facilitate its life cycle support.[291] Another example is that of Britain which makes its procurement decisions in a 'make' or 'buy' format. This kind of methodology is highly practical especially for a country which imports military equipment and simultaneously builds it indigenously as well.[292] In fact, even India under the Defence Acquisition Procedure (DAP) 2020 categorised the procurement and acquisition of military equipment under 'Buy' and 'Buy and Make' in addition to the setting up of Innovations for Defence Excellence (iDEX) to support start-ups in this sector.[293]

Transition to Technology-Based Procurement

The battlefield of today is characterised by technological advancements such as artificial intelligence and unmanned systems; as a result, the QR-based model cannot maintain operational readiness. Therefore, it is only right that technology is incorporated in the procurement model as well as it would help to adopt cutting-edge technologies and ensure that the armed forces are more ready to respond to threats in a dynamic way. The defence supply chains are becoming more complex especially since the supply chains for defence organisations involve moving parts across various countries, which if not done aptly runs the risks of slow delivery of critical equipment and supply chain shocks.[294] The TBP model emphasises the importance of goals such as battlefield capabilities or improved communications. This not only results in a shortened procurement timeline but also helps in integrating incremental changes in the defence acquisition procedure. A technology-based approach helps in aligning with the rapid pace of innovation and advancements which further increase the operational readiness of the armed forces.[295]

Additionally, the TBP model also helps the private sector, especially the tech-focused industries, to collaborate and engage in the defence sector as they refrained from doing so initially because of the rigid structure of the QR model. The TBP model helps in expanding the supplier base in order to deliver the products with sophisticated capabilities. For instance, Ekstrom et al., in his work, '*Towards a purchasing portfolio model for defence procurement – A Delphi study of Swedish defence authorities*' proposes a two-stage segmentation model which is based on four homogenous segments vis-a-vis routine, operational risk, delivery risk and strategic supplies. In the case of routine supplies, there are higher chances in the market's ability to deliver the products on time and as a result there is minimum impact on the operational capability of the Swedish Armed Forces. Operational risks include those products which, although the market can deliver on time, could result in a higher risk in case of any failure. Third, for the delivery risks, the chances of the market to deliver it on time are low but in case it doesn't, the impact on the operational capability is also low. Finally, strategic supplies are those which can't be left to chance and are critical to enhance the operational capability of the Swedish armed forces.[296]

Countries throughout the world are reforming their procurement models, especially in defence. A recent example of this could be the recent policy chapter published by the UK Ministry of Defence titled, *Integrated Procurement Model – Driving pace in delivery of Military Capability.*[297] With respect to technology, it calls for being informed from the very start on factors such as the industrial base, export ability of any product and technology so as to design resilient supply chains. In order to tackle the emerging geopolitical challenges, the policy considers the options of delivering 'minimum deployable capability' rather than waiting for long which otherwise might be too long. With this policy, the UK is looking to adapting rapidly to the technology opportunities and evolving threats by incorporating their technological know-how in their design philosophy to meet the export challenge. This policy aims to work on its methodology to come up with the most apt way to cater to spiral development, technological advancement and procurement method which is not complex.[298]

Some of the key features of the TBP model include real-time data integration which helps the procurement agencies to quickly make informed decisions by considering market trends, risk factors and capabilities of the supplier which further helps in minimising any delay in procurement and helps to tackle outdated technology. Unlike the QR-based model which is static, the TBP model is more agile as it allows the defence forces to maintain operational advantage by swiftly adopting new technologies and reducing procurement cycles. It helps equipment production to be expanded and upgraded as and when required. Moreover, the technology-based procurement has various advantages such as encouraging innovation throughout the procurement cycle which helps in incorporating all emerging technologies as they develop.[299] It also attracts multiple suppliers to push for a market which is more competitive and innovation driven. Most importantly, it improves the operational readiness of the defence forces as it can adapt the latest technologies without any lengthy delays.

Implementation Framework for Technology-Based Procurement

In contemporary times, the defence industry a TBP model which is structured and is comprehended as a phased approach. In addition to this, it also includes policy reforms and stakeholder engagement. For instance, incorporating cutting-edge technology in a weapons system is crucial and this can only happen through collaboration with strategic partners.[300]

Figure 7.2: TBP Model: Implementation Framework

Technology-based Procurement (TBP) Model - Implementation Framework	**Phased Approach**	Planning
		Execution
		Evaluation
	Stakeholder Engagement	Leadership
		Procurement Teams
		Technology Providers
		End-users
	Policy and Regulatory reforms	Flexible Policies
		Cyber Security Standards
		Private Sector Collaboration

Compiled by the author.

As illustrated in Table 7.2, a structured approach is essential in order to optimise the resources, manage risks and transition to a TBP model. This framework can further be categorised as Phased approach, Stakeholder engagement and Policy and regulatory frameworks. A phased approach can further be divided into planning, execution and evaluation. The planning phase sets the foundation for TBP. It establishes the objectives, timelines, and resource allocations. This phase allows defence agencies to conduct a comprehensive needs assessment, wherein TBP can bring immediate and long-term benefits. This phase involves market research to understand the present technologies and potential industry partners. To engage the technology providers enables defence agencies to gauge the feasibility of integrating innovative solutions and form an outline of procurement strategies that are adaptable to the evolving capabilities.[301] In this phase, strategic roadmaps can be developed outlining short-term and long-term milestones. These effective roadmaps would present measurable benchmarks that enable stakeholders to track progress, identify challenges and implement corrective measures as prescribed. Another important plan is financial assistance needed, as TBP models often involve incremental funding to support an agile procurement cycle. By breaking it down into phases, defence agencies can allocate resources more efficiently reducing financial strain and allowing more agility in response to emerging technologies.[302] The execution phase emphasises on active engagement with vendors, iterative testing and real-time adaptability. This phase would allow defence agencies to implement agile procurement practices, facilitating continuous testing and refinement of technologies throughout their development. One of the options is to go for modular contracts as they ensure the updating of equipment as the new technology becomes available. It allows the defence forces to quickly and efficaciously respond to the ever-changing operational landscape. It also enables the agencies to monitor progress and performance metrics during the procurement cycle to take data driven decisions. It is the adaptability during this phase that helps the defence agencies to remain dynamic and adapt to new technologies without restarting the entire procurement process as was the case with stringent specifications of the QR-based model. The third phase under this approach is the evaluation phase wherein the primary focus is laid on assessment of the performance of the procured technologies. The factors that are considered are its scalability, adaptability, and performance which further help the defence agencies in making informed decisions about any future procurements. This phase also constitutes the valuable insights of the end-users which serve as feedback and helps in improving usability and efficaciousness of the any acquisitions in the future.

In addition to the phased approach, another factor to successfully transition to a TBP model is effective stakeholder engagement. The primary stakeholders in defence procurement include defence agencies, civilian leadership, technology providers, and the end-users and all these stakeholders play a significant role in implementing any model successfully. Leadership is crucial in defence acquisitions because it is responsible for the funding and adequate policy support through continuous commitment. Leaders with the defence agencies and the government can help in pushing for the TBP model by emphasising its benefits as it is cost-efficient and bolsters innovation. In order to incorporate technological advancement, the technological providers become equally important in the planning and execution processes as they facilitate steady integration. Moreover, the role of procurement teams is significant as it is their knowledge and expertise that allows for greater incorporation of cutting-edge technologies in the field of defence. Finally, end-users also form the crucial part of the procurement process as the acquired products and technologies should be in consonance with the needs and demands of the military personnel. The feedback provided by the end-users is critical as it enhances the overall effectiveness of the TBP model.[303]

Policy and regulatory framework forms another important pillar of the comprehensive framework of the TBP model as it is these frameworks that bolster innovation and push for modular contracting. Traditionally, the acquisition procedure laid emphasis on strict compliance on specifications which were often restrictive in nature; however, the TBP model calls for continuous improvement by encouraging incremental funding and a flexible contract. This type of procurement model helps defence agencies to procure the components of the project as and when they become available rather than waiting for the completion of the whole project. Another factor to be taken into consideration is alignment of cyber-security standards with that of the TBP model as incorporating technology in the procurement process means the involvement of real-time data and vulnerable technologies; therefore, the policies should be such that both the suppliers and the defence agencies adhere to regular cyber security assessment in order to sustain robustness in the procurement process. While the capabilities of the public sector have significantly improved in the twenty-first century collaboration with private sectors is the need of the hour as it would bring expertise in defence acquisition. In order to encourage private sector collaboration, the government should work on coming up with a single window to accelerate approvals, reduce bureaucratic delays and simultaneously promote tech-start-ups. For instance, in the USA, the Federal Acquisition Regulation supports rapid acquisition through programs like the Defence Innovation Unit and encourages innovation by allowing flexible contracting options.[304]

Hence, implementing a TBP model requires phased adoption, active stakeholder engagement, and supportive policy reforms that are conducive to agile, innovative and modern defence needs procurement. While the shift from a QR-based model to a TBP model is sought after, this transition also presents several challenges that defence organisations must address to ensure effective implementation. The first challenge is to get the traditional stakeholders to adopt the TBP model as they are accustomed to the QR-based approach. Defence procurement has been QR-based since long; therefore, incorporating technology in the process is bound to encounter resistance. A few reasons for this resistance could be the vulnerability and unpredictability of a technology-based model and familiarity with the already existing model.[305] The second challenge is data security concerns which have a direct impact on incorporating technology in any defence acquisition procedure. Defence agencies manage a lot of sensitive information, so incorporating technology would increase the risks of data breaches. In fact, inclusion of any extern tech company would further heighten the risk; therefore, adequate security protocols should be enforced. Finally, for the technology to work effectively, the workforce should be proficient and skilled in comprehending modular contracts, real-time data, emerging technologies and so on. This challenge calls for adequate training and skill development in order to fully utilise the benefits of the TBP model (Rendon & Rendon, 2016).

Risk Mitigation Strategies

To address the risks and challenges to successful TBP implementation, a structural risk mitigation approach is essential. Firstly, a gradual change in management strategy would be highly effective; the phased implementation allows stakeholders to adapt progressively, easing the transition from traditional QR-based procurement. Further, early involvement of procurement teams and leadership, along with fostering a culture of innovation, can further reduce resistance to some extent. The leaders can build stakeholder confidence and support by communicating the benefits of a TBP model, such as faster acquisition cycles and increased flexibility. Secondly, data security risks can be mitigated by integrating robust cyber security measures throughout the TBP process. Defence agencies should establish strict cyber security standards for vendors, ensuring that integrated technology meets high-security benchmarks and helps to navigate through data breaches. The integrated procurement model would acquire a better military capability.[306] Also, regular cyber security assessments, along with vendor compliance with government data protection protocols, become extremely crucial. Real-time monitoring systems can also help detect and address potential threats quickly, minimising vulnerabilities tied to digital integration.[307] With respect to skill development, which is another essential risk mitigation measure, training programs in agile procurement, modular contracts, and digital tools should be available to all procurement personnel. Partnering with technology vendors for specialised training can enhance team capabilities, especially in managing innovative technologies and real-time data. Cross-functional skill development, blending technical and procurement expertise, enables teams to effectively navigate TBP's demands.[308] The defence procurement procedure has often been amended more frequently than weapons systems and serves merely as a procedural guide with flexible interpretations. Therefore, focus should be on civil-military fusion, with works on cyberspace, Artificial Intelligence, Space, Robotics, and so on, leveraging India's substantial technological and knowledge resources.[309] To conclude, addressing the challenges of technology-based procurement requires thoughtful change management, strengthened cyber security practices, and targeted skill development.

Conclusion

The adoption of a technology-based procurement model necessitates a strategic, phased approach to maximise its efficacy and minimise challenges. Defence agencies should first push for incremental changes; for instance, the entire transition could initially start with pilot programs in order to refine the model and tailor it according to India's strategic requirements and defence acquisition landscape. This would help stakeholders to familiarise themselves with the TBP process based on real-time feedback. Second, the twenty-first century has seen a phenomenal increase in information technology in almost all sectors, therefore, collaboration with experts in the private sector become critical for a successful defence procurement process as it would promote innovation. Third, utilising technology has its consequences, primary being its vulnerability to cyber threats. Therefore, strict data protection should be put in place. And lastly, as already stated, all these incremental changes are devoid of foundations if the government does not invest in skill development. To conclude, the transition to a TBP model is a transformative step to modernise defence procurement as it would help defence forces to enhance their operational readiness and aim for a long-term success in a rapidly evolving security landscape.

Chapter Eight

Envisioning the Way Ahead: A Blueprint for Ammunition Self-Reliance

Introduction

India's ammunition ecosystem stands at a decisive inflection point. Over the past decade, sustained governmental support, the emergence of defence industrial corridors, higher foreign investment ceilings, and the gradual inclusion of private industry have collectively created a momentum for defence indigenisation. Yet ammunition, despite being a core operational requirement, remains a domain where India continues to grapple with critical vulnerabilities, particularly in raw materials, key components, advanced technologies, and testing infrastructure. As outlined in earlier chapters, the Indian defence manufacturing landscape has matured considerably, but the ammunition sector still reflects a patchwork of legacy systems, regulatory constraints, and import dependencies. These limitations pose strategic risks in a security environment marked by volatility across India's extended neighbourhood.

In this context, a strategic blueprint becomes essential not merely to address present deficiencies but to shape the contours of a future-ready ammunition ecosystem. Ammunition self-reliance demands far more than increasing domestic production. It requires a coordinated architecture of R&D capability, advanced manufacturing platforms, skilled human capital, resilient supply chains, and a regulatory environment that incentivises innovation rather than constraining it. Indian agencies such as DRDO, Munitions India Limited (MIL) and other DPSUs have gradually expanded their technological portfolios through guided munitions, precision artillery, and extended-range ammunition. However, the pace of R&D-to-production conversion remains slow. Simultaneously, private sector participation, though expanding, continues to face hurdles in licensing, procurement continuity, quality certification, and access to advanced technologies.

The purpose of this chapter, therefore, is to offer a directional framework for the road ahead. While India has made significant strides reflected in rising domestic production capacity, improved private participation, expanding export ambitions, and better integration between policy and industry, self-reliance in ammunition remains an evolving project. This chapter synthesises the current position of India's ammunition landscape, diagnoses structural and operational gaps, and identifies core strategic pillars that must underpin future efforts. It then outlines an actionable roadmap that stretches across short-, medium-, and long-term horizons supported by institutional reforms, modernisation of ordnance factories, industry-academia collaboration, and diversified production architectures. This blueprint recognises that defence self-reliance is inseparable from India's pursuit of broader strategic autonomy. As India seeks greater agency within the global security order, the ability to develop, manufacture, certify, and export world-class ammunition will determine not only its operational readiness but also its geopolitical leverage. Thus, this chapter consolidates the structural vision and capacity-building agenda required to transition towards self-reliance, while the next chapter builds directly upon this foundation by detailing the technological and innovation pathways necessary for realising that vision.

India's Current Position in the Ammunition Ecosystem

India's ammunition ecosystem today reflects a landscape of significant progress, persistent structural constraints, and emerging opportunities shaped by shifting geopolitical and technological currents. Historically, India relied heavily on foreign suppliers from Britain and Russia in the Cold War era to Israel and the USA in the present due to the inability of domestic public-sector entities to meet the full spectrum of the requirements of the armed forces. While this dependence has gradually reduced, critical vulnerabilities remain. The Indian Army still procures between [1] 6,000–8,000 crore worth of ammunition annually; however, as recent reforms have expanded domestic capacity, the Army has announced its intent to halt all major ammunition imports from

2025-26, except in cases of low-volume or economically non-viable production. This policy shift reflects growing confidence in the capabilities of domestic industry, which can now manufacture nearly 150 of the 175 ammunition types used across the services.[310]

The evolution of India's defence export posture also mirrors this transition from import-dependence to outward engagement. Earlier, exports have evolved into a more structured and ambitious framework following policy instruments such as the Defence Procurement Procedure (2002), Defence Production Policy (2011), and the Defence Production and Export Promotion Policy (2020). India's current contribution to the $ 30-billion global ammunition market remains below 1 per cent, but government ambitions target a rise to 5–10 per cent within five years, and up to 30 per cent in the longer term, contingent on quality enhancement and competitive pricing. This shift is further reinforced by broader macroeconomic and institutional reforms across India's defence manufacturing ecosystem. Liberalisation of FDI norms, corporatisation of the erstwhile Ordnance Factory Board into specialised DPSUs, and the creation of defence industrial corridors in Uttar Pradesh and Tamil Nadu represent structural changes that seek to deepen industrial capability and attract private investment. Together, these developments have diversified India's ammunition manufacturing base, with leading private firms such as Bharat Forge, Solar Industries, Adani Defence, and L&T entering the ammunition domain introducing competition, efficiency, and innovation. Despite this momentum, India's ammunition sector is constrained by supply chain vulnerabilities, especially for critical raw materials. Copper, antimony, tungsten, nitrocellulose, and toluene remain heavily import-dependent. Domestic refining for defence-grade inputs remains limited, and disruptions, whether geopolitical or commercial, pose significant risks to production continuity. Legacy ordnance factories continue to face issues of modernisation, throughput limitations, inconsistent quality control, and outdated process flows. Private industry, on the other hand, encounters regulatory bottlenecks, financing challenges, long gestation periods, and restricted access to cutting-edge technologies.

These limitations stand in contrast to global benchmarks. Leading producers such as the USA, Russia, EU states, Israel, and China operate through highly integrated, technologically advanced, and quality-assured ecosystems where innovation, supply chain resilience, and user-industry connectivity are tightly synchronised. India's benchmarking against these systems reveals considerable gaps in precision manufacturing, testing, material science capacity, and cycle-time optimisation. Nevertheless, recent reforms and capabilities, when viewed alongside India's rising defence budgets, modernisation priorities, and expanding geopolitical engagements suggest that the foundations for a competitive ammunition ecosystem are taking shape. The challenge now lies in harmonising these disparate capabilities into a unified, technology-driven, export-competitive entity capable of meeting India's operational needs and securing its broader quest for strategic autonomy.

The strategic rationale for strengthening India's ammunition self-reliance rests fundamentally on the need to insulate national defence preparedness from external shocks. In a security environment defined by contested borders, grey-zone coercion, and rapid escalation risks, dependence on foreign suppliers for critical ammunition exposes India to potential vulnerabilities arising from geopolitical tensions, supply chain disruptions, sanctions regimes, or fluctuating global markets. Self-reliance therefore becomes an instrument of strategic autonomy, enabling India to maintain operational readiness and sustain prolonged military contingencies without the uncertainty of external supply. It also ensures that the armed forces have assured access to high-quality, customised, and mission-specific ammunition aligned with Indian operational doctrines, terrain requirements, and climatic conditions. At the same time, ammunition self-reliance serves a broader strategic-economic purpose. By embedding advanced manufacturing, materials engineering, testing infrastructure, and research ecosystems within the domestic industrial base, India strengthens its long-term technological capabilities and reduces structural dependencies across the defence value chain. The shift from a buyer-dependent model to a producer-driven model simultaneously enhances India's export competitiveness, amplifies its defence diplomacy, and positions the country as a credible contributor to regional security architectures. In essence, ammunition self-reliance is not merely a manufacturing objective but a strategic imperative that links national security, economic resilience, and geopolitical influence into a single coherent trajectory.

Priority Sectors and Key Focus Areas

India's armed forces have long grappled with a persistent ammunition dilemma rooted in their heavy dependence on imported munitions, a vulnerability that becomes acute during political or military crises with adversaries such as China and Pakistan. While successive reforms have aimed to strengthen procurement and modernise production, gaps in research and development, quality assurance, and institutional capacity continue to impede the transition from dependence to autonomy. Addressing these gaps requires a concentrated focus on priority sectors that collectively underpin India's journey towards ammunition self-reliance.

Figure 8.1: Priority Sectors for Ammunition Self-Reliance: A Capability Pillar Model

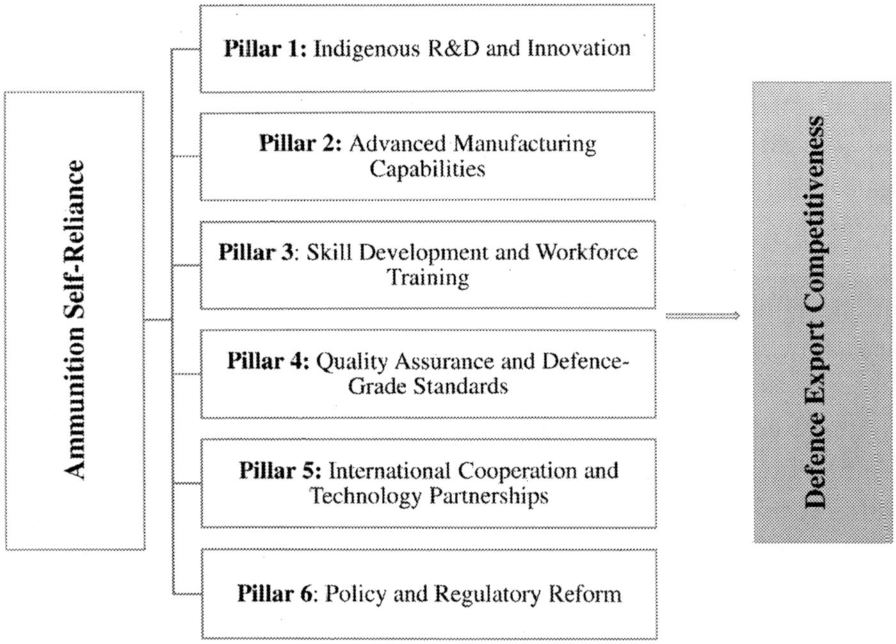

Ammunition Self-Reliance

Pillar 1: Indigenous R&D and Innovation

Pillar 2: Advanced Manufacturing Capabilities

Pillar 3: Skill Development and Workforce Training

Pillar 4: Quality Assurance and Defence-Grade Standards

Pillar 5: International Cooperation and Technology Partnerships

Pillar 6: Policy and Regulatory Reform

Defence Export Competitiveness

Defence Export Competitiveness

Strengthening Indigenous Research & Development (R&D)

To foster the development of indigenous advanced ammunition technologies, there is a pressing need to substantially increase the funding and resources available to the Defence Research and Development Organisation (DRDO).

Enhanced financial support would empower the DRDO to conduct extensive research on smart munitions, precision-guided munitions, and next-generation explosives. Furthermore, setting up specialised R&D centres within the DRDO dedicated to ammunition technology would promote innovation and specialisation.

Public–private partnerships remain indispensable for overcoming the persistent gap between laboratory research and industrial application. The government should create structured mechanisms to encourage collaboration between the DRDO, academic institutions, and the private sector to pool diverse expertise and resources. This could be achieved through joint research projects with defined milestones and accountability frameworks, ensuring effective fund and resource utilisation. To drive innovation, the government could introduce competitive grants, tax incentives, and awards for private companies and start-ups focused on cutting-edge ammunition technology. Establishing defence technology incubators and innovation hubs would provide these start-ups with essential infrastructure and mentorship, thus speeding up technological development.

These initiatives reflect recent efforts like the launch of the Innovations for Defence Excellence (iDEX) framework, which supports start-ups and innovates in defence technology, and the establishment of technology clusters under the DRDO for focused research in critical areas such as artificial intelligence and robotics applied to modern munitions.

Enhancing Manufacturing Capabilities

It is crucial to upgrade the technological base of state-owned ordnance factories which is essential for improving efficiency, safety, and precision. Integrating digitalisation, automation, and Industry 4.0 practices can minimise defects, reduce human error, and shorten production cycles. Aligning these modernisation efforts with global best practices is essential for maintaining competitiveness. Simplifying the regulatory frameworks that govern the defence manufacturing sector is key to encouraging private sector involvement. Relaxing restrictions on foreign direct investment (FDI) and offering subsidies or tax incentives to private firms investing in defence manufacturing could drive growth. Additionally, allowing more private sector companies into ammunition production can help diversify the manufacturing base and introduce competitive dynamics.

The creation of dedicated defence industrial clusters, equipped with modern facilities and shared resources, is beneficial for fostering innovation and reducing production costs. These clusters should encompass testing ranges, R&D centres, and training facilities, thereby creating a comprehensive ecosystem for defence production. This clustering approach encourages collaboration among different stakeholders, which can lead to synergistic advancements. These strategies are exemplified by recent initiatives such as the 'Make in India' program, which has been actively promoting the modernisation of ordnance factories and the development of defence industrial corridors in states like Tamil Nadu and Uttar Pradesh. These corridors aim to create an integrated supply chain for defence manufacturing and stimulate technological innovation through close-knit collaboration among industry players.

Skill Development and Training

It is essential to develop specialised training programs in partnership with academic institutions and industry experts to prepare personnel for roles in advanced manufacturing, quality control, and R&D. Collaborative training programs involving academia, DRDO, DPSUs, and private manufacturers should focus on advanced manufacturing, materials science, explosives handling, quality assurance, and digital process control. Offering certification programs that focus on specialised skills in ammunition technology can standardise competence levels across the industry, thereby improving the quality of the work force. The government should promote continuous learning and skill enhancement through workshops, seminars, and online courses that focus on emerging ammunition technologies. Establishing partnerships with international institutions to integrate global best practices and innovations into Indian training programs would further strengthen the local skill base.

Recent initiatives like the Skill India mission exemplify these strategies by offering targeted training programs in collaboration with defence companies such as Hindustan Aeronautics Limited (HAL) and Bharat Electronics Limited (BEL). These programs are designed to align with the specific needs of the defence sector, enhancing the readiness and capability of the workforce.

Quality Assurance and Standards

Ensuring consistent, defence-grade quality across ammunition batches is foundational to operational readiness. Robust, standardised quality control frameworks supported by independent audits, modern inspection systems, and real-time data analytics are essential. A national digital repository for quality issues and corrective actions would support continuous improvement and enable cross-learning across plants. Assisting domestic manufacturers in acquiring relevant certifications and accreditations can boost their credibility and marketability. The creation of a national accreditation body for defence manufacturing standards would streamline this process.

Leveraging International Cooperation

Negotiating technology transfer agreements with leading defence manufacturers can accelerate the adoption and indigenisation of advanced ammunition technologies. These agreements should include training for Indian engineers and technicians. Encouraging joint ventures with international defence firms can share risks and rewards. Such ventures should introduce new technologies and manufacturing techniques to India, and improve domestic capabilities. Collaborating with international research institutions and defence organisations can keep Indian manufacturers up-to-date with global trends and innovations in ammunition technology. Participating in global defence forums and exhibitions can also facilitate knowledge exchange and highlight Indian capabilities.

Promoting Defence Exports

Market research to identify potential export markets for Indian-made ammunition is critical. A strategic plan for entering these markets, including marketing campaigns and participation in international defence expos, can enhance exports. Simplifying export regulations and supporting manufacturers in navigating international markets can increase export efficiency. A single-window clearance system for defence exports would minimise bureaucratic delays and ease transactions. Organising defence expos and trade missions to demonstrate India's defence production capabilities can forge global partnerships. A government body dedicated to promoting and supporting defence exports can provide market intelligence and logistical support to manufacturers.

Focus on Sustainable and Green Technologies

Investing in the development of eco-friendly ammunition that minimises environmental impact aligns with global sustainability objectives. Partnerships with institutions focusing on sustainable defence technologies can introduce expertise and best practices. Complying with environmental regulations and reducing carbon footprints in defence manufacturing are imperative. Adopting green technologies and practices, such as utilising renewable energy sources and minimising waste, promotes sustainability.

Strengthening Policy and Regulatory Framework

Developing a clear and comprehensive policy that outlines the government's vision, goals, and strategies for achieving self-reliance in defence production is essential. This policy should set specific targets and timelines for various aspects of defence manufacturing, including ammunition technology. Simplifying and speeding up regulatory approvals for defence projects can reduce bureaucratic obstacles and delays. Implementing a transparent and efficient process for defence production licences and contracts is necessary. Consistent defence policies provide a stable and predictable environment for manufacturers and investors. Avoiding frequent changes in policies and regulations ensures that long-term planning and investments remain unaffected.

Structural and Operational Complexities in Establishing Ammunition Manufacturing

Establishing an ammunition manufacturing facility in India is an arduous undertaking shaped by a convergence of technical, regulatory, safety, financial, and institutional challenges. Although an increasing number of Indian firms have expressed interest in entering the ammunition sector, the practical realities of setting up a compliant, secure, and technologically advanced factory reveal structural bottlenecks that few firms are fully prepared for. Table 8.2 summarises the major challenge clusters.

Table 8.1: Key Challenges in Setting up Ammunition Manufacturing Facilities in India

Challenge Area	*Core Issues*	*Implications for Industry*
Technical Complexities	High-precision engineering requirements; specialised materials; stringent process control; continuous quality assurance	High technological barriers; need for advanced machinery, research expertise, and consistent batch-level quality
Regulatory Hurdles	Multi-layered licensing and permits; safety & environmental clearances; complex export controls	Long approval timelines; compliance burden; impediments for SMEs and new entrants
Safety & Security Risks	Handling explosives; risk of accidental detonation; strict facility security requirements	High operational risk; need for specialised training, SOPs, and secure infrastructure
Economic Constraints	Heavy capital investment; high operational costs; market fluctuations; supply chain vulnerabilities	Profitability pressures; difficulty for firms to scale; financial instability without assured orders
Workforce & R&D Gaps	Shortage of skilled labour; limited R&D investment; weak academia–industry collaboration; IP protection issues	Slow innovation cycle; dependence on foreign technology; limited indigenous design capability

Note: Compiled by Author

Following the challenges summarised in Table 8.2, it becomes evident that the establishment of an ammunition manufacturing facility in India is shaped by a combination of structural and operational constraints that intersect across technology, regulation, safety, economics, and human capital. The technological threshold for ammunition production remains exceptionally high. Manufacturing energetic materials, primers, fuzes, shell bodies, or precision-guided components demands advanced engineering capabilities and fine-tuned process control. Many new entrants lack access to such machinery, specialised metallurgical knowledge, or the ability to sustain rigorous batch-level quality assurance, making indigenous production difficult to scale consistently. Regulatory processes constitute another major constraint. Ammunition manufacturing sits at the junction of defence licensing, explosives regulation, industrial safety, and environmental compliance, resulting in a web of approvals that few firms navigate smoothly. The absence of predictable timelines and the multiplicity of agencies involved create delays that disproportionately affect smaller companies. Even after production begins, firms must adhere to stringent rules governing storage, transport, and export, which add to operational complexity.

Safety and security concerns further heighten the difficulty of establishing such facilities. The inherent risks associated with handling explosive compounds require specialised infrastructure, controlled environments, and a workforce trained in hazard mitigation. At the same time, the sensitivity of ammunition demands high levels of physical security to prevent theft, pilferage, or sabotage. These dual demands make it necessary for firms to invest heavily in protective systems and emergency management mechanisms. The economic dimensions of ammunition manufacturing also pose challenges. The sector requires significant capital outlay on land, blast-resistant structures, automated production lines, and testing facilities followed by high recurring costs. Market fluctuations linked to defence procurement cycles, along with supply chain disruptions for inputs like nitrocellulose or specialised alloys, further compound the financial risks. This discourages private sector investment unless long-term orders are assured. Lastly, the workforce and R&D ecosystem remain underdeveloped. India faces a shortage of specialists in propulsion chemistry, energetic materials, advanced machining, and quality testing. Limited investment in R&D and weak collaboration between DRDO, academia, and industry continues to restrict innovation. The challenge is magnified by the lack of robust intellectual property protection mechanisms, reducing incentives for firms to develop proprietary technologies.

Charting the Path Forward

The transition from ammunition import dependency to comprehensive self-reliance requires a phased, institutionally coordinated, and technologically forward-looking roadmap. India's ammunition ecosystem is marked by fragmented production capacities, uneven R&D depth, and limited indigenisation of critical subsystems, all of which restrict strategic autonomy. A long-term national strategy must therefore align policy vision, research infrastructure, manufacturing capability, quality assurance, skilled manpower, and regulatory reform into a coherent sequencing framework. This section outlines the ten central pillars of the self-reliance roadmap—policy direction, R&D strengthening, manufacturing expansion, indigenisation, certification, human capital, innovation, regulatory facilitation, sustainability, and oversight—supported by short-, medium-, and long-term milestones that together define the trajectory of India's ammunition transformation.

Table 8.3 consolidates this step-by-step roadmap by grouping the core activities into ten strategic pillars, each reflecting a critical requirement for building a self-reliant ammunition ecosystem.

Table 8.2: Step-by-Step Roadmap for Self-Reliance in Ammunition Manufacturing

Theme	*Actions*
Policy and Strategic Vision	• **Formulate a National Policy:** Establish a clear policy promoting self-reliance in ammunition with defined objectives, timelines, and stakeholder responsibilities. • **Set Long-Term Vision:** Create a 10–15 year roadmap for transition from import dependence to full domestic production of conventional, niche, and advanced ammunition. • **Focus on Key Technologies:** Identify priority areas such as smart munitions, precision-guided ammunition, and advanced propellants aligned with future battlefield needs.
Research and Development (R&D) Ecosystem	• **Strengthen Public Sector R&D Institutions:** Enhance DRDO's role in pioneering ammunition technologies through funding and expert staffing. • **Collaborate with Academia:** Promote joint research with universities and technical institutes in materials science, electronics, and weapon systems. • **Encourage Private Sector R&D:** Offer incentives like tax breaks and grants to boost private R&D in smart ammunition, guidance systems, and advanced explosives.
Develop Domestic Manufacturing Capabilities	• **Upgrade Existing Facilities:** Modernise ordnance factories and private units through automation and advanced materials handling. • **Build New Facilities:** Establish state-of-the-art manufacturing units capable of producing ammunition from small arms to heavy artillery. • **Promote PPPs:** Encourage joint ventures between government entities and private firms (domestic and international) to leverage expertise.
Indigenisation of Components	• **Develop Critical Subsystems:** Focus on indigenous production of casings, fuzes, propellants, and warheads to reduce dependency. • **Leverage Local Supply Chains:** Strengthen domestic suppliers for raw materials, electronics, and precision machining; integrate MSMEs into defence production. • **Advance Material Science:** Invest in lightweight composites and smart materials to enhance performance and cost-efficiency

Quality Assurance and Certification	• **Establish Robust Testing Facilities:** Set up or upgrade firing ranges, environmental labs, and failure-analysis centres. • **Adopt International Standards:** Align domestic ammunition production with global military standards (e.g., NATO) to build credibility and enable exports.
Human Resource Development	• **Skilling Programs:** Train engineers, scientists, and technicians in ammunition design, manufacturing, and quality control through partnerships with institutes and defence universities. • **Encourage Technical Expertise:** Promote R&D careers through scholarships, internships, and fellowships in ammunition technologies.
Fostering Innovation and Start-Ups	• **Defence Innovation Hubs:** Establish incubators for start-ups and SMEs focusing on smart ammunition, AI-driven targeting, and eco-friendly explosives. • **Defence Grants and Competitions:** Launch national innovation challenges, grants, and competitions to encourage breakthrough technologies.
Regulatory and Export Facilitation	• **Streamline Licensing and Approvals:** Simplify licensing, manufacturing, and procurement procedures to accelerate private sector participation. • **Focus on Exports:** After meeting domestic needs, promote ammunition exports through a dedicated export promotion council.
Sustainability and Environmental Responsibility	• **Develop Green Ammunition:** Innovate non-toxic, biodegradable materials to reduce environmental impact. • **Reduce Waste and Pollution:** Implement strict environmental norms across production facilities to minimise hazardous waste.
Regular Reviews and Audits	• **Set up Oversight Bodies:** Create a defence production board for continuous monitoring and evaluation of progress. • **Adapt to Changing Needs:** Update the strategy regularly to respond to technological advances, battlefield dynamics, and global developments.

To operationalise the ten strategic pillars presented above, the roadmap is sequenced across short-, medium-, and long-term milestones. These milestones structure the transition process, ensure measurable progress, and align institutional efforts with clearly defined timelines. The phased approach also enables continuous modernisation, incremental capacity building, and a progressive shift toward advanced ammunition technologies. The recommended milestones are as follows:

Short-Term (1–3 Years)

- Set up R&D partnerships with academia and the private sector.
- Begin upgrading existing production facilities.
- Focus on indigenising key subsystems and components.

Medium-Term (4-7 Years)

- Establish new, state-of-the-art ammunition production units.
- Achieve self-reliance in conventional ammunition types.
- Launch export initiatives for niche technologies.

Long-Term (8-15 Years)

- Reach self-reliance in advanced, smart ammunition tech.
- Integrate domestic supply chains for all critical components.
- Become a global exporter of advanced ammunition.

Together, these phased milestones provide a structured pathway for building a robust, innovative, and globally competitive ammunition manufacturing ecosystem.

Modernisation of Ordnance Factories: A Strategic Imperative

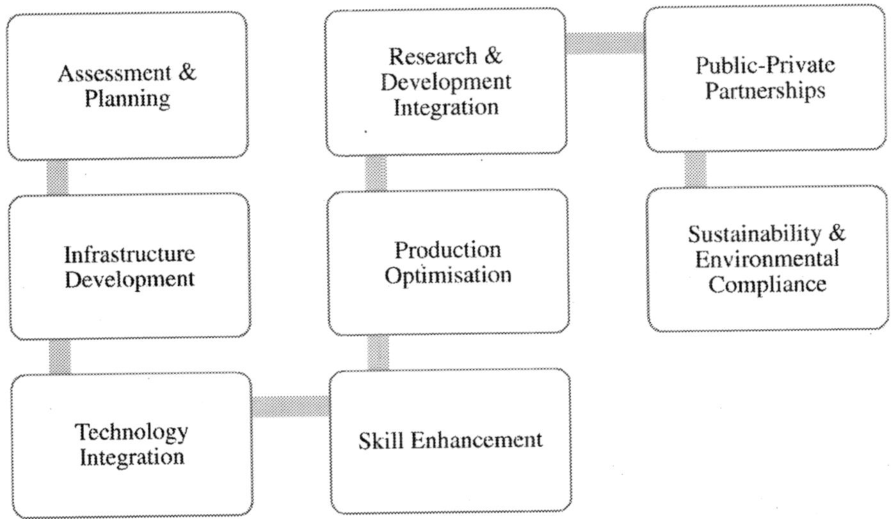

Modernising India's ordnance factories is essential for strengthening the country's defence industrial base and ensuring sustained self-reliance in ammunition manufacturing. Given their historical structure and uneven technological progression, ordnance factories require a systematic transformation that spans infrastructure, workforce capabilities, technology adoption, production processes, and long-term sustainability. The modernisation effort begins with a comprehensive assessment and planning exercise that evaluates existing infrastructure, machinery, technology, manpower, and production capacities. This audit enables a transparent gap analysis against present and future ammunition requirements and forms the basis for a detailed technology roadmap. Planning at this stage also includes evaluating the skill profile of the workforce and determining specific training requirements for operating modern equipment and advanced production systems.

Following assessment, the second priority is infrastructure development. Upgradation of existing buildings, workshops, and storage facilities is required to meet current safety and production standards, while new production lines must be established for specialised ammunition such as precision-guided munitions and advanced artillery shells. Infrastructure modernisation must also incorporate energy-efficient technologies to reduce long-term operational costs and meet environmental requirements. Building on upgraded infrastructure, the next component is technology integration. Automation and robotics must be increasingly deployed to enhance efficiency, consistency, and workplace safety. Digital manufacturing systems including CAD/CAM, PLM, and ERP need to be embedded throughout design, production, and supply chain management. Enhanced quality control mechanisms, such as automated inspection and testing platforms, are essential for ensuring reliability. At the same time, investment in reverse engineering capabilities will help develop indigenous alternatives to imported technologies and reduce external dependencies.

A modernised production ecosystem also requires a skilled workforce. Skill enhancement is therefore a central pillar of factory reform. Comprehensive training programmes should equip employees with the ability to handle advanced machinery and digital systems, while a culture of continuous learning ensures that personnel remain aligned with evolving industry standards. Workforce expansion through the recruitment of trained professionals in engineering, manufacturing, and quality control complements these initiatives and strengthens institutional depth. As the workforce evolves, production processes must also be optimised. The adoption of lean manufacturing principles can minimise waste and increase productivity, while supply chain modernisation improves the timely availability of raw materials and components. Advanced production planning and scheduling tools further ensure efficient resource utilisation and stable throughput.

Parallel to production reforms, dedicated research and development capabilities must be cultivated within the ordnance factory ecosystem. Establishing in-house R&D centres allows factories to contribute directly to the development of new ammunition technologies. Collaboration with academia, research institutions, and private industry promotes technology transfer and supports the creation of innovative solutions tailored to operational requirements. Intellectual property emerging from these efforts should be systematically protected to support long-term competitiveness and indigenous innovation. Public-private partnerships offer additional pathways to accelerate modernisation. Strategic partnerships with private sector companies bring in external expertise, investment, and technological inputs. Joint ventures for ammunition production and research expand capacity while offset clauses in defence contracts can be leveraged for technology transfer and domestic industrial growth.

Sustainability constitutes the final dimension of modernisation. Ordnance factories must adhere to stringent environmental regulations and adopt sustainable practices in production processes. Efficient waste management systems minimise environmental impact, while the exploration and integration of green technologies contribute to long-term ecological responsibility. Additional considerations cut across all phases of the modernisation process. Security and safety must remain a priority, given the sensitive nature of materials and processes involved in ammunition manufacturing. Financial sustainability is equally important, requiring prudent resource allocation and cost management. Finally, modernisation must be aligned with India's ambition to tap into the global ammunition market, making export potential an integral part of long-term planning.

Building a Collaborative Ammunition Ecosystem

Building a resilient and self-sustaining ammunition ecosystem requires more than strengthening individual production units; it demands an interconnected framework in which private industry, public-sector entities, research institutions, and regulatory agencies operate in a coordinated manner. The effectiveness of India's ammunition manufacturing base depends on how well these actors collaborate, share capacities, and address systemic bottlenecks that have historically limited private-sector participation. Challenges related to regulation, finance, technology access, operational capability, and market structure underscore the need for a more integrated approach. At the same time, improved production-sharing models, structured partnerships, technology-transfer mechanisms, and industry-academia cooperation provide pathways for enhancing efficiency, innovation, and indigenisation. A collaborative ecosystem thus forms the foundation on which India can expand domestic capacities, reduce external dependence, and build a competitive and future-ready ammunition industry.

Addressing Concerns of Private Industries

Indian private industries engaged in ammunition manufacturing face a series of entrenched challenges that collectively restrict their ability to contribute meaningfully to the defence production ecosystem. Regulatory barriers remain the most persistent, with complex and time-consuming licensing procedures, multi-agency approvals, and cumbersome export permissions creating delays and uncertainty for firms seeking to scale or diversify. These issues are compounded by inconsistent procurement policies, frequent shifts between domestic and foreign sourcing preferences, and unclear norms governing FDI in defence, all of which undermine investor confidence and disrupt long-term planning. Even when private players secure contracts, the traditional preference for public sector undertakings and delays in government payments continue to constrain their operational stability and cash flow.

Financial constraints further weaken private sector participation. Ammunition manufacturing requires substantial capital investment in advanced machinery, specialised infrastructure, and stringent safety systems—costs that are prohibitive for many small and medium enterprises. Limited access to credit, the perception of defence manufacturing as a high-risk sector, and hesitancy among financial institutions and private investors to support long-gestation defence projects make it difficult for companies to mobilise the resources needed to expand production. The inconsistent flow of government orders adds to this uncertainty, leaving firms with underutilised capacity and eroding their ability to plan for sustained growth.

Technological barriers also impede competitiveness. Restricted access to advanced foreign technologies, limited opportunities for international collaboration and insufficient indigenous R&D capacity leave many private firms operating with outdated or incomplete technological capabilities. Their dependence on imported raw materials, electronic subsystems, and high-precision components further exposes them to supply-chain vulnerabilities, especially during periods of geopolitical tension. At the operational level, shortages of specialised skilled labour—particularly in materials science, explosives handling, and precision engineering—combined with inadequate testing and validation infrastructure, make it difficult for private companies to meet the stringent quality, safety, and environmental standards required for defence production. Infrastructure limitations in logistics and transportation exacerbate delays, creating inefficiencies across the production cycle.

Competitive dynamics reinforce these structural constraints. Large PSUs benefit from legacy relationships, established production lines, and preferential access to government contracts, making it difficult for newer private entrants to gain a meaningful market share. Limited governmental support for defence exports restricts the ability of private firms to tap international markets and achieve economies of scale, especially in a globally competitive environment dominated by established defence producers. The broader industrial ecosystem remains fragmented, with weak linkages between industry, academia, and research institutions, and insufficient collaboration among private players themselves. This fragmentation leads to duplication of effort, delays innovation, and prevents the emergence of a cohesive, scalable industrial base capable of meeting national ammunition requirements. Overcoming these challenges will require a more supportive regulatory framework, predictable procurement, improved access to technology and finance, and stronger collaborative networks spanning government, industry, and academia to enable a genuinely self-reliant ammunition manufacturing ecosystem.

Adopting a Shared Production and Distribution Model

Creating a shared production and distribution model for components, propellants, and explosives requires a coordinated framework that leverages the complementary strengths of private industry and ordnance factories while ensuring quality, efficiency, and security across the ammunition supply chain. One pathway is a structured Public–Private Partnership framework that formalises collaboration through clear divisions of labour, enabling private industries to manufacture specific components while ordnance factories undertake final assembly and integration, supported by joint R&D initiatives to advance propellant and explosive technologies. A component-sharing consortia model offers another collaborative structure, pooling resources under a unified management system and operating through a centralised procurement and distribution hub responsible for quality control and standardized production protocols. Sub-contracting and vendor development mechanisms can expand private-sector participation by allowing firms to supply designated components under a tiered model, backed by targeted training and certification programmes and real-time digital supply-chain integration. Technology-transfer and licensing arrangements further deepen collaboration by enabling ordnance factories to share critical technologies under controlled licensing agreements, supported by joint IP management offices and capacity-building initiatives to ensure high-quality, scalable production. Integrated production clusters provide additional opportunities by co-locating private and public facilities within shared industrial zones, thereby reducing logistics costs, enhancing security, enabling shared utilities, and fostering collaborative innovation centres for R&D in propellants and explosives. A joint quality-assurance and certification body can reinforce these models by establishing unified standards, conducting regular audits, and institutionalising feedback mechanisms for continuous improvement. Strategic joint ventures between private firms and ordnance factories, supported through shared equity, specialised production lines, and targeted export strategies, further strengthen the ecosystem by synchronising resources and enabling India to meet both domestic demand and emerging global opportunities. Together, these collaborative models offer a comprehensive approach to integrating production, technology, and quality assurance, laying the foundation for a resilient and self-reliant ammunition manufacturing ecosystem.

Exploring Joint Ventures in Ammunition Manufacturing

Joint ventures in ammunition manufacturing represent an important pathway for integrating advanced technology, specialised expertise, and proven defence-production practices into India's evolving ammunition ecosystem. Potential international partners bring distinct competencies: Rafael Advanced Defence Systems offers capabilities in precision-guided munitions and smart weapon systems; Lockheed Martin contributes extensive experience in aerospace, defence systems, and precision-guided ammunition suitable for air defence; Thales provides technological strengths in munitions, electronic warfare, and advanced sensors; BAE Systems brings expertise in artillery ammunition, tank rounds, and integration of next-generation technologies; Rheinmetall AG offers a strong portfolio in medium- and large-calibre ammunition and modern manufacturing processes, and; General Dynamics Ordnance and Tactical Systems adds substantial experience in small arms ammunition, artillery shells, and specialised tactical munitions. Within the domestic landscape, public-sector entities such as Munitions India Limited and Advanced Weapons and Equipment India Limited provide institutional infrastructure, production capacity, and established linkages with the armed forces, enabling collaborative ventures that blend public-sector experience with private-sector agility. The potential models for such joint ventures range from technology-transfer and licensing agreements allowing domestic production of advanced ammunition under foreign technical guidance to joint R&D initiatives that develop next-generation ammunition suited to India's specific operational requirements. Export-oriented partnerships also offer opportunities to position India as a competitive global supplier by leveraging cost efficiencies and strategic geographic advantages. Ultimately, successful joint ventures will depend on selecting partners whose technological capabilities complement domestic strengths, prioritise meaningful technology transfer, and align with the broader objectives of defence indigenisation and long-term self-reliance, thereby enabling the creation of a robust ammunition manufacturing ecosystem that serves both national and export markets.

Industry and Academia Collaboration

A structured and phased model of collaboration between industry and academia is essential for advancing ammunition technologies in a coherent and sustainable manner. The first phase is Foundation Building, which focuses on creating the initial institutional and intellectual groundwork for cooperation. This involves identifying key stakeholders, mapping industrial challenges alongside academic research strengths, and establishing shared research priorities across domains such as materials science, propulsion systems, and manufacturing processes. It also emphasises the creation of knowledge-transfer mechanisms such as workshops, conferences, and publications that help both sides understand each other's capabilities and needs.

The second phase is Collaborative Research, which centres on deepening the partnership through joint scientific and technological activities. This phase includes launching collaborative research projects, developing funding mechanisms to support them, enabling talent exchange through internships and faculty sabbaticals, and establishing clear intellectual-property management frameworks that protect and incentivise joint innovation. The third phase is Technology Transfer and Commercialisation, which focuses on converting research outputs into deployable industrial solutions. This is achieved through the establishment of specialised technology-transfer offices, the development and testing of prototypes, pilot-scale production runs, and measures that encourage industrial adoption of academic research.

The fourth phase is Skill Development and Training, which concentrates on strengthening the human capital needed to sustain an advanced ammunition ecosystem. This involves designing industry-relevant curricula, running targeted skill-enhancement programmes, supporting faculty development, and creating mentorship channels between industry experts and academic institutions. The fifth and final phase is Long-Term Partnership, which focuses on institutionalising the collaboration so that it becomes durable and future-oriented. This includes forming strategic alliances, establishing joint centres of excellence, advocating enabling policy frameworks, and carrying out continuous evaluations to refine and adapt the collaboration as requirements evolve.

Across all phases, the partnership is anchored in key technology domains such as advanced materials, improved propellant and propulsion systems, precision manufacturing, simulation and modelling tools, modern quality-control methods, and the development of environmentally responsible production practices. Taken together, this phased approach ensures that industry-academia collaboration remains systematic, scalable, and aligned with the long-term needs of India's ammunition manufacturing ecosystem.

Conclusion

A coherent ammunition ecosystem requires more than isolated reforms; it demands the alignment of policy intent, institutional capability, technological depth, and collaborative mechanisms across the entire manufacturing landscape. This chapter has shown that India's progress towards ammunition self-reliance is shaped by simultaneous movements vis-à-vis modernising legacy structures, expanding private-sector participation, strengthening regulatory clarity, and embedding research-driven innovation into production processes. These elements point towards a sector undergoing transition where incremental improvements are gradually establishing the foundation for a more resilient and competitive industrial base.

What emerges clearly is that self-reliance is ultimately a systems challenge. It depends on how effectively India can synchronise its production capacities with user requirements, technological advancements, and global industry standards. The frameworks discussed ranging from phased modernisation and indigenisation pathways to shared production models, PPPs, and joint ventures illustrate the types of institutional arrangements needed to overcome fragmentation, accelerate learning curves, and reduce technological dependence. Equally important is the role of human capital, testing infrastructure, quality assurance, and supply-chain integration, which together determine whether the sector can scale sustainably and absorb advanced technologies.

This chapter therefore provides a strategic direction rather than a final prescription. It maps the structural conditions that must evolve, the partnerships that must deepen, and the capabilities that must be cultivated for India to move from partial dependence to credible autonomy in ammunition manufacturing. Yet the viability of this trajectory ultimately rests on India's ability to navigate rapid technological change and compress development cycles in an industry where innovation is both capital-intensive and time-sensitive. Accordingly, the next chapter turns to the technological and innovation pathways that will define the sector's future trajectory. It examines the emerging technologies, production architectures, and institutional innovation models that can enable India not only to secure domestic requirements but also to position itself as a producer of advanced, high-value, and export-ready ammunition systems.

Chapter Nine

Roadmap and Innovation Pathways

Introduction

India's pursuit of ammunition self-reliance cannot rest on policy intent alone; it must be anchored in the capacity to transform that intent into dependable, high-performance manufacturing. The gaps identified earlier, such as import dependence, legacy production lines, fragmented innovation efforts, and slow translation of research into field-ready systems highlight the distance between strategic ambition and industrial reality. Bridging this distance requires more than incremental improvements. It calls for a decisive shift towards technologies, supply chains, and institutional practices capable of sustaining a modern ammunition ecosystem.

The global munitions domain is already in the midst of such a transition. Automation, digital manufacturing, advanced materials, and new energetic chemistries are reshaping how ammunition is designed and produced. For India, these shifts present both an opportunity and a warning. While conventional capabilities have strengthened over time, the demands of contemporary warfare vis-à-vis precision, range, survivability, sustainability, and rapid adaptability require a level of technological depth that traditional manufacturing models cannot deliver. Additive manufacturing, nano-materials, next-generation propellants, and materials engineering offer pathways to address many of India's long-standing vulnerabilities, from precision deficits to supply-chain bottlenecks.

However, technology alone is insufficient without the operational scaffolding that sustains it. The dependence on critical raw materials such as copper, antimony, tungsten, toluene, and nitrocellulose demonstrates how quickly industrial progress can be constrained by external shocks. A resilient ammunition ecosystem must therefore rest on assured access to essential inputs, efficient logistics, and manufacturing clusters that bring research, production, testing, and user feedback into one continuous loop. Without these foundations, advanced technologies risk remaining isolated experiments rather than becoming reliable, repeatable capabilities.

Equally essential is an institutional capacity to push the boundaries of innovation. The pace of global defence R&D shows that meaningful breakthroughs emerge from agile, high-risk, high-reward environments rather than conventional bureaucratic systems. Models such as a DARPA-like DRONA entity, a Talpiot-inspired talent programme like Project Aviyna, and an Ammunition Innovation Unit to connect private innovation with military needs demonstrate how India could compress development cycles and close the gap between laboratory and production line. These technological, operational, and institutional elements form the core of India's transition from a fragmented manufacturing landscape to one capable of delivering advanced, dependable, and strategically autonomous ammunition. As this is the concluding chapter, the focus now turns to how these pathways can translate strategic intent into durable capability moving India closer to a self-reliant, competitive, and future-ready ammunition ecosystem.

Emerging Technologies in Ammunition Manufacturing

Ammunition manufacturing is entering a period of significant technological change, shaped by advances in materials science, digital manufacturing, and energetic chemistry. For decades, conventional production methods were sufficient to meet operational needs. Today, however, modern warfare demands far greater levels of precision, reliability, adaptability, and control. Requirements such as reduced collateral damage, extended ranges, improved accuracy, and operational stealth have made older manufacturing models increasingly inadequate. This shift compels a rethinking of how ammunition is designed, engineered, and produced.

Within this broader transformation, three technological domains stand out for their potential to reshape India's capabilities and support its long-term goal of self-reliance. Additive manufacturing commonly known as 3D printing opens possibilities that traditional machining cannot match, from rapid prototyping to intricate geometric designs that optimise weight, balance, and performance. Nano-materials, engineered at the molecular scale, offer pathways to stronger, lighter, and more efficient munitions by enhancing projectile penetration, increasing the energy density of propellants, and enabling improved fragmentation characteristics. Next-generation propellants, using advanced energetic materials and refined chemical formulations, address operational needs related to range, safety, smoke and flash signature reduction, and ballistic consistency.

Individually, each of these technologies offers a distinct performance advantage; collectively, they represent a shift in how ammunition can be conceptualised and manufactured. They move beyond incremental upgrades and point towards a fundamentally different technological landscape, one in which India can reduce long-standing dependencies, accelerate development cycles, and build ammunition aligned with contemporary battlefield conditions. The subsections that follow examine each technological frontier in greater detail, focusing on their applications, benefits, challenges, and relevance to India's evolving defence manufacturing ecosystem.

Additive Manufacturing (3D Printing) for Ammunition

Additive manufacturing (AM), or 3D printing, presents a significant departure from conventional ammunition production by enabling components to be built layer by layer rather than shaped through subtractive or forging processes. This approach allows the creation of highly complex geometries that traditional machining often cannot achieve, offering considerable potential for both design optimisation and rapid development. In ammunition manufacturing, AM supports a wide spectrum of applications. It enables the production of intricate components such as fuzes, primers, and sabots with internal structures tailored for performance; facilitates lightweighting by generating optimised geometries and allows component customisation for specific ammunition types. Beyond end-use parts, AM is particularly valuable in producing tooling and fixtures, making rapid prototyping possible and significantly reducing lead times during development cycles. The technology can also produce metal elements such as bullet jackets, cartridge cases, and limited projectile components, as well as polymer-based parts like bullet tips, sabots, and spacers.

Despite its advantages, AM faces several constraints that shape its feasibility for large-scale ammunition production. The range of materials that can be reliably processed remains limited, and not all AM-compatible metals or polymers meet the strength, durability, or ballistic requirements essential for munitions. Production using AM can also be slower and more expensive than traditional high-volume methods, especially when manufacturing large quantities. Quality control is another critical concern, as ammunition demands exceptionally tight tolerances and reliability, requiring rigorous verification of AM outputs. Additionally, the sector is governed by strict regulatory standards, which AM processes must fully satisfy before components can enter production pipelines.

These limitations, however, do not diminish the transformative potential of additive manufacturing. Its design flexibility makes it possible to achieve levels of optimisation that conventional techniques cannot match, enabling rapid iteration and reducing the time required to field new ammunition types. AM can also strengthen supply chain resilience by enabling localised production of components that might otherwise be vulnerable to global disruptions. The technology's capacity for customisation further supports specialised operational requirements. Although significant challenges remain, continued research, improvements in AM materials, and maturation of printing technologies are likely to expand the role of additive manufacturing within ammunition production. In the long term, AM is positioned to become an important complement rather than a replacement to traditional manufacturing, contributing to a more agile, responsive, and self-reliant ammunition ecosystem.

Nano-materials in Ammunition Manufacturing: A Potential Game-Changer

Nano-materials, owing to their distinctive properties at the molecular and atomic scale, offer substantial potential to reshape the performance and design of modern ammunition. Their ability to combine high strength, controlled behaviour, and enhanced energetic characteristics makes them particularly valuable in applications where precision, efficiency, and reliability are paramount. In projectile design, nano-structured materials can significantly enhance penetrative capability by increasing hardness and density; embedding tungsten or uranium nano-particles within structural matrices enables deeper penetration and improved terminal effects. At the same time, the strength-to-weight advantages of nano-materials allow projectiles to be lighter without compromising structural integrity, thereby improving range and velocity. Controlled fragmentation is another notable benefit, as nano-materials can be engineered to produce predictable fragmentation patterns aligned with specific operational requirements.

Nano-materials also offer important advantages in propellant formulations. Their ability to increase energy density translates into higher muzzle velocities and extended ranges, while the precision with which they can be engineered enables fine control over burn rates. This supports mission-specific ballistic profiles and greater consistency in performance. Additionally, nano-material-based propellants can reduce visible and infrared smoke signatures, improving concealment for both the weapon system and the user, an increasingly important consideration in modern combat environments.

Fuze technology similarly benefits from nano-material integration. Enhanced sensitivity and reliability can be achieved through nano-scale components that respond more precisely to environmental and target conditions. Miniaturisation is a key advantage, enabling the development of smaller yet more capable fuze assemblies. In some cases, nano-materials can support more advanced functionalities, including improved timing, sensing, or activation characteristics that contribute to smarter and more adaptive ammunition systems. The incorporation of nano-materials into ammunition, however, comes with significant challenges. Achieving consistent and reliable material synthesis at the nano-scale remains complex, and integrating these materials into existing ammunition components requires sophisticated engineering to ensure that performance improvements do not compromise safety or durability. Handling nano-materials poses its own set of safety concerns, necessitating strict adherence to environmental and occupational standards. Cost remains a major limiting factor, as the production of nano-materials and related processing technologies can be expensive and difficult to scale for mass production.

Despite these challenges, several classes of nano-materials hold strong promise for ammunition applications. Carbon nanotubes offer exceptional strength-to-weight ratios and thermal conductivity; graphene provides remarkable flexibility and structural resilience; metal nano-particles contribute enhanced hardness, strength, and catalytic behaviour; and ceramic nano-particles bring high temperature resistance and durability. As research and manufacturing processes continue to mature, these materials are likely to play an increasingly central role in next-generation ammunition design, offering India significant opportunities to improve performance, reduce weight, and enhance the reliability of its munitions ecosystem.

Establishing a Reliable and Robust Ammunition Supply Chain

A reliable and resilient supply chain is central to sustaining ammunition production, particularly in an environment where operational readiness depends on uninterrupted access to high-quality materials and components. The first step in strengthening India's ammunition supply chain lies in understanding its foundational elements. This begins with a comprehensive mapping of all essential raw materials, components, and sub-assemblies, accompanied by a clear categorisation based on their criticality, availability, and degree of import dependence. Such clarity enables targeted interventions, especially for materials that are both indispensable and vulnerable to external disruptions.

Reducing dependence on imports requires a deliberate push towards domestic sourcing. Encouraging domestic production of critical components, identifying capable suppliers, and fostering long-term relationships through contracts, capacity-building initiatives, and consistent quality assurance are essential. A well-developed domestic supplier base not only enhances self-reliance but also reduces exposure to geopolitical and market-related uncertainties. Nevertheless, imports will continue to play a role, making import management equally important. Diversifying international suppliers, conducting regular risk assessments, maintaining strategic stockpiles, and streamlining customs and logistics procedures help mitigate global supply chain shocks and reduce delays.

Quality assurance must span the entire supply chain. Establishing rigorous quality standards, implementing robust inspection and testing systems, and conducting periodic supplier audits ensure that every material entering the production line meets the specifications required for ammunition safety and reliability. Alongside quality, supply chain visibility plays a critical role. Digital tools that enable real-time tracking of materials, data analytics that identify emerging bottlenecks, and collaborative platforms that connect suppliers, manufacturers, and logistics providers contribute to a more transparent, predictable, and responsive ecosystem.

Risk mitigation must be embedded within supply chain planning. Mapping the entire supply chain allows vulnerabilities to be identified early, while contingency plans provide structured responses to disruptions caused by natural disasters, geopolitical tensions, or supplier failures. Dual sourcing for critical items further strengthens resilience by ensuring that production is not jeopardised by the failure of a single supplier.

Infrastructure remains another pillar of supply chain reliability. Efficient transportation networks such as roads, railways, and ports are essential for timely movement of materials across production sites. The development of strategically located warehousing facilities supports better inventory management, reduces lead times, and enhances the sector's ability to respond quickly to fluctuations in demand.

Finally, government support forms the enabling framework for all these efforts. Policies that offer tax incentives, subsidies, or simplified regulatory procedures can attract greater investment in domestic production. Public–private partnerships can help bridge capacity gaps, encourage technological upgrades, and promote the long-term stability of the ammunition supply chain. Overall, a robust supply chain for ammunition requires coordinated action across sourcing, quality control, risk mitigation, infrastructure, and policy support; this reinforces the others to create a secure and efficient foundation for India's ammunition manufacturing ecosystem.

Next Generation Propellants in Ammunition Manufacturing

The modernisation of ammunition manufacturing is closely tied to advances in propellant technology. Next-generation propellants offer the possibility of improved range, greater precision, enhanced safety, and reduced environmental impact attributes that have become increasingly important as contemporary battlefields demand higher performance with lower operational risks. Central to this evolution are several key performance parameters. Propellants with higher energy density can significantly increase the lethality and effective range of ammunition without adding weight. Equally important is reduced sensitivity to shock, friction, and heat, which enhances safety during transport, storage, and handling. Lower smoke and flash signatures contribute to improved survivability by minimising the visual and infrared detection of firing positions. Consistency in ballistic behaviour including delivering predictable pressure curves and muzzle velocities directly improves accuracy. Environmental considerations are also becoming prominent, as propellant formulations with lower toxicity and reduced emissions align with long-term sustainability requirements.

Multiple technological approaches underpin these advances. Nano-composites allow scientists to fine-tune burning rates, mechanical strength, and overall energy output by embedding nano-materials within propellant matrices. New energetic materials can offer superior performance characteristics that go beyond the limitations of legacy formulations. Additives provide another means of tailoring propellant behaviour by modifying temperature sensitivity, mechanical resilience, or combustion profiles. Hybrid technologies that combine elements of solid and liquid propellants introduce opportunities for balancing safety, flexibility, and performance in novel ways. Each of these approaches opens specific pathways towards more efficient, reliable, and adaptable ammunition.

However, the development and adoption of next-generation propellants also involve significant challenges. Safety concerns remain paramount, as new formulations must be rigorously tested to ensure they do not introduce unforeseen risks during manufacturing or field use. Cost is another constraint, since advanced materials and complex production processes can raise overall ammunition prices, limiting scalability. Compatibility poses an additional barrier, as propellants must align with the characteristics of existing weapon systems and manufacturing lines to avoid costly redesigns. Environmental implications, despite improvements in some areas, still require careful assessment to meet both operational and regulatory expectations.

Integrating new propellant technologies into ammunition manufacturing therefore demands a structured approach. Continued investment in dedicated research and development is essential for refining formulations and evaluating their suitability across different ammunition types. Pilot-scale production facilities can help test and adjust emerging technologies before transitioning them to full-scale manufacturing. Rigorous quality control systems are necessary to validate consistency, reliability, and safety, given the critical role propellants play in ammunition performance. Finally, workforce training ensures that personnel involved in the production and handling of advanced propellants possess the specialised skills required to manage new materials and processes safely and effectively. Together, these elements shape the trajectory of next-generation propellant development, offering India the opportunity to enhance performance while strengthening the broader ammunition ecosystem.

Ensuring Availability of Critical Raw Materials for Ammunition Manufacturing

The availability of key raw materials required for ammunition production remains a challenge for India. Essential materials like copper, antimony, and toluene are critical, yet India relies heavily on imports to meet its needs. This dependency poses risks, especially in times of geopolitical uncertainty and economic fluctuations. Copper is essential for making bullet casings, but India's domestic production falls short of demand. This means India has to import large quantities, which can make us vulnerable to price hikes and supply disruptions. Antimony is a crucial element used in bullets and primers to enhance their performance. Unfortunately, India lacks domestic sources and depends almost entirely on imports from China and Russia. Used to produce TNT, toluene is a vital component in explosive charges. While India does have some domestic production capacity, it isn't enough to fully support the defence sector. Strengthening our petrochemical infrastructure can help bridge this gap. Materials like lead, tungsten, nitrocellulose, and other explosive ingredients are critical for various ammunition types. While India has lead reserves, refining it to defence-grade quality is still a challenge. Scaling up domestic production and improving processing capabilities is crucial to reducing dependence on imports.

To ensure India's ammunition needs are met independently, a focused and strategic approach is necessary. Investing in the exploration and extraction of key minerals like copper and antimony will be a game-changer. Encouraging partnerships between the government and private sector can help develop our mining industry and make India less dependent on imports. Establishing facilities for producing critical materials such as toluene and nitrocellulose within the country will strengthen our defence ecosystem. Encouraging innovation and technology transfer will further enhance production capacity. Simplifying regulatory processes and offering incentives like tax breaks or subsidies can encourage businesses to invest in ammunition-related industries. Streamlining bureaucratic approvals will accelerate domestic production. Developing indigenous alternatives to imported materials and improving existing processes through R&D is essential. Collaboration between defence research institutions and private industries will be key to achieving this. While we work on enhancing domestic production, creating stockpiles of critical materials can help mitigate potential supply chain disruptions. Additionally, sourcing from multiple countries instead of relying on a single supplier will reduce risks. Encouraging cooperation between the government, defence forces, and private industry can drive efficiency and innovation. Leveraging the strengths of both sectors will ensure sustainable ammunition production. Engaging in strategic alliances with resource-rich nations can provide India access to advanced technologies and a steady supply of materials while we work on developing our domestic capabilities.

Integrated Cluster Model for Niche Ammunition Manufacturing in India

India's transition towards advanced and self-reliant ammunition production requires a manufacturing ecosystem that is simultaneously collaborative, technologically agile, and operationally integrated. The proposed integrated cluster model offers a structured pathway to achieve this by bringing together public-sector expertise, private-sector innovation, academic research capabilities, and the operational insights of the Indian Army. At the institutional level, the cluster is anchored by a dedicated governance mechanism along with the Ammunition Manufacturing Cluster Council (AMCC) supported by a Cluster Coordination Office (CCO) designed to ensure coherence, oversight, and seamless communication across agencies. This apex body includes representatives from the Ministry of Defence, the Department of Defence Production, DRDO, the Indian Army and Army Design Bureau, public-sector units such as Munitions India Limited and Bharat Dynamics Limited, leading academic institutions, and emerging start-ups developing niche ammunition technologies. Functionally, the CCO serves as the administrative and operational backbone of the cluster, enabling day-to-day coordination between government bodies, industry, academia, and the armed forces.

Geographic integration is a defining strength of this model. By situating cluster hubs within established defence industrial regions such as Bengaluru, Hyderabad, Pune, or Nashik, the model embeds manufacturing facilities, R&D laboratories, and testing infrastructure within a single ecosystem. Co-located public and private manufacturing units benefit from proximity to research institutions, enabling rapid prototyping, continuous user feedback, and scalable production. The roles of individual stakeholders within this cluster are both complementary and interdependent. Public-sector units and ordnance factories form the manufacturing backbone, contributing production capacity, institutional experience, and the ability to scale high-volume requirements. Their modernisation through advanced technologies is essential for producing precision-guided, smart, and next-generation ammunition. Private defence firms inject innovation and agility into the ecosystem, while joint ventures between PSUs and private companies support co-development of niche ammunition domains. SMEs and start-ups further enrich the cluster by offering specialised capabilities in electronics, materials, AI, and subsystems often overlooked in large-scale industrial setups.

The cluster equally relies on the scientific and human capital of academia. Technical institutions such as IITs, NITs, and IISc contribute research in materials, explosives, and precision systems, while also nurturing specialised talent pipelines for ammunition design and manufacturing. Formal technology transfer mechanisms ensure that laboratory research translates into deployable products, and sponsored research programmes supported by the Indian Army or defence industry help align academic work with battlefield requirements. The DRDO and associated defence laboratories provide the cluster with strategic R&D leadership, especially in precision-guided munitions, smart ammunition, and advanced energetic materials. Their collaboration with private industry and academia is intended to accelerate prototyping cycles, which are then tested and refined in partnership with the Indian Army.

The Indian Army itself occupies a central role as the end-user and final evaluator of all ammunition developed within the cluster. Through continuous feedback loops, early-stage design inputs, and structured user trials, the Army ensures that technological innovation remains firmly grounded in operational realities. Integrating Army test ranges and simulation environments into the cluster allows for real-time evaluation, minimising delays between design, testing, and deployment. To sustain momentum and innovation, the cluster model incorporates collaborative platforms such as defence innovation hubs, joint research projects, centres of excellence, and biannual knowledge exchange forums. These mechanisms are designed to catalyse research, encourage cross-institutional collaboration, and maintain technological currency. Financial and policy incentives ranging from the utilisation of defence manufacturing corridors in Uttar Pradesh and Tamil Nadu to tax incentives, subsidised infrastructure, and interest-free loans reinforce the commercial viability of niche ammunition development. Public–private partnerships extend the financial risk-sharing necessary for high-cost R&D projects.

A sophisticated testing and quality assurance framework further anchors the model. Centralised testing facilities within each cluster assess ballistic performance, environmental resilience, safety, and reliability, while specialised laboratories evaluate advanced electronics and smart ammunition systems. Integrating Indian Army user trials into the production pipeline ensures that performance standards remain mission-oriented and continuously validated. The model is designed for both sustainability and scalability. Manufacturing setups are expected to meet domestic requirements while also positioning India as a competitive exporter to markets across Asia, Africa, and Latin America. A dedicated Defence Export Promotion Council and export-supportive infrastructure would help translate technological achievements into global market presence.

Overall, this integrated cluster model advances a coherent, collaborative, and innovation-driven approach to ammunition manufacturing. By consolidating research, production, testing, and user involvement within a shared ecosystem, it reduces dependency on imports, accelerates technology absorption, strengthens national security, and elevates India's long-term potential as a global producer of advanced and niche ammunition systems.

Figure 9.1: Integrated Cluster Model for Niche Ammunition Manufacturing in India

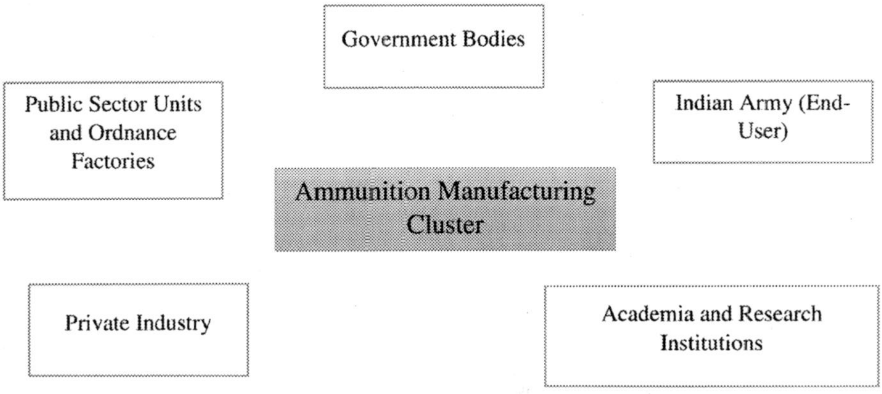

This visual representation of the Integrated Cluster Model illustrates the ecosystem-based approach necessary for advancing niche ammunition manufacturing in India. At the centre of the diagram is the Cluster Hub, the operational core where research, prototyping, testing, and manufacturing converge. Surrounding this hub are the key institutional pillars that collectively sustain the ecosystem. Governance is provided by the AMCC and the CCO, which ensure strategic coherence and coordination across ministries, regulatory bodies, and defence institutions. The scientific and technological backbone is formed by the DRDO and specialised defence laboratories, while public-sector units and ordnance factories contribute large-scale manufacturing capabilities. Private industry, along with SMEs and start-ups, injects innovation, agility, and specialised component expertise. Academic institutions strengthen the model through research contributions and talent development, supported by structured mechanisms for technology transfer. The Indian Army, positioned as the end-user, provides continuous operational feedback and validates prototypes through user trials, ensuring alignment between technological development and battlefield needs. Together, these interconnected nodes demonstrate the model's emphasis on collaboration, co-location, and iterative refinement that are essential features for building a self-reliant, high-tech ammunition manufacturing ecosystem.

Pioneering R&D Models for Cutting-Edge Ammunition Innovations

India's pursuit of self-reliance in advanced ammunition technologies demands R&D structures that are faster, more agile, and more specialised than the country's existing institutional arrangements. While the DRDO and public-sector units remain central to defence innovation, the rapid pace of technological changes globally; materials engineering, energetics, precision systems, and AI requires complementary frameworks capable of driving high-risk research, nurturing elite scientific talent, and accelerating the transition from laboratory concepts to deployable ammunition systems. Drawing on successful international models such as DARPA in the USA, Talpiot in Israel, and DIU's rapid innovation pathways, this section proposes three mutually reinforcing institutional mechanisms tailored to India's requirements: DRONA, a DARPA-like high-risk research organisation focused exclusively on next-generation ammunition; Project Aviyna, an elite Talpiot-style programme to develop mission-oriented scientific and engineering leaders; and the Ammunition Innovation Unit (AIU), India's equivalent of DIU for rapid technology absorption and military-industry integration. Together, these models offer a comprehensive R&D architecture capable of accelerating breakthrough ammunition technologies and supporting India's long-term strategic autonomy.

Table 9.1: Distinct Roles of India's Three Proposed Innovation Models

Model	*Global Inspiration*	*Core Purpose*	*What it resolves in India's Ammunition Innovation Ecosystem*
DRONA (Defence Research Organisation for Next-Gen Ammunition)	DARPA (USA)	To conduct high-risk, high-reward frontier research in advanced materials, energetics, smart ammunition, and disruptive manufacturing processes.	Overcomes slow research cycles, limited breakthrough R&D, fragmented innovation pathways, and the absence of a specialised agency dedicated to next-generation ammunition.
Project Aviyna (India's Talpiot-style elite technical corps)	Talpiot Program (Israel)	To cultivate an elite cadre of mission-oriented scientists, engineers, and military technologists capable of leading defence innovation programmes.	Addresses shortages of specialised leadership talent, weak military–science integration, and the lack of structured pathways to develop long-term technical expertise in ammunition systems.
AIU (Ammunition Innovation Unit)	DIU (USA)	To rapidly scout, evaluate, prototype, and integrate emerging technologies from industry, start-ups, and academia into defence manufacturing and ammunition programmes.	Mitigates slow absorption of new technologies, weak military-industry connectivity, bureaucratic delays, and the lack of a rapid-deployment mechanism connecting R&D outputs to production lines.

The comparative framework underscores that the three proposed institutional mechanisms vis-à-vis DRONA, Project Aviyna, and the Ammunition Innovation Unit (AIU) perform distinct yet mutually reinforcing roles in strengthening India's ammunition innovation ecosystem. DRONA provides the high-risk, frontier research capacity required to generate disruptive breakthroughs; Project Aviyna cultivates the specialised scientific and military talent needed to sustain such innovation over the long term; and AIU ensures that emerging technologies are rapidly evaluated, prototyped, and absorbed into manufacturing pipelines. Together, these models establish a layered architecture in which advanced research, talent development, and rapid deployment operate in a coordinated manner, closing the gaps that have long slowed India's progress in next-generation ammunition development. Building on this structural overview, the following subsections examine each model in detail, outlining their organisational logic, operational functions, and the specific capability gaps they are designed to address within India's evolving ammunition ecosystem.

DRONA (Defence Research Organisation for Next-gen Ammunition)

The DRONA model envisions a DARPA-type institution dedicated exclusively to next-generation ammunition development in India. It is conceived as an autonomous, mission-driven agency under the Ministry of Defence with the singular mandate of pursuing high-risk, high-reward research that conventional structures often cannot accommodate. At its core, DRONA would function as the national engine for breakthrough innovation in advanced energetics, materials, manufacturing, and ammunition system design. Anchored by an advisory board comprising defence scientists, military leaders, and industry experts, the organisation would ensure that all research trajectories remain aligned with operational priorities and the broader national security agenda.

The primary objective of DRONA is to create an ecosystem where cutting-edge research in materials science, energetics, smart ammunition, and sustainable manufacturing converges with the practical needs of India's defence forces. By fostering deep collaboration among PSUs, private industry, academic institutions, and research laboratories, DRONA aims to integrate the fragmented innovation landscape that currently slows technological advancement. Its mandate includes cultivating capabilities for rapid prototyping and iterative testing so that new designs can transition from laboratory concepts to field evaluation with minimal delay. This approach directly addresses the long-standing gap between R&D and deployable products that has constrained India's ammunition modernisation.

To support these ambitions, DRONA would be equipped with a dedicated and stable funding apparatus that draws primarily from the defence budget while also incentivising private sector participation through co-investment and targeted subsidies. Competitive innovation grants would further attract research institutions, start-ups, and specialised companies working on disruptive approaches to ammunition manufacturing. The research portfolio would span advanced materials such as high-strength alloys, composites, and nano-materials; precision and smart ammunition with embedded sensors and AI; sustainable manufacturing methods including additive manufacturing; and efforts to build resilient supply chains for critical components.

Operationally, DRONA would adopt a milestone-based project management structure, forming specialised, cross-disciplinary teams for each initiative. These teams would move through defined stages of design, prototyping, evaluation, and field testing, with the Indian Armed Forces integrated into the process from the outset. Continuous evaluation and feedback loops would allow for iterative refinement, while clear frameworks for intellectual property management would facilitate technology transfer to India's defence manufacturers without compromising innovation ownership. DRONA would also prioritise dual-use technologies that can stimulate broader industrial development.

A key pillar of the model is capacity building. DRONA would collaborate with leading academic institutions to develop specialised training programmes, research fellowships, and advanced courses in ammunition technology and defence manufacturing. This would strengthen India's long-term talent base and ensure that scientific and engineering expertise is continuously replenished. At the same time, structured performance metrics and monitoring mechanisms would evaluate the impact of DRONA's initiatives on innovation output, production efficiency, and battlefield effectiveness, creating a culture of accountability and continuous improvement. International collaboration would form another strategic dimension. By building partnerships with friendly nations and defence organisations, DRONA could exchange knowledge, benchmark best practices, and create opportunities for exporting advanced ammunition technologies. Its success, however, would depend on supportive regulatory reforms including streamlined approvals and procurement policies that prioritise domestically developed systems.

Overall, the DRONA model provides India with a focused, agile, and innovation-driven institutional pathway that complements the broad-based but slower research ecosystem led by DRDO and defence PSUs. By introducing speed, specialisation, and risk-tolerant research culture, DRONA fills a critical structural gap and positions India to make decisive advances in next-generation ammunition development.

Project Aviyna: Similar to Israeli Talpiot Program

Project Aviyna represents an elite, talent-driven innovation pathway modelled on Israel's highly successful Talpiot programme, adapted specifically to strengthen India's ammunition manufacturing ecosystem. While DRONA focuses on breakthrough research and institutional capability, Project Aviyna addresses the equally critical human-capital dimension by cultivating a cadre of technically exceptional, strategically oriented leaders capable of driving innovation across military, industrial, and research domains. Designed as a multi-year, immersive programme drawing participants from the top one per cent of India's technical universities, defence academies, and R&D institutions, Project Aviyna seeks to create a specialised knowledge community positioned at the intersection of advanced science, military requirements, and industrial production.

Structured over three to four years, the programme integrates advanced academic education, military exposure, and industry immersion into a coherent training pipeline. Small cohort sizes enable rigorous mentorship, facilitate personalised development, and replicate the intensity that defines Talpiot's success in Israel. Selection relies on a stringent, multi-stage evaluation process involving aptitude tests, technical assessments, psychological screening, and interviews conducted by leaders from the military, academia, and the defence sector. By admitting candidates who combine technical excellence, leadership potential, and a strong commitment to national defence, Project Aviyna seeks to build a talent pool uniquely equipped for next-generation ammunition development.

Once inducted, participants undergo an advanced, multidisciplinary curriculum grounded in ammunition design, novel manufacturing technologies, materials science, systems engineering, and AI applications in defence. This academic component is complemented by hands-on R&D assignments within DRDO laboratories, defence PSUs, and private manufacturing units. The integration of basic and advanced military training ensures that participants develop a lived understanding of operational environments, logistical constraints, and tactical realities—knowledge that is essential for designing ammunition aligned with battlefield requirements. Rotational internships across public and private manufacturing establishments, along with optional short-term international exposure, further ensure that participants gain a realistic understanding of production ecosystems and global defence standards.

Central to Project Aviyna is its emphasis on research-led innovation. Each participant, or team, undertakes a capstone project focused on designing new ammunition technologies or improving existing manufacturing processes. These projects, conducted under the guidance of mentors from the military, academia, and industry, are directly aligned with the operational and strategic needs of the Indian Armed Forces. Innovation clusters connected to the broader ammunition ecosystem provide spaces for prototyping, experimentation, and interdisciplinary problem-solving. Upon completion, graduates assume dual roles serving as technical officers within the Indian Armed Forces and simultaneously functioning as scientific and industrial liaisons with defence R&D and manufacturing entities. This dual-placement structure ensures a continuous exchange of knowledge and strengthens institutional integration across the defence innovation landscape. The programme is designed to prepare participants for long-term leadership trajectories, positioning them as future decision-makers capable of shaping India's ammunition modernisation and broader defence-industrial policy.

Project outcomes would be evaluated through measurable indicators such as technological outputs, contributions to defence self-reliance, and the long-term career impact of graduates. Regular programme reviews and feedback mechanisms ensure adaptability and alignment with shifting defence priorities. Sustained government support through dedicated funding, streamlined policy frameworks, and clear institutional pathways for alumni integration is essential for ensuring the programme's viability and strategic relevance. Overall, Project Aviyna offers India a transformative mechanism for cultivating deep scientific expertise and operationally attuned leadership in defence innovation. By seamlessly blending advanced education, military orientation, and industrial exposure, the model ensures that India develops the human capital required to remain at the forefront of ammunition technology and defence manufacturing excellence.

Ammunition Innovation Unit

The proposed Ammunition Innovation Unit (AIU) represents an operationally agile, industry-facing innovation mechanism modelled on the US Defence Innovation Unit (DIU), adapted specifically to accelerate the infusion of emerging technologies into India's ammunition manufacturing ecosystem. While DRONA provides high-end, exploratory research capacity and Project Aviyna cultivates specialised human capital, AIU serves as the implementation arm that bridges the gap between technological potential and production-ready solutions. Its mandate is explicitly centred on rapid adoption, prototyping, and deployment of advanced technologies, ensuring that India's ammunition industry remains responsive to evolving operational requirements and global innovation cycles.

Structurally, AIU would operate under the Ministry of Defence, maintaining close functional alignment with the Department of Defence Production and the DRDO. Led by a director with demonstrated expertise in defence technology and innovation, the unit would draw leadership from the military, industry, and technical domains, reflecting its cross-sectoral mission. Its overarching objective is to accelerate the adoption of advanced technologies in ammunition manufacturing by facilitating structured collaboration between the armed forces, defence manufacturers, start-ups, and research institutions. This includes identifying emerging technologies, enabling their evaluation through specialised hubs, and supporting their transition from concept to prototype and from prototype to scalable manufacturing.

The AIU's core functions consolidate the entire innovation pipeline from technology scouting to operational deployment. The unit would maintain comprehensive technology radar, scouting innovations, both domestically and internationally, with particular attention to start-ups, SMEs, and academic labs working on advanced materials, AI-enabled design, automation, and other frontier fields. Dedicated evaluation hubs, established in collaboration with DRDO and leading academic institutions, would assess the feasibility, manufacturability, and operational relevance of these technologies. Once a technology demonstrates promise, AIU's innovation labs equipped for rapid prototyping, additive manufacturing, AI-driven modelling, and advanced materials testing would enable accelerated development cycles. Close coordination with the Indian Armed Forces ensures that field trials, feedback loops, and operational validation occur at pace, allowing iterative refinement and shortening the development-to-deployment timeframe.

Public-private partnerships form a central pillar of the AIU model. The unit would administer flexible, milestone-based innovation contracts to private firms, including start-ups, to develop specific technological solutions. By providing shared platforms for collaboration among manufacturers, technology firms, and the military, AIU would encourage co-development models that distribute risk and leverage specialised expertise. Complementing this is a dedicated innovation fund to support scaling efforts, combined with grants and competitions designed to stimulate creativity across India's broader technology ecosystem. The AIU would also manage intellectual property generated through its initiatives, ensuring that IP licensing and technology transfer pathways facilitate commercialisation, dual-use applications, and industrial growth.

Collaboration is built into the institutional design of AIU. Engagement with the Indian Armed Forces ensures that innovation agendas remain aligned with operational needs; partnerships with major defence manufacturers facilitate rapid scale-up; and collaborations with academic institutions deepen access to cutting-edge research and skilled talent. International linkages would allow India to learn from allied innovation ecosystems and pursue joint ventures that deliver technology transfer and capacity-building outcomes. AIU would also integrate closely with existing institutions complementing DRDO's long-cycle research, working alongside a future DRONA-like entity, and linking with national initiatives such as Start-up India to widen the innovation base.

Monitoring mechanisms are essential for maintaining organisational agility. The AIU would employ clear metrics to assess technology adoption rates, the number of innovations developed, patents produced, and the operational impact of deployed technologies. Agile project management practices and regular reviews ensure that the unit remains responsive to shifting priorities and can recalibrate efforts as required by national defence imperatives. Regulatory and policy support underpin the effectiveness of the AIU model. Streamlined approval processes, supportive IP frameworks, and export-enabling policies are critical for ensuring rapid deployment and broader commercial viability of innovations. Outreach initiatives, including innovation challenges, hackathons, and defence-technology conferences would broaden participation, increase public-private engagement, and help normalise a culture of experimentation across the defence manufacturing ecosystem.

In essence, the Ammunition Innovation Unit serves as the connective tissue linking research breakthroughs, skilled talent, and industrial capability. By acting as a catalyst for rapid prototyping, collaborative development, and technology absorption, AIU strengthens India's ability to integrate cutting-edge solutions into ammunition manufacturing. Its operational agility, multi-sectoral partnerships, and mission-driven structure position it as a critical enabler of India's ambition to achieve self-reliance in defence manufacturing while keeping pace with global technological trajectories.

Conclusion

Achieving self-reliance in ammunition manufacturing is ultimately a question of strategic design, technological depth, and institutional coherence. The preceding chapters have demonstrated that India's ammunition ecosystem cannot be strengthened through manufacturing reforms alone; it requires an innovation-driven architecture that integrates advanced technologies, resilient supply chains, and agile R&D structures. The technological pathways examined in this chapter including additive manufacturing, nano-materials, next-generation propellants, and advanced materials engineering illustrate how India can shift from incremental improvement to genuine capability transformation.

These frontiers directly address long-standing vulnerabilities such as import dependence, precision deficits, slow prototyping cycles, and fragile inputs-based supply chains.

Yet technology by itself does not create self-reliance. The integrated cluster model shows that manufacturing excellence emerges only when public industry, private firms, academia, R&D laboratories, and the Indian Army function within a shared ecosystem characterised by real-time feedback, codified collaboration, and common innovation objectives. This chapter's institutional models such as DRONA, Project Aviyna, and the Ammunition Innovation Unit further demonstrate that India's ammunition self-reliance will depend on building high-risk research capability, developing specialised human capital, and ensuring rapid absorption of new technologies. Together, these mechanisms form a coherent innovation pipeline that spans frontier research, talent cultivation, prototyping, deployment, and eventual scale-up.

In essence, the pathway to self-reliance in ammunition manufacturing is multidimensional. It requires sustained investment in indigenous R&D, stable policy direction, predictable procurement frameworks, capability-driven manufacturing ecosystems, and continuous technological renewal. More importantly, it demands institutional architectures capable of overcoming the inertia associated with legacy systems. If implemented with continuity and strategic clarity, the measures outlined across this work can significantly enhance India's defence preparedness, strengthen its strategic autonomy, and position the country as a credible and competitive producer of advanced ammunition. The journey towards self-reliance is complex, but with coherent technological, operational, and organisational reforms, India can build an ammunition ecosystem that is resilient, innovative, and globally benchmarked.

Endnotes

1. "Self-Reliance not an option but a necessity says Rajnath" (17 June 2023). *Deccan Herald.* Retrieved from https://www.deccanherald.com/india/self-reliance-is-not-an-option-but-a-necessity-says-rajnath-singh-1228585.html
2. "PM launches 'Make in India' global initiative" (25 September 2014). PMINDIA. Retrieved from https://www.pmindia.gov.in/en/ news_updates/pm-launches-make-in-india-global-initiative/
3. Ministry of Defence, Government of India. (2022). 'Aatmanirbhar Bharat Initiative in Defence Production'. (1 April 2022). Press Information Bureau. Retrieved from https://pib.gov.in/Pressreleaseshare.aspx? PRID=1812297
4. Jaisinghani, M. 'Defending the World'. *Defence Manufacturing in India - Companies & Investment.* (n.d.). Invest India. Retrieved from https:// www.investindia.gov.in/sector/defence-manufacturing
5. Wezeman, P.D. et al. (2024). 'Trends in International Arms Transfers, 2023' (March 2024). SIPRI Fact Sheet. SIPRI. Retrieved from https://www.sipri.org/sites/default/files/2024-03/fs_2403_at_2023.pdf
6. Ibid., p. 9.
7. Suman, M. (2019). 'Make in India and the defence sector: progress and challenges' (10 July 2019). India Foundation. Retrieved from https://indiafoundation.in/articles-and-commentaries/make-in-india-andthe-defence-sector-progress-and-challenges/
8. Ibid.
9. Cowshish, A. (2020). 'Why is the Ministry of Defence so committed to Forming Committees?' 10 September 2020. *The Wire.* Retrieved from https://thewire.in/government/ministry-of-defence-committeereports
10. Ibid.
11. Suman, M. (2019). 'Make in India and the defence sector: progress and challenges' (10 July 2019). India Foundation. Retrieved from https://indiafoundation.in/articles-and-commentaries/make-in-india-andthe-defence-sector-progress-and-challenges/
12. Stockholm International Peace Research Institute (SIPRI). (2021). "Arms Transfers Database." Retrieved from https://www.sipri.org/databases/armstransfers
13. Bitzinger, R.A. (2011). 'The Defence Industry in the Post-Transformational World: Implications for the United States and Global Security.' *Journal of Strategic Studies*, 32(4), 513-536.
14. Katz, Y. (2020). *The Weapon Wizards: How Israel Became a High-Tech Military Superpower.* St. Martin's Press.

15. Pant, H.V. (2019). 'India's Emerging Defence Industry: Challenges and Prospects.' *International Affairs*, 95(4), 853-871.
16. KPMG. (2018). Indian Defence Sector: The Way Forward. Retrieved from https://home.kpmg/in
17. Jayakumar, P.B. "The $130 Billion Battle for India's Defence Pie", *FortuneIndia*, March 7, 2023. Retrieved from https://www.fortuneindia.com/long-reads/the-130-billion-battle-for-indias-defence-pie/111829
18. Ministry of Defence. (2020). Defence Production and Export Promotion Policy (DPEPP) 2020. Government of India. Retrieved from https://www.mod.gov.in
19. "The Defence Procurement Procedure", Lok Sabha Secretariat, 2016. Retrieved from https://loksabhadocs.nic.in/Refinput/New_Reference_Notes/English/The%20Defence%20Procurement%20Procedure.pdf
20. Ministry of Defence. (2021, July 26). Private players in defence manufacturing sector. June 15, 2022. Retrieved from https://pib.gov.in/PressReleaseIframePage.aspx?PRID=1739049
21. Press Information Bureau. (2020). Government of India. Retrieved from pib.gov.in.
22. Singh, S.V. (2023). 'Policy Recommendations for achieving India's Defence Export Ambitions'. (23 November 2023). ORF Issue Brief, No. 676, Observer Research Foundation. Retrieved from https://www.orfonline.org/research/policy-recommendations-for-achieving-india-sdefence-export-ambitions
23. Ibid.
24. Assocham India. (2014). Self-Reliance in Defence Production: The Unfinished Agenda. Pricewaterhouse Coopers
25. Press Information Bureau. "Another major boost to Atmanirbharta in defence: Ministry of Defence signs five major capital acquisition contracts worth Rs 39,125.39 crore," March 1, 2024.
26. Ministry of Defence India (2021). "Defence Equipments and Make in India Scheme". *Press Information Bureau.* Retrieved from https://www.pib.gov.in/PressReleasePage.aspx?PRID=1780866
27. Ministry of Defence. (2021, July 26). Private players in defence manufacturing sector. June 15, 2022. Retrieved from https:// pib.gov.in/PressReleaseIframePage.aspx?PRID=1739049
28. Ministry of Defence, Government of India. (2024, July 17). Defence Ministry notifies Fifth Positive Indigenisation List of 346 items for DPSUs. *Press Information Bureau.* Retrieved from https://www.pib.gov.in/PressReleasePage.aspx?PRID=2033571
29. Press Information Bureau. (2022). "Ministry of Defence – Year End Review 2022." Retrieved from https://pib.gov.in/PressReleasePage.aspx?PRID=1884353
30. DRDO. (2021). "Small Arms and Ammunition". Retrieved from https:// www.drdo.gov.in/drdo/sites/default/files/technology-focus- document/TF_Oct_2021.pdf
31. Kumar, A. & Singh, P. (2022). *Miniaturization in Defence Electronics.* IEEE Transactions on Electronics, 61(4), 415-422.
32. Rao, V.; Sharma, P. & Kumar, R. (2021). 'Sensor Integration in Precision Guided Munitions.' *Journal of Military Science and Technology*, 37(2), 88- 99.
33. Patel, S. & Verma, M. (2022). 'Collaboration in Defence Research and Development.' *Strategic Analysis*, 46(1), 78-90.

34. Mehta, R. & Singh, V. (2022). *Communication Systems for Smart Ammunition. Defence Technology Review*, 18(2), 55-63.
35. Raman, V. & Gupta, M. (2021). 'Next-Generation Propellants: Challenges and Opportunities.' *Propellants, Explosives, and Pyrotechnics*, 46(1), 19-29.
36. Shukla, R. & Banerjee, S. (2022). 'Material Science Innovations in Propellant Formulations'. *Journal of Materials Science*, 57(4), 1124-1136.
37. Mishra, R. & Tiwari, S. (2021). Safety and Stability of Propellants: A Review. *Journal of Energetic Materials*, 39(5), 245-258.
38. Srivastava, M. & Kumar, S. (2022). 'Lightweight Materials for Ammunition Components.' *Materials Today*: Proceedings, 47(1), 98-105.
39. Pandey, N. & Sharma, K. (2021). 'Wear-Resistant Materials in Ammunition Manufacturing.' *Materials Science and Engineering*, 42(3), 321-329.
40. Verma, R. & Singh, P. (2021). 'Corrosion Resistance in Military Applications'. *Journal of Applied Materials and Technologies*, 56(2), 67-78. ../../arush/Music/freelancing/bj/Indian Defence Industry-A Global Reach
41. Chakrabarti, R. & Bose, S. (2021). Intellectual Property Challenges in Defence Technology. *Journal of Intellectual Property Rights*, 26(3), 115-127.
42. Rao, K. & Nair, S. (2021). 'Talent Acquisition in the Indian Defence Sector.' *Journal of Defence Studies*, 15(1), 14-31.
43. Sharma, D. & Gupta, A. (2021). 'Infrastructure Development for Defence Technology.' *Defence Infrastructure Journal*, 12(3), 64-73.
44. Patel, S. & Verma, M. (2022). 'Collaboration in Defence Research and Development.' *Strategic Analysis*, 46(1), 78-90.
45. Anand J.C. (2022). "India's R&D spends amongst the lowest in the world: NITI Aayog study". *The Economic Times.* Retrieved from https://economictimes.indiatimes.com/news/india/indias-rd-spends-amongst-the-lowest-in-the-world-niti-aayog-study/articleshow/93024586.cms?from=mdr
46. Saxena, N. (2020). 'Regulatory frameworks in India's defence sector.' *Journal of Regulatory Affairs,* 12(1), 30-39.
47. KPMG. (2021). *India's Defence Manufacturing Sector: Opportunities and Challenges.* KPMG Reports.
48. Bhandari, V.B. (2019). *Introduction to Machine Design.* Tata McGraw-Hill Education.
49. Gupta, A. & Mehta, R. (2020). 'Geographical challenges in setting up manufacturing units in India.' *Economic and Political Weekly,* 55(18), 24- 30.
50. Chopra, S. & Singh, P. (2021). 'Logistics and supply chain management in India's defence sector.' *Journal of Defence Studies,* 15(2), 123-140.
51. Joshi, S. (2020). 'Energy and water resource management in industrial sectors.' *Journal of Environmental Management,* 264, 110477.
52. Deloitte. (2020). *The Indian Defence Industry: Strategic Opportunities and Challenges.* Deloitte Insights.
53. KPMG. (2021). *India's Defence Manufacturing Sector: Opportunities and Challenges.* KPMG Reports.
54. Mahapatra, D. & Mishra, P. (2019). 'Raw material price volatility and its impact on the

manufacturing sector.' *Journal of Industrial Economics,* 67(4), 798-814.

55. Sharma, A. & Kumar, S. (2021). 'Advanced manufacturing technologies in the defence sector.' *Journal of Manufacturing Processes,* 62, 230-245.
56. Singh, R. & Joshi, A. (2020). 'Skill development in India's defence manufacturing.' *Journal of Defence Management,* 10(2), 67-78.
57. Ghosh, S. & Banerjee, P. (2021). 'R&D challenges in India's defence manufacturing sector.' *Defence Science Journal,* 71(1), 45-56.
58. Ministry of Defence. (2021). Defence Procurement Procedure (DPP) 2021. Government of India.
59. Ranganathan, V. (2021). 'Regional security dynamics and defence manufacturing in India.' *Strategic Analysis,* 45(3), 256-271.
60. Saxena, N. (2020). 'Regulatory frameworks in India's defence sector.' *Journal of Regulatory Affairs,* 12(1), 30-39.
61. Jones, A. (2021). *The Evolution of the UK's Defence Industry.* Oxford University Press.
62. Smith, J. (2022). *Brexit and the UK's Defence Sector: A Comprehensive Analysis.* Cambridge University Press.
63. Jones, A. (2021). *The Evolution of the UK's Defence Industry.* Oxford University Press.
64. Smith, J. (2022). *Brexit and the UK's Defence Sector: A Comprehensive Analysis.* Cambridge University Press.
65. Kumar, S. (2023). *India's Defence Production and Modernization.* Routledge. Kundu, O. (2021) 'Risks in Defence Procurement: India in the 21st Century', *Defence and Peace Economics,* Vol. 32, Issue 3.
66. Sharma, R. (2024). *The Role of Private Sector in India's Defence Industry.* Springer.
67. Rajan, P. (2023). 'Challenges and Prospects in India's Ammunition Industry.' *Defence Studies Journal,* 29(3), 45-67.
68. Kumar, S. (2023). *India's Defence Production and Modernization.* Routledge. Kundu, O. (2021) 'Risks in Defence Procurement: India in the 21st Century', *Defence and Peace Economics,* Vol. 32, Issue 3.
69. Sharma, R. (2024). *The Role of Private Sector in India's Defence Industry.* Springer.
70. Rajan, P. (2023). 'Challenges and Prospects in India's Ammunition Industry.' *Defence Studies Journal,* 29(3), 45-67.
71. Jones, A. (2021). *The Evolution of the UK's Defence Industry.* Oxford University Press.
72. Kumar, S. (2023). *India's Defence Production and Modernization.* Routledge. Kundu, O. (2021) 'Risks in Defence Procurement: India in the 21st Century', *Defence and Peace Economics,* Vol. 32, Issue 3.
73. Smith, J. (2022). *Brexit and the UK's Defence Sector: A Comprehensive Analysis.* Cambridge University Press.
74. Rajan, P. (2023). 'Challenges and Prospects in India's Ammunition Industry.' *Defence Studies Journal,* 29(3), 45-67.
75. Sharma, R. (2024). *The Role of Private Sector in India's Defence Industry.* Springer.
76. Gokhale, N. (2021). 'The Untold Story of LCA Tejas Journey.' Bharat Shakti. Retrieved from https://bharatshakti.in/the-untold-story-of- lca-tejas-journey/
77. Chawla, A.K. (2022). 'The Re-Birth of Vikrant: A Triumph of Indigenisation.' *SPS Naval*

Forces. Retrieved from https://www.spsnavalforces.com/story/?id=809&h=The-Re-Birth-of-Vikrant-andndash;-A-Triumph-of-Indigenisation#:~:text= Legacy%20of%20Ins%20Vikrant &text=The%20ship%20remained%20laid%20up,Belfast%20on%20March%204%2C% 2019 61.

78. Kulkarni, S. (2025). 'Story of BrahMos: the 'fire and forget', stealthy cruise missile India likely used against Pakistan. *The Indian Express*. Retrieved from https://indianexpress.com/article/explained/brahmos-missile-pakistan-sindoor-speed-range-9996781/

79. National Institute for Defence Studies (NIDS), 'Strategic Autonomy in the Indian Defence Sector,' 2020.

80. Ministry of Defence, Government of India. 'Annual Report, 2020-2021'. Retrieved from https://mod.gov.in/annual-report-archive

81. Confederation of Indian Industry (CII). 'Economic Impact of Defence Manufacturing,' 2019.

82. Institute for Defence Studies and Analyses (IDSA), 'India's Defence Industrial Base: Capabilities and Challenges,' 2021.

83. Ministry of Defence, Government of India. (2022). 'Annual Report 2021- 22'. www.mod.gov.in.

84. Confederation of Indian Industry (CII). 'Defence'. Retrieved from https:/ /www.cii.in/sectors.aspx?enc=prvePUj2bdMtgTmvPwvisYH+5EnGjyGXO9hLECvTuNvhsHyQdbr0qayHmED87nB1

85. 'Annual Report 2021-22.' Retrieved from https://mod.gov.in/annual-report; BrahMos Aerospace. 'BrahMos Supersonic Cruise Missile.'

86. Kapoor, N. (2021). 'India's Defence Sector: Opportunities and Challenges.' *Journal of Defence Studies*, 15(1), 47-65.

87. Ministry of Commerce and Industry. 'Annual Report 2021-2022'. Retrieved from https://commerce.gov.in/wp-content/uploads/2022/02/ English-Annual-Report-2021-22-Department-of-Commerce.pdf

88. Ministry of Defence. (2020). 'Defence Production and Export Promotion Policy (DPEPP)' 2020. Government of India. Retrieved from https:// www.mod.gov.in

89 'A study reveals how India can achieve $5 billion defence export goal,' *The Economic Times*, June 17, 2024. Retrieved from https://economic times.indiatimes.com/news/defence/a-study-reveals-how-india-can- achieve-5-billion-defence-export-goal/articleshow/111059109.cms?from=mdr

90. 'Defence Production and Export Promotion Policy', PIB, 2020. Retrieved from https://pib.gov.in/PressReleasePage.aspx?PRID=1643194

91. Behera, L.K.. 'The State of India's Public Defence Industry', *ORF*, October 26, 2023. Retrieved from https://www.orfonline.org/research/the-state-of-indias-public-sector-defence-industry

92. Smith, C. (1994) 'India's *Ad Hoc* Arsenal: Direction or Drift in Defence Policy?' SIPRI. Retrieved from https://www.sipri.org/sites/default/ files/files/books/SIPRI94Smith.pdf

93. Behera, L.K.(2023). 'The State of India's Public Defence Industry', *ORF*, October 26, 2023. Retrieved from https://www.orfonline.org/research/the-state-of-indias-public-sector-defence-industry

94. *The Economic Times*, (2022). Retrieved from https://economictimes.india times.com/news/

economy/policy/on-this-day-in-1991-a-landmark- budget-that-changed-indias-fortunes/articleshow/93090439. cms?fro m=mdr

95. Hilali, A.Z. (2001).'"India's Strategic Thinking and Its National Security Policy', *Asian Survey*, 41:5, pp. 737–764. Retrieved from https://library.fes.de/ libalt/journals/swetsfulltext/14218805.PDF
96. Department of Defence Production, Government of India. (n.d.). 'Defence Production and Export Promotion Policy (DPEPP) 2020'. ddpmod.gov. Retrieved from https://www.ddpmod.gov.in/sites/default/files/ pdfupload/DraftDPEPP.pdf
97. Singh, S.V. (2023). 'Policy Recommendations for achieving India's Defence Export Ambitions'. (23 November 2023). ORF Issue Brief, No. 676, Observer Research Foundation. Retrieved from https://www.orfon line.org/research/policy-recommendations-for-achieving-india-s- defence-export-ambitions
98. '$5 billion export target by 2025: Modi govt's push to turn India into world's defence manufacturing hub.' *The Times of India*, 2023. Retrieved from http://timesofindia.india times.com/articleshow/97874264.cms? utm_source=contentofinterest&utm_medium=text&utm_ campaign=cppst
99. Kumar, A. & Bharadwaj, T. (2024). 'One Year of the INDUS-X: Defence Innovation between India and the U.S.', Carnegie India. Retrieved from //carnegieindia.org/research/2024/06/one-year-of-the-indus- x-defence-innovation-between-india-and-the-us?lang=en¢er=india
100. DRDO. (2021). *Guidance Systems Development in India.* Defence Research and Development Organisation Annual Report.
101. Solanki, V. (2024). 'India's increased defence and security engagement with Southeast Asia.' *IISS.* Retrieved from https:// www.iiss.org/en/online-analysis/online-analysis/2024/04/indias-increased-defence-and-security-engagement-with-southeast-asia/
102. Peri, D. 'India gifts missile corvette *INS Kirpan* to Vietnam', *The Hindu.* Retrieved from https://www.thehindu.com/news/ national/india-gifts-missile-corvette-ins-kirpan-to-vietnam/article66986653.ece
103. Choudhary, D.R. (2022). 'In a first, India to export BrahMos Missile to the Philippines', *The Economic Times*, January 15, 2022. Retrieved from https://economictimes.indiatimes.com/news/defence/in-a-first- india-to-export-brahmos-missile-to-philippines/articleshow/8890 8287.cms?from=mdr
104. Mishra, A. (2023). 'Boosting India-Africa defence and security partnership', *ORF.* Retrieved from https://www.orfonline.org/expert-speak/ boosting-india-africa-defence-and-security-partnership
105. Badri-Maharaj, S. (2016, June). 'The Mauritius-India Naval Relationship: Naval Diplomacy 2.0.' *IDSA.* Retrieved from https://www.idsa.in/ africatrends/the-mauritius-india-naval-relationship%3A-naval- diplomacy
106. Ministry of External Affairs. (2024). "India-Seychelles Bilateral Relations." (2024, March). MEA. Retrieved from https://www.mea.gov.in/Portal/ForeignRelation/IndiaSeychells24. pdf
107. Ministry of External Affairs. (2024). 'India-Mozambique Bilateral Relations.' Retrieved from https://www.hcimaputo.gov.in/page/india-mozambique-relations/ #:~:text=INS%20Kesari%20visited%20Maputo%20in,boats%2C%20military%20 equipment%20and%20accessories
108. 'Invest in R&D for India to keep pace with evolving world: Rajnath Singh' (12 September

2023). *Business Standard.* Retrieved from https:// www.business-standard.com/india-news/invest-more-in-r-d-for- india-to-keep-pace-with-evolving-world-rajnath-to-domestic-defence-firms-123091200936_1.html

109. 'India, Saudi Arabia explore new avenues of defence cooperation,', (2024). *The Economic Times.* Retrieved from https://economictimes.india times.com/news/defence/india-saudi-arabia-explore-new-avenues- of-defence-cooperation/articleshow/107500475.cms?from=mdr.
110. Kaushik, K. & Roy, S. (2021) 'India, Russia sign 4 deals; New Delhi brings up China aggression,' *Indian Express.* Retrieved from https://indianexpress.com/article/india/22-meeting-india-russia- sign-4-deals-new-delhi-brings-up-china-aggression-7659987/
111. 'India, France agree to expand partnership in defence, security,', *Indian Express*, 2021. Retrieved from https://indianexpress.com/article/ india/india-france-agree-to-expand-partnership-in-defence-security- 7610677/
112. Kutty, S.N. & Basrur, R. (2021). 'The QUAD: What it is – and what it is not', *The Diplomat*, March 2021. Retrieved from https:// thediplomat.com/2021/03/the-quad-what-it-is-and-what-it-is-not/
113. Shukla, A. (2024). 'India's FY24 defence exports jump record 32.5%, touch Rs 21,083 crore,', *Business Standard*, April 2024. Retrieved from https:// www.business-standard.com/industry /news/india-s-defence- exports-jump-record-32-5-touch-rs-21-083-crore-12404010 1000_1.html
114. 'The Indian Economy: A Review,', Department of Economic Affairs, 2024. Retrieved from https://dea.gov.in/sites/default/files/The%20Indian %20Economy-A%20Review_Jan%202024.pdf
115. 'Defence exports touch record Rs 21,083 crore in FY 2023-24, an increase of 32.5% over last fiscal; Private sector contributes 60%, DPSUs - 40%.', PIB, 1 April 2024. Retrieved from https://pib.gov.in/PressReleseDetail m.aspx?PRID=2016818
116. Ibid.
117. Suman, M. (2019). 'Make in India and the defence sector: progress and challenges' (10 July 2019). India Foundation. Retrieved from https:// indiafoundation.in/articles-and-commentaries/make-in-india-and- the-defence-sector-progress-and-challenges/
118. Ibid.
119. Cowshish, A. (2020). 'Why is the Ministry of Defence so committed to Forming Committees?' 10 September 2020. *The Wire.* Retrieved from https://thewire.in/government/ministry-of-defence-committee- reports
120. Ibid.
121. Suman, M. (2019). 'Make in India and the defence sector: progress and challenges' (10 July 2019). India Foundation. Retrieved from https:// indiafoundation.in/articles-and-commentaries/make-in-india-and- the-defence-sector-progress-and-challenges/
122. 'Trends in International Arms Transfers,', SIPRI, 2023, March 2024. Retrieved from https:/ /www.sipri.org/publications/2024/sipri-factsheets/trends-international-arms-transfers-2023.
123. https://www.sipri.org/sites/default/files/2024-03/fs_2403_at_2023.pdf
124. Ibid.
125. Ministry of Defence. (2023). Defence Annual Report 2022-23. Government of India.p64. Retrieved from https://mod.gov.in/sites/default/files/ DEFENCE%20AR%202022-

23%20LOW.pdf

126. Ibid.
127. SIPRI Yearbook 2020: Armaments, Disarmament, and International Security. Stockholm International Peace Research Institute. Retrieved from https://www.sipri.org/yearbook/2020
128. Behuria, A.K. (2018). 'Defence Exports as an Instrument of National Security: An Overview', *Journal of Strategic Studies*, Vol. 41, Issue 1-2.
129. Singh, S.V. (2023). 'Policy Recommendations for achieving India's Defence Export Ambitions,' (23 November 2023). ORF Issue Brief, No. 676, Observer Research Foundation. Retrieved from https://www.orfon line.org/research/policy-recommendations-for-achieving-india-s- defence-export-ambitions
130. Aggarwal, Arpit. Ministry of Defence, Government of India. (2020). Defence Acquisition Procedure (DAP) 2020. Retrieved from https:// www.mod.gov.in
131. Singh, S.V. (2023). 'Policy Recommendations for achieving India's Defence Export Ambitions'. (23 November 2023). ORF Issue Brief, No. 676, Observer Research Foundation. Retrieved from https://www.orfon line.org/research/policy-recommendations-for-achieving-india-s- defence-export-ambitions
132. Ministry of Defence (2024). DefConnect 2024: Raksha Mantri launches ADITI scheme to promote innovations in critical & strategic defence technologies. *Press Information Bureau.* Retrieved from https://www.pib.gov.in/PressReleasePage.aspx?PRID=2011171
133. Shukla, A. (2024). 'India's FY24 defence exports jump record 32.5%, touch Rs 21,083 crore,' *Business Standard*, April 2024. Retrieved from https:// www.business-standard.com/ industry /news/india-s-defence-exports-jump-record-32-5-touch-rs-21-083-crore-124040 101000_1.html
134. 'Defence Production and Export Promotion Policy,' PIB, 2022. Retrieved from https:// pib.gov.in/PressReleasePage.aspx?PRID=1809580
135. Reddy, S. (2021). 'Collaborative Pathways for Defence R&D towards Atmanirbharta.' *Synergy*. Retrieved from https://cenjows.in/wp- content/uploads /2022/02/15-Dr-Sateesh-Reddy.pdf
136. Research and Markets. (2023). Ammunition Manufacturing Market in India 2023.
137. Wresearch. (2024). India Weapons and Ammunition Market (2024-2030). 'Year-ender: 2023 witnesses record defence exports, all-time high productions,' *The Economic Times*, December 2023. Retrieved from https://m.economictimes.com/news/defence/year-ender-2023-witnesses-record-defence-exports-all-time-high-productions/articles how/1062595 61.cms
138. Army Technology. (2023). World's biggest arms importer India is pursuing defence "indigenisation."
139. 'IIT Madras to spearhead development of India's first Indigenous 155mm Smart Ammunition'. (6 February 2024). *The Economic Times*. Retrieved from https:// economictimes.indiatimes.com/news/defence/iit- madras-to-spearhead-development-of-indias-first-indigenous-155mm- smart-ammunition/articleshow/107462407.cms?from=mdr
140. *The Hindu Business Line*. (2023). IIT Madras and Munitions India Limited partnership.
141. Army Technology. (2023). World's biggest arms importer India is pursuing defence "indigenisation."

142. Research and Markets. (2023). Ammunition Manufacturing Market in India 2023.
143. Behera, L.K. (2012). 'India's Ordnance Factories: A Performance Analysis.' *Quantum Technologies and Military Strategies*, 6 (2), 63-77.
144. Neihsial, N. (2009). 'Outsourcing and Vendor Development in the Indian Ordnance Factories.' *Journal of Defence Studies*, 3 (3), 75-90.
145. Yadav, A. (2025). '10 years of missile development: How India's defence tech has evolved.' *WION.* Retrieved from https://www.wionews.com/photos/10-years-of-missile-development-how-india-s-defence-tech-has-evolved-1762165532520/1762165532521
146. Menon, S. 'Self-Reliance in Defence Production: India's Strategies and Challenges.' *Defence Studies*, vol. 18, no. 3, 2018, pp. 321-335.
147. Kumar, A. & Singh, P. (2022). Miniaturization in Defence Electronics. *IEEE Transactions on Electronics*, 61(4), 415-422.
148. Khare, A. (2023). 'Technology Development Fund: Opportunities and Challenges.' *MP-Institute for Defence Studies and Analyses.* Retrieved from https://www.idsa.in/publisher/issuebrief/technology-development-fund-opportunities-and-challenges
149. Saxena, N. (2020). 'Regulatory frameworks in India's defence sector.' *Journal of Regulatory Affairs,* 12(1), 30-39.
150. SIPRI (1988). 'Arms Production in the Third World: An Analysis of Decision-making.'
151. Joshi, V. (1992). 'The Dynamics of Indian Defence Production.' In *Defence Economics in India.*
152. Rajagopalan, S. (1990). 'India's Defence Industry: A Case Study in Industrial Development.' *Journal of Strategic Studies.*
153. Behera, L.K. (2008, January 8). 'Private Sector Participation in Indian Defence Industry.' *IDSA Comments.* Manohar Parrikar Institute for Defence Studies and Analyses. Retrieved June 6, 2022.
154. Ministry of Defence. (2024). FDI in Defence Sector. *Press Information Bureau.* Retrieved from https://www.pib.gov.in/PressReleasePage.aspx?PRID=2004475
155. Ministry of Defence. (2021, July 26). Private players in defence manufacturing sector. June 15, 2022. Retrieved from https:// pib.gov.in/PressReleaseIframePage.aspx?PRID=1739049
156. Maheshwari, S. (2004). 'Diversification of Defence-Based Industries in India.' In A. Markusen, S. Digiovanni, & M. C. Leary (eds.), *From Defence to Development: International Perspectives on Realizing the Peace Dividend* (pp. 179-200). New York: Routledge.
157. Khan, J.A. & Shaikh, N. (2018). 'Defence Production in India: A Commercial Approach to Self- Reliance.' *Aayushi International Interdisciplinary Research Journal*, 5 (2).
158. Ministry of Defence. (2016). Defence Procurement Procedure 2016 Capital Procurement. Retrieved from https://www.mod.gov.in/sites/default/files/dppm.pdf_0.pdf
159. Choudhary, D.R.. 'In a first, India to export BrahMos Missile to the Philippines,' *The Economic Times*, January 15, 2022. Retrieved from https://economictimes.indiatimes.com/news/defence/in-a-first- india-to-export-brahmos-missile-to-philippines/articleshow/88908287.cms?from=mdr
160. Joshi, M. (2012). 'India's Defence Industrial Base: A Quest for Self-Reliance.' *China Report*, vol. 48, no. 4, 2012, pp. 357-371.
161. Pant, H.V & Bommakanti, K. (2024). 'India's Defence Exports: Continuing Defence

Reforms is Critical.' *Observer Research Foundation.* Retrieved from https://www.orfonline.org/research/indias-defence-exports-continuing-defence-reforms-is-critical

162. Mishra, D. (2019, January 4). 'India's Gradual Transition from 'Defence Market to 'Export Hub'. Retrieved from https://www.vifindia.org/ article/2019/january/04/india-s-gradual-transition-from-defence- market-to-export-hub
163. 'India posts record Rs 13,000 crore worth defence exports in 2021-22' (2022). *The Economic Times.* Retrieved from https://economictimes.indiatimes.com/news/defence/india-posts-record-rs-13000-crore-worth-defence-exports-in-2021-22/articleshow/92752080.cms?from=mdr
164. Gopal, V. (2021). 'The case for Nurturing Military Scientists in the Indian Army.' *Observer Research Foundation Occasional Paper.* Retrieved from https://www.orfonline.org/public/uploads/posts/pdf/20240630145855.pdf
165. Chakrabarti, R., & Bose, S. (2021). 'Intellectual Property Challenges in Defence Technology.' *Journal of Intellectual Property Rights*, 26(3), 115-127.
166. Mehta, R. & Singh, V. (2022). 'Communication Systems for Smart Ammunition.' *Defence Technology Review*, 18(2), 55-63.
167. Singh, D. (2017). 'Strategic Partnership with Private Players: An Overview. Retrieved from https://www.indiandefencereview.com/news/ strategic-partnership-with-private-players-an-overview/
168 'A study reveals how India can achieve $5 billion defence export goal,' *The Economic Times*, June 17, 2024. Retrieved from https://economic times.indiatimes.com/news/defence/a-study-reveals-how-india-can- achieve-5-billion-defence-export-goal/articleshow/111059109.cms?from=mdr
169. Ministry of Defence, Government of India. (2021). 'Seven new companies, carved out of OFB, dedicated to the Nation on the occasion of Vijaydashmi'. (15 October 2021). Press Information Bureau. Retrieved from https://pib.gov.in/PressReleasePage.aspx?PRID=1764148
170. Mann, R.S. (2020). 'Need for a Defence Industrial Ecosystem for Atmanirbharta in Defence.' Retrieved from https://www.indiandefen cereview.com/news/need-for-a-defence-industrial-ecosystem-for- atmanirbharta-in-defence/
171. Ordnance Factory Board. (2020). 'History of Ordnance Factories.' Retrieved from https://ofb.gov.in
172. Raghavan, V.R. (2010). 'India's Defence and Security Challenges: A Historical Perspective.' *Journal of Defence Studies*, 4(2), 1-20.
173. Ministry of Defence, Government of India. (2018). Defence Production Policy 2018. Retrieved from https://mod.gov.in
174. DRDO (Defence Research and Development Organisation). (2020). Annual-Report 2019-2020. Retrieved from https://www.drdo.gov.in
175. Ibid.
176. Shukla, A. (2017). 'Private Sector Participation in India's Defence Production: Challenges and Opportunities.' *Journal of Defence Studies*, 11(3), 23-45.
177. Peri, D. (2019). 'Army gets first batch of Dhanush, home-made Bofors artillery guns, from OFB.' *The Hindu.* Retrieved from https://www.thehindu.com/news/national/army-gets-desi-bofors-in-home-made-dhanush-howitzer/article26769308.ece

178. Ministry of Defence, Government of India. (2018). Defence Production Policy 2018. Retrieved from https://mod.gov.in
179. FICCI (Federation of Indian Chambers of Commerce & Industry). (2020). Boosting Defence Exports: A Strategic Roadmap. Retrieved from https://ficci.in
180. 'Achieving Self-Reliance through Indigenous R&D by DRDO/Industry.' (2020). *vifindia.org.* [VIF Task Force Report II] New Delhi. Retrieved from https://www.vifindia.org/sites/default/files/Achieving-Self- Reliance-through-Indigenous-RandD-by-DRDO-Industry-part-II.pdf
181. Ministry of Defence (2025). Make in India Powers Defence Growth. *Press Information Bureau.* http://pib.gov.in/PressReleasePage.aspx?PRID=2116612
182. Ministry of Defence (2019). India to achieve USD 26 Billion Defence Industry by 2025: Raksha Mantri. *Press Information Bureau.* Retrieved from https://www.pib.gov.in/newsite/PrintRelease.aspx?relid=193256
183. Goh, G.D. et al. (2018). 'Additive manufacturing in unmanned aerial vehicles (UAVs): Challenges and potential.' *Aerospace Science and Technology*, 72, 223-234.
184. Mizokami, K. (2019). 'The Army's Next Bullet Is Designed to Pierce 'Next- Gen' Body Armour.' *Popular Mechanics*. Retrieved from https:// www.popularmechanics.com
185. Karp, A. (2016). 'Greener Guns: Reducing the Environmental Impact of Small Arms.' *Small Arms Survey*, 2016(2), 12-23.
186. Bogue, R. (2017). 'Growth in the Internet of Things sensor market.' *Sensor Review*, 37(4), 425-430.
187. Nave, R. (2020). 'Modern Ammunition Manufacturing Techniques.' *Manufacturing Today*, 10(4), 34-39.
188. Ferguson, J. (2019). 'Precision Manufacturing in Ammunition Production.' *Journal of Defence Engineering*, 22(3), 215-229.
189. Griffiths, J. (2017). 'Advances in Artillery Technology.' *Defence Review*, 33(2), 45-58.
190. Sutton, G.P. & Biblarz, O. (2017). *Rocket Propulsion Elements*. John Wiley & Sons.
191. Defence Manufacturing Institute. (2021). 'Smart Manufacturing in Defence.' Retrieved from https://www.defencemanufacturing institute.org
192. Ibid.
193. Bogue, R. (2017). 'Growth in the Internet of Things sensor market.' *Sensor Review*, 37(4), 425-430.
194. National Institute of Standards and Technology (NIST). (2020). 'NIST Standards in Defence.' Retrieved from https://www.nist.gov
195. European Defence Agency (EDA). (2020). 'European Defence Standards Reference System.' Retrieved from https://eda.europa.eu
196. Rheinmetall A.G. (2021). 'Ammunition.' Retrieved from https:// www.rheinmetall.com
197. Nexter. (2020). 'Nexter Munitions.' Retrieved from https://www.nexter- group.fr
198. Leonardo S.p.A. (2021). 'Products and Capabilities.' Retrieved from https://www.leonardocompany.com
199. Saab. (2021). 'Land Systems and Products.' Retrieved from https:// www.saab.com
200. European Defence Agency (EDA). (2020). 'European Defence Standards Reference System.' Retrieved from https://eda.europa.eu
201. Stockholm International Peace Research Institute (SIPRI). (2021). 'Trends in International

Arms Transfers,' 2020. Retrieved from https:// www.sipri.org/publications/2021/sipri-fact-sheets/trends- international-arms-transfers-2020

202. Foss, C. (2018). 'Russia's Defence Industry: A Research Guide to the 2018 Literature.' *Defence Studies*, 18(1), 72-85.
203. Ibid.
204. Ibid.
205. Kruijff, M. (2015). 'Material Requirements for Ammunition Production.' *Journal of Materials Science*, 50(12), 4210-4220.
206. Cheung, T.M. (2018). '*China's Emergence as a Defence Technological Power.*' Routledge.
207. Ibid.
208. Ibid.
209. FICCI (Federation of Indian Chambers of Commerce & Industry). (2020). 'Boosting Defence Exports: A Strategic Roadmap.' Retrieved from https://ficci.in
210. Shukla, A. (2020). 'India's Struggles with Precision-Guided Munitions.' *Journal of Defence Studies*, 14(3), 45-67.
211. Sinha, R. (2019). 'Modernization of Ordnance Factories: Challenges and Prospects.' *Journal of Defence Production*, 11(2), 23-35.
212. Singh, R. (2016). 'Pulgaon Depot Explosions: A Tragic Reminder of Quality Control Lapses.' *The Hindu*. Retrieved from https://www.thehindu. com
213. Shukla, A. (2020). 'India's Struggles with Precision-Guided Munitions.' *Journal of Defence Studies*, 14(3), 45-67.
214. Sinha, R. (2019). 'Modernization of Ordnance Factories: Challenges and Prospects.' *Journal of Defence Production*, 11(2), 23-35.
215. DRDO (Defence Research and Development Organisation). (2020). Annual-Report 2019-2020. Retrieved from https://www.drdo.gov.in
216. Singh, R. (2016). 'Pulgaon Depot Explosions: A Tragic Reminder of Quality Control Lapses.' *The Hindu*. Retrieved from https://www.thehindu. com
217. Chaudhary, A. (2018). 'Delays in Ammunition Procurement Affecting Indian Army's Readiness.' *Defence News India*. Retrieved from https://www.defencenewsindia.com
218. Shukla, A. (2020). 'India's Struggles with Precision-Guided Munitions.' *Journal of Defence Studies*, 14(3), 45-67.
219. Directorate of Ordnance (Coordination and Services). Government of India. 'History' (n.d.). Retrieved from https://ddpdoo.gov.in/pages/history
220. Ordnance Factory Board. (2020). 'History of Ordnance Factories.' Retrieved from https://ofb.gov.in
221. Sinha, R. (2019). 'Modernization of Ordnance Factories: Challenges and Prospects.' *Journal of Defence Production*, 11(2), 23-35.
222. 'Achieving Self-Reliance through Indigenous R&D by DRDO/Industry' (2020). *vifindia.org*. [VIF Task Force Report II] New Delhi. Retrieved from https://www.vifindia.org/sites/default/files/Achieving-Self- Reliance-through-Indigenous-RandD-by-DRDO-Industry-part-II.pdf
223. Behera, L.K. (2024). 'India's Defence Industry: Achievements and Challenges.' *Observer Research Foundation*. Retrieved from https://www.orfonline.org/research/india-s-defence-industry-achievements-and-challenge

224. Bharat Forge (2021). 'Defence Capabilities.' Retrieved from https:// www.bharatforge.com/ defence.
225. L&T. (2021). 'L&T Defence.' Retrieved from https://www.larsentoubro.com/defence/
226. TATA Advanced Systems. 'Our Products & Services'. Retrieved from https:// www.tataadvancedsystems.com/
227. Kalyani Strategic Systems Ltd. (n.d.) About. Retrieved from https://www.kssl.in/
228. Kruijff, M. (2015). 'Material Requirements for Ammunition Production.' *Journal of Materials Science*, 50(12), 4210-4220.
229. Jain, R. (2019). 'Challenges in Securing Raw Materials for Ammunition Production.' *Materials Today*, 21(4), 34-40.
230. Nave, R. (2020). 'Modern Ammunition Manufacturing Techniques.' *Manufacturing Today*, 10(4), 34-39.
231. Ferguson, J. (2019). 'Precision Manufacturing in Ammunition Production.' *Journal of Defence Engineering*, 22(3), 215-229.
232. Chaudhary, A. (2018). 'Delays in Ammunition Procurement Affecting Indian Army's Readiness.' *Defence News India*. Retrieved from https://www.defencenewsindia.com
233. Ministry of Defence, Government of India. (2021). 'Seven new companies, carved out of OFB, dedicated to the Nation on the occasion of Vijaydashmi'. (15 October 2021). Press Information Bureau. Retrieved from https://pib.gov.in/PressReleasePage.aspx?PRID=1764148
234. Bharat Forge (2021). 'Defence Capabilities.' Retrieved from https:// www.bharatforge.com/ defence
235. Ministry of Defence, Government of India. (2021). 'Annual Report 2020-2021.' Retrieved from https://mod.gov.in
236. Sinha, R. (2019). 'Modernization of Ordnance Factories: Challenges and Prospects.' *Journal of Defence Production*, 11(2), 23-35.
237. FICCI (Federation of Indian Chambers of Commerce & Industry). (2020). 'Boosting Defence Exports: A Strategic Roadmap.' Retrieved from https://ficci.in
238. Shukla, A. (2020). 'India's Struggles with Precision-Guided Munitions.' *Journal of Defence Studies*, 14(3), 45-67.
239. Ministry of Defence, Government of India. (2021). 'Annual Report 2020-2021.' Retrieved from https://mod.gov.in
240. Shukla, A. (2020). 'India's Struggles with Precision-Guided Munitions.' *Journal of Defence Studies*, 14(3), 45-67.
241. Sinha, R. (2019). 'Modernization of Ordnance Factories: Challenges and Prospects.' *Journal of Defence Production*, 11(2), 23-35.
242. Bharat Forge. (2021). 'Defence Capabilities.' Retrieved from https:// www.bharatforge.com/ defence
243. Shukla, A. (2020). 'India's Struggles with Precision-Guided Munitions.' *Journal of Defence Studies*, 14(3), 45-67.
244. Bharat Forge. (2021). 'Defence Capabilities.' Retrieved from https:// www.bharatforge.com/ defence
245. Sinha, R. (2019). 'Modernization of Ordnance Factories: Challenges and Prospects.' *Journal of Defence Production*, 11(2), 23-35.

246. FICCI (Federation of Indian Chambers of Commerce & Industry). (2020). 'Boosting Defence Exports: A Strategic Roadmap.' Retrieved from https://ficci.in
247. Jain, R. (2019). 'Challenges in Securing Raw Materials for Ammunition Production.' *Materials Today*, 21(4), 34-40.
248. Ibid.
249. Sinha, R. (2019). 'Modernization of Ordnance Factories: Challenges and Prospects.' *Journal of Defence Production*, 11(2), 23-35.
250. Singh, R. (2016). 'Pulgaon Depot Explosions: A Tragic Reminder of Quality Control Lapses.' *The Hindu*. Retrieved from https://www.thehindu. com
251. Sinha, R. (2019). 'Modernization of Ordnance Factories: Challenges and Prospects.' *Journal of Defence Production*, 11(2), 23-35.
252. Singh, R. (2016). 'Pulgaon Depot Explosions: A Tragic Reminder of Quality Control Lapses.' *The Hindu*. Retrieved from https://www.thehindu. com
253. Shukla, A. (2020). 'India's Struggles with Precision-Guided Munitions.' *Journal of Defence Studies*, 14(3), 45-67.
254. FICCI (Federation of Indian Chambers of Commerce & Industry). (2020). 'Boosting Defence Exports: A Strategic Roadmap.' Retrieved from https://ficci.in
255. Shukla, A. (2020). 'India's Struggles with Precision-Guided Munitions.' *Journal of Defence Studies*, 14(3), 45-67.
256. Bogue, R. (2017). 'Growth in the Internet of Things sensor market.' *Sensor Review*, 37(4), 425-430.
257. Chaudhary, A. (2018). 'Delays in Ammunition Procurement Affecting Indian Army's Readiness.' *Defence News India*. Retrieved from https://www.defencenewsindia.com
258. Kruijff, M. (2015). 'Material Requirements for Ammunition Production.' *Journal of Materials Science*, 50(12), 4210-4220.
259. Jain, R. (2019). 'Challenges in Securing Raw Materials for Ammunition Production.' *Materials Today*, 21(4), 34-40.
260. Karp, A. (2016). 'Greener Guns: Reducing the Environmental Impact of Small Arms.' *Small Arms Survey*, 2016(2), 12-23.
261. Hancock Jr., S.R. (1998). *The Ammunition Supply Chain and Intermodalism: from Depot to Foxhole*. [Master's Thesis]. Naval Postgraduate School, United States Navy. Retrieved from https://apps.dtic.mil/sti/tr/pdf/ ADA343623.pdf
262. Ibid.
263. Ibid., p. 11.
264. Ibid., pp. 11-19.
265. Ibid., p. 49.
266. Ibid., pp. 49-72.
267 'Ammo India 2024: Make in India – Make for the world.' (2024). *FICCI* and *KPMG*. Retrieved from https://assets.kpmg.com/content/dam/kpmg/in/pdf/ 2024/08/ammo-india-2024-make-in-india-make-for-the-world.pdf
268. Blue Waterforces. (2024). 'Understanding the ammunition supply chain in naval operations.' *BWF Editorial*. Retrieved from https://bluewaterforces.com/ ammunition-supply-chain/
269. Girardi, B. et al. 92023). 'Strategic raw materials for Defence.' *The Hague Centre for Strategic*

Studies. Retrieved from https://hcss.nl/wp-content/uploads/2023/ 01/Strategic-Raw-Materials-for-Defence-2023-HCSS.pdf

270. Gaustad, G., Krystofik, M. Bustamante, M. & Badami, K. (2018). 'Circular economy strategies for mitigating critical material supply issues.' *Resources, Conservation and Recycling.* Vol. 135. pp. 24-33. Retrieved from https:// doi.org/10.1016/j.resconrec.2017.08.002
271. Pavel. C.C. & Tzimas, E. (2016). 'Raw materials in the European defence industry.' *JRC Science for Policy Report.* EUR 27542. Retrieved from https:// setis.ec.europa.eu/system/files/2021-02/raw_materials_in_the_ euro pean_defence_industry.pdf
272. European Commission. (2024). EU secures access to diversified, affordable, and sustainable supply of critical raw materials. ec.*europa.eu* [Press Release] https://ec.europa.eu/commission/presscorner/detail/en/ ip_24_2748
273. 'Ammo India 2024: Make in India – Make for the world.' (2024). *FICCI* and *KPMG.* Retrieved from https://assets.kpmg.com/content/dam/kpmg/in/pdf/ 2024/08/ammo-india-2024-make-in-india-make-for-the-world.pdf
274. Andrew-Speed, P. & Hove, A. (2023). 'China's rare earths dominance and policy responses.' *The Oxford Institute for Energy Studies.* Paper: CE7. Retrieved from https:// www.oxfordenergy.org/wpcms/wp-content/uploads/2023/ 06/CE7-Chinas-rare-earths-dominance-and-policy-responses.pdf
275. 'Ammo India 2024: Make in India – Make for the world.' (2024). *FICCI* and *KPMG.* Retrieved from https://assets.kpmg.com/content/dam/kpmg/in/pdf/ 2024/08/ammo-india-2024-make-in-india-make-for-the-world.pdf
276. Jacob, B. (2024). 'Ammunition Management in Modern Warfare: Analysing recent Conflicts and Strategic Implications.' *United Service Institution of India.* Retrieved from https:// www.usiofindia.org/publication-journal/Ammunition- Management-in-Modern-Warfare-Analysing-Recent-Conflicts-and- Strategic-Implications.html
277. Ministry of Defence, Government of India. (2024). 'Marching towards Atmanirbharta: India's Defence revolution.' Press Information Bureau, Delhi. Retrieved from https://pib.gov.in/PressReleasePage.aspx?PRID=2069090
278. Andrew-Speed, P. & Hove, A. (2023). 'China's rare earths dominance and policy responses.' *The Oxford Institute for Energy Studies.* Paper: CE7. Retrieved from https://www.oxfordener gy.org/wpcms/wp-content/uploads/2023/ 06/CE7-Chinas-rare-earths-dominance-and-policy-responses.pdf
279. Gaustad, G.; Krystofik, M.; Bustamante, M. & Badami, K. (2018). 'Circular economy strategies for mitigating critical material supply issues.' *Resources, Conservation and Recycling.* Vol. 135, Pp. 24-33. Retrieved from https:// doi.org/10.1016/j.resconrec.2017.08.002
280. Ministry of Defence, Government of India. (2024). 'Marching towards Atmanirbharta: India's Defence revolution,' Press Information Bureau, Delhi. Retrieved from https://pib.gov.in/PressReleasePage.aspx?PRID=2069090
281. Vicente, P.L. (2024). 'Additive Manufacturing in Defence.' *European Defence Matters.* Retrieved from https://eda.europa.eu/webzine/issue14/cover-story/additive-manufacturing-in-defence
282. Jacob, B. (2024). 'Ammunition Management in Modern Warfare: Analysing recent Conflicts and Strategic Implications.' *United Service Institution of India.* Retrieved from https:// www.usiofindia.org/publication-journal/Ammunition- Management-in-Modern-Warfare-

Analysing-Recent-Conflicts-and- Strategic-Implications.html

283. Kleeman, F.C. & Essig, M. (2013). 'A providers' perspective on supplier relationships in performance-based contracting.' *Journal of Purchasing and Supply Management.* Vol. 19, No. 3, pp. 185-198.
284. Suman, M. (2006). 'Weapons Procurement: Qualitative Requirements and Transparency in Evaluation.' *Strategic Analysis.* Retrieved from https://www.idsa.in/ system/files/ strategiccommetns_msuman_1206.pdf
285. Moswetsi, W. (2007). 'Investigating e-commerce adoption in the procurement processes of the Botswana Defence Force: A Qualitative Study.'
286. Bedi, R. (2021). 'Not just the MoD, the military's QR overreach is also culpable for impeding modernisation.' *The Wire.* Retrieved from https://thewire.in/ security/indian-military-qr-overreach-modernisation
287. Behera, L.K. (2011). 'A Critical Review of Defence Procurement Procedure 2011.' New Delhi: IDSA.
288. Dhir, R.K. (2010). 'Challenges of Capability Definition and Cost efficient QR Formulation.' *Journal of Defence Studies.* Vol. 4, No. 1, P. 55. January. Retrieved from https:/ /demo.idsa.in/ system/files/jds_4_1_rkdhir.pdf
289. Iyer, M.K.K. (2017). 'Can we do away with service Qualitative Requirements?' *Centre for Land Warfare Studies.* Issue Brief. Retrieved from https://www.claws.in/ static/IB106_Can-We-Do-Away-with-Service-Qualitative-Requirements.pdf
290. Suman, M. (2006). 'Weapons Procurement: Qualitative Requirements and Transparency in Evaluation.' *Strategic Analysis.* Retrieved from https://www.idsa.in/ system/files/ strategiccommetns_msuman_1206.pdf
291. Ibid.
292. Ibid.
293. *Defence Acquisition Procedure* (2024). Make in India. Retrieved from https://www.make inindia.com/defence-acquisition-procedure.
294. Carter, S. (2024). 'Simplifying defence procurement: The power of cloud based S2P.' *CPO Strategy.* Retrieved from https://cpostrategy.media/blog/2024/10/ 31/simplifying-defence-procurement-the-power-of-cloud-based-s2p/
295. Rendon, J.M. & Rendon, R.G. (2016). 'Procurement fraud in the US Department of Defence: Implications for contracting processes and internal controls.' *Managerial Auditing Journal.* Retrieved from https://www.researchgate.net/ publication/303977178_ Procurement_ fraud_in_ the_US_Department_ of_Defence_Implications_ for_contracting_ processes_and_internal_ controls
296. Ekstrom, T.; Hilletofth, P. & Skoglund, P. (2021). 'Towards a purchasing portfolio model for defence procurement – A Delphi study of Swedish defence authorities.' *International Journal of Production Economics.* Vol. 233. (March 2021). Retrieved from https:// www.sciencedirect.com/science/article/ pii/S0925527320303455
297. 'Integrated Procurement Model; Driving pace in the delivery of Military Capability.' Ministry of Defence (2024). Report. Retrieved from https:// assets.publishing.service.gov.uk/media/ 65e07110cf7eb16adff57ff4/ Integrated_Procurement_Model.pdf
298. Ibid.

299. Borky, J.M. & Bradley, T.H. (2018). 'Protecting Information with Cybersecurity.' In *An Effective Model-Based Systems Engineering.* (ed.) *Springer Nature.* pp. 345-404. Retrieved from https:// link.springer.com/chapter/10.1007/978-3-319-95669-5_10
300. Shekhar, C. (2012). 'Procurement Strategy and Modernisation of Defence Forces.' *Journal of the United Service Institution of India.* Vol. CXLI, No. 588. Retrieved from https:// www.usiofindia.org/publication-journal/procurement- strategy-and-modernisation-of-defence-forces.html
301. Rendon, J.M. & Rendon, R.G. (2016). 'Procurement fraud in the US Department of Defence: Implications for contracting processes and internal controls.' *Managerial Auditing Journal.* Retrieved from https://www.researchgate.net/ publication/303977178_ Procurement_ fraud_in_ the_US_Department_ of_Defence_Implications_for_contracting_ processes_and_internal_ controls
302. Ekstrom, T.; Hilletofth, P. & Skoglund, P. (2021). 'Towards a purchasing portfolio model for defence procurement – A Delphi study of Swedish defence authorities.' *International Journal of Production Economics,* vol. 233. (March 2021). Retrieved from https:// www.sciencedirect.com/science/article/ pii/S0925527320303455
303. Ali, Y. et al. (2018). 'Through Life Cycle Management on Defence Acquisition Planning.' *Economic and Social Development.* Retrieved from https:// www.proquest.com/openview/ a348cf71c6b0171da5f1c351d3cb4309/ 1?pq-origsite=gscholar&cbl=29577
304. Rendon, J.M. & Rendon, R.G. (2016). 'Procurement fraud in the US Department of Defence: Implications for contracting processes and internal controls'. *Managerial Auditing Journal.* Retrieved from https://www.researchgate.net/ publication/303977178_ Procurement_ fraud_in_ the_US_Department_ of_Defence_Implications_for_contracting_ processes_and_internal_ controls
305. Ali, Y. et al. (2018). 'Through Life Cycle Management on Defence Acquisition Planning.' *Economic and Social Development.* Retrieved from https:// www.proquest.com/openview/ a348cf71c6b0171da5f1c351d3cb4309/ 1?pq-origsite=gscholar&cbl=29577
306. 'Integrated Procurement Model; Driving pace in the delivery of Military Capability.' Ministry of Defence (2024). Report. Retrieved from https:// assets.publishing.service.gov.uk/media/ 65e07110cf7eb16adff57ff4/ Integrated_Procurement_Model.pdf
307. Borky, J.M. & Bradley, T.H. (2018). 'Protecting Information with Cybersecurity.' In *An Effective Model-Based Systems Engineering..* (ed.) Springer Nature. pp. 345-404. Retrieved from https:// link.springer.com/chapter/10.1007/978-3-319-95669-5_10
308. Ekstrom, T., Hilletofth, P. & Skoglund, P. (2021). 'Towards a purchasing portfolio model for defence procurement – A Delphi study of Swedish defence authorities.' *International Journal of Production Economics.* vol. 233. (March 2021). Retrieved from https:// www.sciencedirect.com/science/article/ pii/S0925527320303455
309 Shankar, P.R. (2020). Atma Nirbharta and Defence Procurement. *Gunners Shot.* Retrieved from https://gunnersshot.com/2020/06/07/atma-nirbharta-and-defence-procurement-by-lt-gen-p-r-shankar/comment-page-1/
310. 'Indian Army to Indigenize 100% Ammunition Procurement by FY 2025-26" (2024).' *Knowledge & News Network.* Retrieved from https://knnindia.co.in/news/newsdetails/sectors/ defence/indian-army-to-indigenize-100-ammunition-procurement-by-fy-2025-26

APPENDICES

APPENDIX 1

India's Defence Exports from FY 2017-2024 (in billion Indian Rupees)

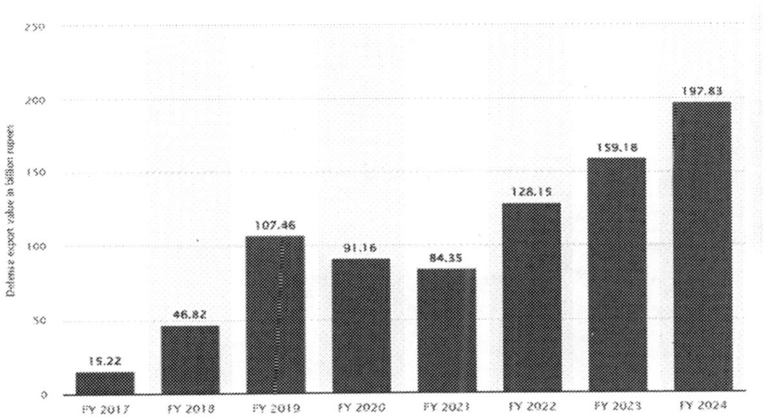

Source: "India's Defence Exports from FY 2017-2024 (in billion Indian Rupees)", https://www.statista.com/statistics/1345048/india-defence-export/. Accessed on 10 May 2024.

APPENDIX 2

Frameworks to Boost Defence Exports

Framework	*Result*
DPEP, 2020	Export & Revenue Benchmarks (2025)
DAP, 2020	Enhanced Domestic Defence Manufacturing
Positive Indigenisation Lists	Market Opportunities for Domestic Defence Manufacturers
Liberalised Export Licensing	Enabling Regulatory Environment
Digital Certifications	Easier Compliance
Role of MEA	Whole-of-Government Approach

Source: Suchet Vir Singh, "Policy Recommendations for Achieving India's Defence-Export Ambitions", ORF, 2023, https://www.orfonline.org/research/policy-recommendations-for-achieving-india-s-defence-export-ambitions.

APPENDIX 3

India's Defence Production

Financial Year	*DPSUs (INR Billion)*	*OFs (INR Billion)*	*Other PSUs and JVs (INR Billion)*	*Private Companies (INR Billion)*	*Total Production (INR Billion)*
2016-17	404.27	148.25	46.98	141.04	740.54
2017-18	434.64	148.29	51.80	153.47	788.20
2018-19	453.87	128.16	55.67	173.50	811.20
2019-20	476.55	92.27	62.95	158.94	790.71
2020-21	467.11	146.35	60.29	172.68	846.43
2021-22	557.90	119.13	72.22	199.20	948.45
2022-23	634.66	169.98	71.37	210.83	1086.84

Source: Ministry of Defence, Government of India.

APPENDIX 4

State-wise Details of Ordnance Factories

Ordnance Factories have ISO 9000-certified Quality Management Systems (QMS) along with National Accreditation Board for Laboratories (NABL) accredited Labs. Items manufactured in ordnance factories are inspected by the Quality Control wing of the concerned ordnance factory during the manufacturing process. Also, there is a surveillance audit and Final Acceptance Inspection (FAI) by the Directorate General of Quality Assurance (DGQA) as second-party Quality Assurance agency. State-wise details of Ordnance Factories are as under:

S.No.	*Factory/Location*	*Major Product (s)*
Telengana		
1.	Ordnance Factory, Medak	Infantry Combat Vehicle
Bihar		
2.	Ordnance Factory, Nalanda, Bihar	Propellant Bi-modular charges System (At Project Stage).
Chandigarh		
3.	Ordnance Cable Factory, Chandigarh	Cables of various types, optical sights
Maharashtra		
4.	Ammunition Factory, Kirkee, Pune	Small Arms ammunition
5.	High Explosive Factory, Pune	Explosives, Initiatory Explosives, Acids and Chemicals, etc.
6.	Ordnance Factory, Chandrapur	Tank Gun Ammunition and Mortar ammunition.
7.	Ordnance Factory, Varangaon	Small Arms ammunition
8.	Ordnance Factory, Bhandara	Propellants and Commercial Explosives
9.	Ordnance Factory, Dehu Road	Various Pyrotechnic compositions
10.	Ordnance Factory, Ambajhari	Ammunition hardware for various ammunitions.
11.	Ordnance Factory, Ambarnath	Brass and Guilding Metal cups of various Calibres for small arms and other ammunition.
12.	Machine Tool Prototype Factory, Ambarnath	Design, development and manufacture of special purpose machine tools and equipment, components and sub-assemblies for A & B vehicles.
13.	Ordnance Factory, Bhusawal	Drums, Barrels, Ammunition boxes.

Madhya Pradesh		
14.	Ordnance Factory, Khamaria, Jabalpur	Small arms ammunition, anti-aircraft ammunition, Heavy calibre anti tank ammunition, bombs, mines, ammunitions for Air Force and Navy.
15.	Ordnance Factory, Itarsi	Propellants of various types, Acid, Sulphuric Acid, Picrite, etc.
16.	Ordnance Factory, Katni	Non-Ferrous Rolled and Extruded sections, cups for small arms ammunitions, Heavy calibre cartridge cases
17.	Gun Carriage Factory, Jabalpur	Carriages for Artillery Guns, Tank Gun Recoil System, Anti-aircraft Gun, Mortars
18.	Vehicle Factory, Jabalpur	Army Transport vehicles
19.	Grey Iron FoundryJabalpur	Automobile casting of Grey and Malleable Iron
Odisha		
20.	Ordnance Factory, Badmal, Bolangir	Tank Gun and Artillery ammunition
Tamil Nadu		
21.	Heavy Alloy Penetrator Project, Tiruchirapalli	Empty Shots for Kinetic Energy ammunition.
22.	Ordnance Factory, Trichy, Tiruchirapalli	Small Arms
23.	Heavy Vehicle Factory, Avadi	Tanks
24.	Engine Factory, Avadi	Engines for Battle Tanks and ICV
25.	Ordnance Clothing Factory, Avadi	All Combat Clothing & Parade Garments, Parachutes
26.	Cordite Factory, Aruvankadu	Propellants of various types.
Uttarakhand		
27.	Ordnance Factory, Dehradun	Sighting and Fire Control instruments for tanks, Fire Control instruments for Guns and Mortars, Binoculars.
28.	Opto Electronic Factory, Dehradun	Precision Opto Mechanical/Electronic Instruments for sighting and fire control for A class vehicles.
Uttar Pradesh		
29.	Ordnance Factory, Muradnagar	Plain Carbon and alloy steel castings for Tanks, ammunitions, and Steel forgings.
30.	Ordnance Factory, Kanpur	Medium & High calibre guns, Shell empties.
31.	Small Arms Factory, Kanpur	Small Arms.
32.	Field Gun Factory, Kanpur	High Calibre Ordnance & Spare Barrels, .32 Revolver
33.	Ordnance Equipment Factory, Kanpur	Leather items, textile items, engineering equipment including mountaineering items.
34.	Ordnance Parachute Factory, Kanpur	Parachutes of different types.
35.	Ordnance Clothing Factory, Shahjahanpur	All Combat Clothing, Textile and Tentage items
36.	Ordnance Equipment Factory, Hazratpur	Tents & other clothing items
37.	Ordnance Factory, Korwa	For production of carbines (At Project Stage).

West Bengal

38.	Gun & Shell Factory, Cossipore	Medium Calibre Guns, Shells & Fuses, pistols and Rocket Launcher
39.	Rifle Factory, Ishapore	Small Arms.
40.	Metal and Steel Factory, Ishapore	Various Ferrous and non-ferrous castings & extrusions, Light/Medium/Heavy Steel Forgings including Gun Barrel Forgings
41.	Ordnance Factory, Dum Dum	Various Precision Machined and Fabricated items for Defence Forces.

Source: "Ordnance Factories", PIB, April 2015, https://pib.gov.in/newsite/printrelease.aspx?relid=118647.

APPENDIX 5

Dissolution of OFB and Creation of Seven Defence PSUs (Corporatisation)

The Union cabinet on 16th Jun 2021, corporatised the functions of 41 production units of the Ordnance Factory Board functioning under the Department of Defence Production, Ministry of Defence. This led to restructuring of OFB into seven PSUs, wholly owned by the Govt. These seven PSU hubs are created to manage and streamline the operations of 41 production units. Each PSU is handling a cluster of Ordnance factories in specified field namely Weapons, Ammunition, Vehicles, Optics, Clothing, Parachutes and Equipment and their new HQ has been created near the cluster of Ordnance factories for smooth management, control, and handling of operations. Details of the PSUs are as under:

S.No	*PSU*	*HQ Location*	*Ordnance Factories under PSUs*
1	Munitions India Ltd (MIL)	Pune	12
2	Adv Wpns and Eqpt India Ltd (AWEIL)	Kanpur	08
3	Armoured Vehs Nigam Ltd (AVNL)	Chennai	05
4	Troop Comforts Ltd (TCL)	Kanpur	04
5	India Optel Ltd (IOL)	Dehradun	03
6	Yantra India Ltd (YIL)	Nagpur	08
7	Gliders India Ltd (GIL)	Kanpur	01

MUNITIONS INDIA LTD (MIL): FACTORIES

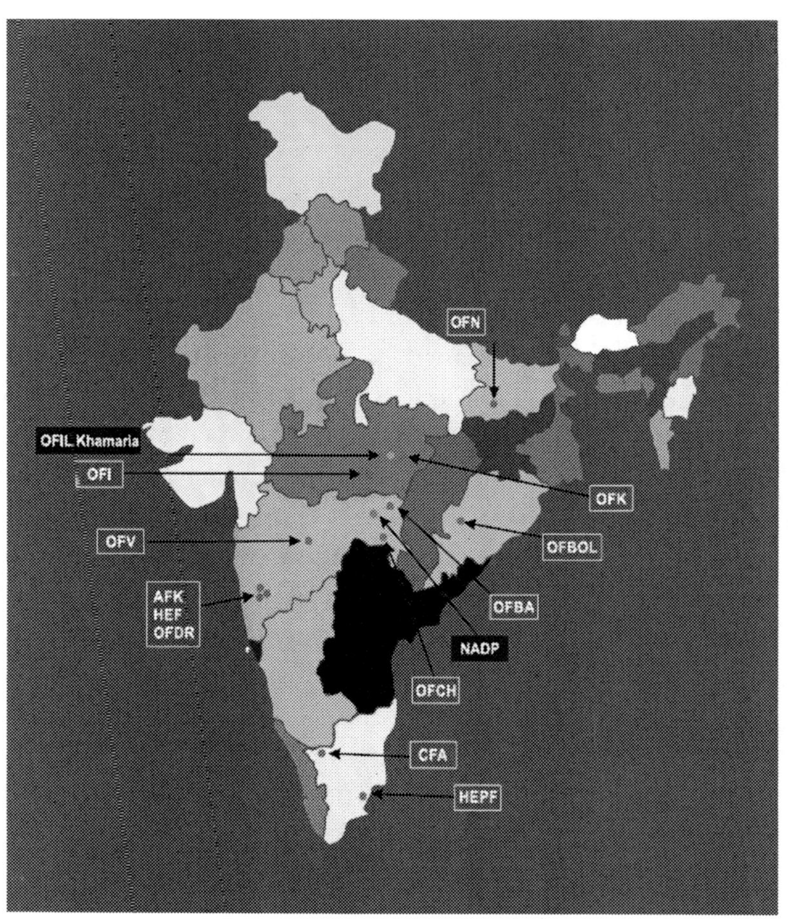

SMALL ARMS AMMUNITION

Cartridge
0.22" Ball

Cartridge
SA 5.56X 45MM

Cartridge
5.56X45MM

Cartridge
SA 7.62 x 39MM
Ball

Cartridge
SA 7.62 x 51MM
Tracer

Cartridge
SA 9X19MM Ball

Cartridge
SA 12 BORE 70MM
Plastic Astram

Cartridge
SA 12.7MM
API

Cartridge
SA 14.5MM
TAPD

LARGE CALIBER AMMUNITION
Shell 155 mm
HE ERFB BT
Shell 155 mm
HE ERFB BB
Shell 155 mm
Illuminating ERFB
Shell 155 mm
HE M77 B
Shell 155 mm
Screening
Smoke ERFB
Shell 155 mm
HE M 107
Charge 9
Charge 8
Charge M4A2
BMCS M91 & M92
3

RCL & TANK AMMUNITION

84 mm
Smoke 469 C

84 mm
TPT 65

84 mm
Heat 651

84 mm
HE 441B

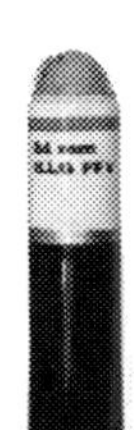
84 mm
Illg 545

84 mm
Heat 751

84 mm
HEDP 502

Round 120mm
FSAPDS

Round 120mm
HESH T 1A

Shell 125 mm
HE 1A

125 mm
FSAPDS

125 mm
SCCC

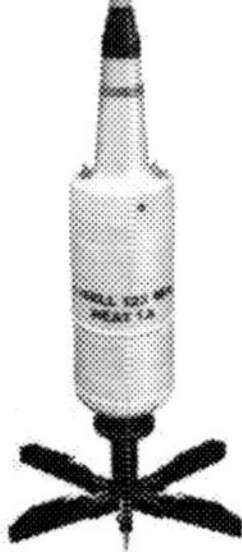
Shell 125 mm
Heat 1A

4

MORTAR BOMB

51mm
HE

51mm
Smoke

51mm
Illuminating

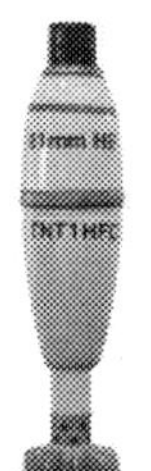

81mm
HE

81mm
Smoke

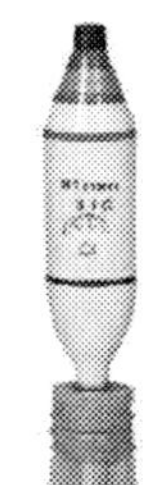

81mm
Illuminating

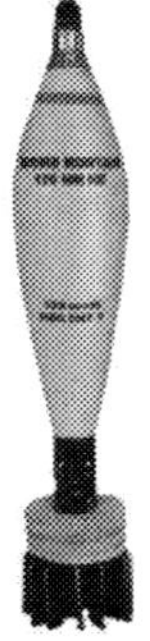

120mm HE

120mm Smoke

120mm
Illuminating

5

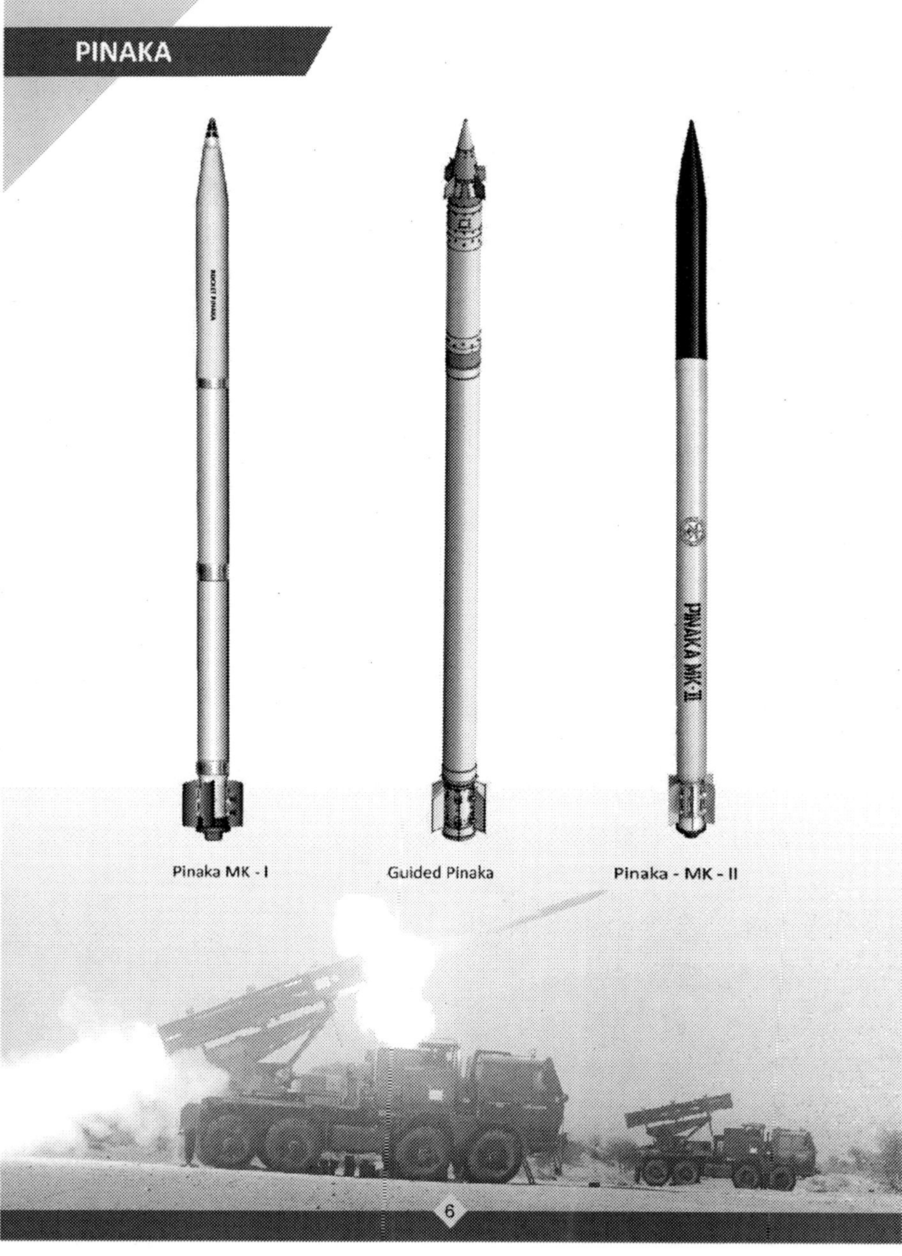
PINAKA
PINAKA MK-II
Pinaka MK - I
Guided Pinaka
Pinaka - MK - II
6

EXPLOSIVES & PROPELLANTS

DNT

TNT

HNS

RDX_TNT

RDX_WAX

TETRYL

PETN

PICRITE